WHITE MAN

STORIES FROM THE REZ

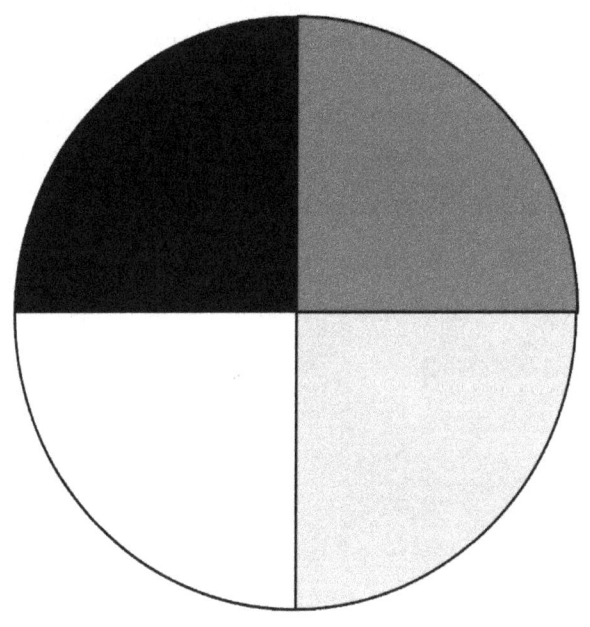

STRIDER BLUE

Copyright © 2020 by Strider Blue

All rights reserved. No part of this publication may be reproduced, distributed, or transmitted in any form or by any means, without prior written permission.

Strider Blue
strider@striderblue.com
Cover design by Strider Blue and Tanja Prokop

striderblue.com
Publisher's Note: This is a work of fiction. Names, characters, places, and incidents are a product of the author's imagination. Locales and public names are sometimes used for atmospheric purposes. Any resemblance to actual people, living or dead, or to businesses, companies, events, institutions, or locales is completely coincidental.

White Man: Stories from the Rez / Strider Blue. -- 1st ed.

Paperback ISBN 978-1-7347940-0-7

Hardcover ISBN 978-1-7347940-1-4

eBook ISBN 978-1-7347940-2-1

Preface

I experienced hundreds of beautiful, amazing, and wonderful people during my time in Indian Country. I miss many of them.

Indian Country, by the way, is an appropriate term. It is politically correct.

Although I don't remember any past lives, I do believe in reincarnation. It makes more sense to me than any other spiritual philosophy. For all I know, I may have been an Indian in one or more of my past lives. For all I know, you may have been a White Man in one of yours.

We're all aware of archetypal themes and characters that transcend culture and time. Many of the following stories and characters are just that—*archetypal*.

Some real people managed to work their way into a few of the stories, mostly on the periphery. Many of them you already know; they're icons from our pop culture. For the rest, please allow me to introduce you.

Whenever I include someone's real name, be it musician, actor, leader, or friend, my intention is to recognize and honor that person.

It's easy to find things to disagree about, to be angry about, to divide us.

In every relationship, I choose to look for what I call a *Point-of-Connection,* a *POC*. It's something that we can both relate to—something that unites us.

I hope you find many POCs in this book.

There's plenty here to be angry about, which may quite possibly be, our first Point-of-Connection. I'm angry, too.

I'm angry about the state of *Our* world.

∞

We're all on a hero's journey. What's yours? What dragons must *you* slay? What others will you befriend? What demons will you conquer? Which will conquer you? What glorious riches await you? Only the life you dare to imagine…the one you breathe into existence.

∞

Forewarning

Attention all passengers. You're about to enter Indian Country. Slow Down! Things don't move as fast around here. Hell, not only do things happen a lot slower in Indian Country, they're just not like what you're used to; well, unless, of course, you're from the Rez. In that case, you know way more than I ever will, so please help enlighten the rest of us.

Before landing, please bring your attention to *Father Sky* above and *Mother Earth* below. Now please recognize the four directions: *East, South, West,* and *North*. They have significance. Lastly, loosen your seat belt, have some fry bread, and enjoy the ride.

Dedication

This book is for Fate.

Contents

Preface I
Forewarning III
Dedication IV
Contents V
Last Day on the Rez 1
First Day on the Rez 11
Day 2—My People Will Judge You 15
Day 3—Meeting the ICW Committee 17
Trash Day 20
Tony 25
Tribal Court 30
White Man 32
Wanda 35
Todd Smoke 38
Lester 41
White Bison 55
Monotone Sue 68
Chain of Command 70
Rookie Mistake 71
Accepting Reality 74
Sasha 87
Lester in Treatment 91

Greasy Weasel	101
Don't Worry Honey, It Happens to All of Us	108
Beyond Judgement	110
Good Will Prevail	117
Elder Dorothy	118
Stan	120
Black Silk	122
Earth Tribe	124
Indian Child Welfare	137
Because Grandma Wanted It	139
New Management	142
Barney Smith	146
Odessa Knight a.k.a. *Full of Herself*	148
Simple Math	153
Making the Rounds	156
Big Thunder	158
Lady	171
Starbright	174
Elephant in the Room	181
Visiting Starbright	183
Nervous Beaver	191
Starlight	195
Where's the Baby?	198
Big Thunder Returns	210
Runaway Randy	217
The Worst Thing You Can Do	229
The White Table	232

Another Grand Opening 234
The Lodge 237
Vision Quest 243
Barney's Confession 246
Snake Eyes 248
A Different Set of Rules 255
Sunshine Who Walks in the Clouds 261
Gentle Owl 266
My Second to Last Day on the Rez 269
Aftermath 273
Regal Eagle 275
First Acknowledgement 276
Exclusion 278
My Personal Call to Action 280
Smoke Signals 282
My Last Communication to the Tribe 283
Moving Forward 284
Finding Closure 286
The Code 291
RhythmQuest 292

Last Day on the Rez

It was Friday morning, just turning towards noon. I was sitting in my office, organizing myself a bit before heading over to the grand opening of the Tribe's new jail. This was clearly another incredible accomplishment for the Tribe, and there were sure to be tons of people, pomp, *and* circumstance. Tribal Members, leaders from the community, and all of Tribal Council (*TC*) would be there. Local politicians and banking executives would receive Pendleton blankets for their role in the project's success.

The Tribe was celebrating *another* multimillion-dollar project come to life. Another "project" that was going to make them even richer. In the last few years alone, they'd spent tens of millions on new construction including the new Youth and Community Center, the Tribal Administration Building, and now the new Law Enforcement/Jail Complex. The County needed more jail space, and the Tribe was perfectly positioned to fulfill that need with their fancy new high-tech facility. They were also preparing to complete a major expansion of the casino and build a new super-sized gas station across the street from it. (Have a few burgers at the casino bar, and you can glean all kinds of information.)

When I came to the Tribe, they already had the casino, but they were just beginning to fortify their program infrastructure. Tribal Members were not even receiving *percap* payments from casino profits yet. The Tribe was busily expanding and developing their departments for everything including law enforcement, medical, dental, IT, social services, childcare—you name it. New employees came both from without and within the Tribe. Most management and professional positions were filled with outsiders. Once these professionals trained the Tribe's own people, they'd be expended.

The casino was just down the road from the Tribal Center, but it was a whole separate entity, another world, so to speak. Their staff and the Tribal staff never intermixed like all the Tribe's other departments, even though the Tribe owned the casino and many Tribal Members worked there. They kept their inner affairs very separate from their public image.

It was amazing to witness the Tribe's progress over the years, particularly for such a small tribe. In addition to their plans for the expansion of the existing casino, they also had plans for a new casino and hotel right along the main highway corridor. They already owned the equivalent of a small town, plus they own property at the mountain and have access to areas that are off-limits to the general public. They're buying up land, homes, and businesses all over the place.

The Indians are getting their land back.

Tribal Members receive numerous benefits including medical, dental, social services, and education. They have access to generous government grants for everything from buying homes to starting businesses. Plus, Tribal Members can fish and sell salmon, and harvest and sell shellfish. They can sell fireworks during the 4th and New Year's, and they can sell wood that they log for cheap from nearby U.S. Government land.

By law, the tribes have *Sovereignty*, and therefore, political rights and powers that no other U.S. Citizen or entity possesses. And then, of course, they get to own casinos. Cha-ching ad infinitum! (tax-free at that)

All this and more, and no one can say a word about it. The subject is taboo because of the horrific history of what has been done, and what continues to be done, to Tribal people. No one gets to talk about it except Tribal Members.

It's truly quite astonishing. The rights of the tribes are to be envied. Bet the *Powers that Be* didn't see that one coming.

Anyway, back to the story...

So, I finished up in my office and was closing the door to leave, when I heard someone enter the front reception area. I stepped down the hall and walked out to greet whomever had just entered the building. I recognized the man from previous encounters. I knew he was a Tribal Member. I had talked to him many times before, but never in a professional capacity.

He told me, "I need to see the voc-rehab lady." I told him she'd already gone over to the ceremony at the jail. He asked if we could go into my office, and then, before I could answer, he started down the hall, entered my office, and then planted himself in front of my desk. I followed him in and sat down. He began to share some stories about what he'd been going through. He seemed like he just needed to talk to someone. He seemed pretty content to talk to me.

I was a Tribal servant. I accepted. Everyone who works for the Tribe is there to serve the Tribal Members. The Tribal Members *are* the Tribe. I showed up for him as expected, and because that is what is in my heart to do.

We sat and talked for a while. I mostly listened and occasionally offered an encouraging word or gesture. After some time, he took a deep breath, straightened up in his chair, and returned a subtle nod. Then he motioned toward the door. I got up to walk him out, and he led the way down the hall to the reception area.

In the hallway he turned and said, "Can I get a ride up to the jail?"

I was happy to help. It was an honor to serve the Tribal Members. I didn't always feel that way. In the beginning I didn't even really understand that it was part of the gig, that is, to be available to help *all* Tribal Members whether they had a child in my program or not. Over time though, I developed a sense of pride for serving them and doing it well. It felt good to be building positive relationships with so many different people in the community. This community really needed the help, and I felt honored to serve them in this capacity. I knew I was having an impact on them, and they were definitely having an impact on me.

We continued talking as we walked out to my *GSA* (government-issued service vehicle) and drove down the street to the new jail.

As I drove him over to attend the ceremony, I felt like I had a small place there in the community, and I sort of belonged, even if just a little. I felt good about my role at the Tribe.

The entrance driveway was lined with cars, and the parking lot was packed. We found a place to park, and then shared some parting sentiments. I walked through the main entrance and followed a series of hallways that led to a courtyard in the middle of the complex. The new compound was beautiful, for a jail. They could certainly house a lot more inmates, employ many more people, and generate significant revenue to the Tribe.

The crowd was primed with excitement. It was very chilly. People huddled around portable outdoor space heaters while they listened to the speeches. Many Tribal leaders and local community leaders spoke. They praised the Chief of Police, who held the event's spotlight, for his incredible vision and leadership in bringing this project to fruition. Having worked closely with the Chief for so many years, I definitely felt proud for him personally, for his family, and for the Tribe as a whole.

Pendleton blankets (non-Tribal owned) were gifted to the VIPs, and then the corrections staff marched in sporting formal uniforms and presented themselves to the crowd. Many new detention officers filled the ranks.

After the speeches, everyone scattered to tour the premises for a little while before reconvening in the dining hall for a catered lunch. The Tribe always served food at their events. It was often the lure to get people to the event; although, this day people seemed genuinely happy and excited to attend.

I walked around greeting and congratulating many of the Tribal leaders and police officers. I had good relationships with many of them from my work in child welfare. I knew many of them from both sides of my job—as my leadership and co-workers, and as family placements and welfare cases. Many were both. Number one rule of *The Code*, hell, the number one rule in Indian Country: *everyone's related*. My child welfare cases were all related to my leadership. Let that sink in a little more. My child welfare cases were *all* related to my leadership. That dynamic created an environment for risky business.

I found a moment to squeeze in the line of people waiting to talk to the Chief so I could share my congratulations personally. I remember the first time I met Chief. I didn't know if I should salute him or shake his hand. I'm never really sure with uniformed officers. I always feel an inclination to salute.

He seemed so happy, and so exhausted. I'd recently walked through a crowd of people to shake the Chief's hand, but, regrettably, that time was to offer condolences at his Lieutenant's funeral. The Lt. also had a significant role in the jail project. He had worked for the Tribe for over 30 years. He was one of the only White Men to be truly accepted by this community. He was surely missed at this ceremony.

I explored some of the facility including the sterile, industrial-style inmate's quarters as well as various offices and transition spaces. It was quite impressive.

Finally, I joined everyone in the crowded dining hall, squeezed into a table for a quick bite, and then headed out to get some more work done. It's good to be seen, make some connections, and move on. *Lingering brews trouble.* It gives people something to talk about. It was part of The Code. I always tried to keep moving.

I walked out to my car and then drove to town to attend a few more appointments. It was almost the end of the day when I finally made it back to the office. My supervisor, Nervous Beaver, was there waiting for me. She asked me to come to her office, so I followed her in. One of the women from Human Resources was already seated in front of her desk. Nervous Beaver walked around her desk and sat down behind it without a word. She avoided my eye contact. She looked pale.

The HR representative introduced herself and told me the HR Director couldn't attend this meeting because her child had an appointment. Then she handed me a sealed envelope.

The gravity of the situation hit me. I felt insulted that the HR Director was not there personally. Like many other people in the community, we'd worked closely together both as co-workers and through my child welfare work.

The HR lady asked me to open the letter. I opened it, started to read it, and then stopped and asked my supervisor, "What's this about?"

She said she didn't know. I told her what it was about. She didn't look surprised, but she did look nervous.

My lip started to quiver. I pleaded to her, "You're supposed to do something or say something... *say something!*"

Looking down, she flatly stated, "I don't know what to do. I can't say anything."

I started to panic. I felt the urge to flee. I told Nervous Beaver I had some things to attend to, and I left. I walked out to my GSA, got in, and drove back towards town.

I knew I needed to leave that scene. I was struggling to face reality. I feared it was only going to get worse if I stayed.

I was in a mild state of shock. Fears were racing through my head. *Fuck! Now what? What the fuck am I supposed to do now? They finally did it. How am I going to tell India?*

Numerous times in the past I'd feared this possibility, but now the reality was staring me in the face. So many times I'd come home from work looking stressed out, and India would ask, "Did you lose your job today?" She asked me that dozens of times. The politics of my work were so extreme that I often found myself in the crosshairs.

For years I told myself if anything like this ever happened, Todd Smoke was going to be the first person I'd call. He was a Tribal Member, we'd been developing our relationship for over eight years, and I'd helped him out a lot over the years. His daughter had been removed from her mother and placed with him, and I was her social worker. She was a very sweet little girl about my son's age.

So, I drove my GSA back into town, pulled over, and looked up Todd's number. I took a deep breath, and then I called him.

He answered on the third ring. He asked me what was going on. I burst into tears. I could barely talk. In between sobs, I struggled to get the words out, "*I just got fired!*"

He responded with a low, grizzly bear tone, "I'm out on the water right now. Let me make some calls and figure out what's going on, and I'll get back to you." I made sure he had my contact info, and then we hung up.

I never heard back from Todd.

Moments after the call, my phone went dead. They'd shut it down. Well, jeez, I was officially fired, and I still had the car and the phone. I knew I needed to take them back to the office. I needed to face reality.

I took a few more deep breaths, gathered myself, and headed back to the office. When I got back to the Rez, I entered the dirt lot across the street from the casino, crossed the lot, and then drove down the row of modular buildings. I parked the GSA at the end of this row, directly in front of the Red and Clean

Café. I walked around the back of the Café to the Indian Child Welfare (*ICW*) modular, entered the building, and then walked down the hall to my office.

I took a quick look around the room. I couldn't even begin to think about packing up my belongings. I dropped the phone and keys on *my* desk, and then turned and walked out to the front reception area. I leaned into the doorway of Harmony's office (the voc-rehab lady), mustered up a smile, and thanked her. She smiled back and empathetically said, "I'm sorry."

I returned back across the gravel lot where I'd just driven in. In the summer this strip would become "Fireworks Alley" with rows of makeshift fireworks shacks lining the gravel parking lot. It's a very happening time at the Tribe—another chance to make money, and it's quite busy every day, all day, the week of the 4th. Of course, the real action happens after dark—the real *troubled* action, that is.

It was just after 5 p.m. The sun was setting. I was in shock. I hadn't even begun to digest what had just transpired. I just walked. I figured it was a more dramatic ending to my story, anyway.

At the edge of the lot, a dirt road led off toward land owned by the Army Base. The Indian Reservation bordered right up against the Army Reservation.

This dirt road paralleled the main rural highway that led toward town. The Army Reservation separated the Tribe from my little town. I could walk part of the way to town on this dirt road vs facing 50 mile-an-hour traffic, with no streetlights or footpath.

I could feel bombs exploding in the distance as I walked. Sometimes in the summer when the soldiers are training, it sounds like a war is happening right next door—machine gun fire and everything. (Well, at least, what I *imagine* war would sound like. I hope I never find out. Ultimate respect to our troops. *Never forget!*)

I walked up onto this dirt mound that covered a huge water tank. I stood there for a moment watching the sun set behind the trees. The orange and red sunlight glimmered through the evergreens lining the hill behind the casino.

I felt a surge of anger. I turned and looked back toward the Tribe. I clenched my fist down by my side, extended my middle finger, and then looked down at it pointing toward the ground. I imagined raising my middle finger at the Tribe and yelling, "Fuck You!!!"

Instead, I took a deep breath, unclenched my fist, and relaxed my fingers. I climbed down the other side of the mound, and continued walking down the dirt road.

I walked for about 100 yards before coming across an Indian man and a young boy who looked about ten years old. I felt a slight pause in my stride. They were just finishing some work on one of the more permanent firework shacks.

I continued walking toward them. I was just about to say hello, when the man quickly, aggressively advanced toward me and started shouting, "You get the fuck off my land mother fucker! I'll call Tribal and get you picked up!"

I stepped back from him and calmly said, "I thought this *was* Tribal land. I'm sorry. I was just trying to stay off the main road." I gestured toward the rush hour traffic speeding by.

"This is *my* land. You just get the fuck out of here *Mother-Fucker*, or I'm gonna—"

"You're gonna what?" I interrupted. I walked toward him and faced him. "Why you gotta be such an asshole about it? You could ask nicely, but you came at me with all this hostility. You've got a big stick up your ass. Fuck you!"

The boy pleaded, "Come on Uncle. Uncle…please…stop."

The man bellowed, "Look what you're doing to my nephew."

"Me? I was just trying to avoid getting hit by a car. I'm sorry if I walked onto your property, but you're the one having a bad influence on your nephew."

He reached down and picked up some rocks.

In disbelief, I questioned, "You're going to throw rocks at me now?"

He paused for a second, and then threw one, way off left.

I humbly conceded. "All right. I'll face the traffic." I turned toward the road to go, while cautiously watching over my shoulder to see if he'd throw another rock or try to attack me. He just stood there, so I headed towards the busy highway.

Then I heard it. "Fucking White Man!"

No, you didn't, I thought.

I know it sounds cliché, but I said, "Oh no you fucking didn't!", and I rocketed toward him like a linebacker. I got in his face and said, "Mother-Fucker, *You!* can get arrested. I can't. Tribal has no power over me. Fuck you and your frickin' stick up your ass!"

He raised his arms and moved in to attack. I gave him a hard shove, two hands solid into his chest, causing him to lose balance and stumble back. He regained his balance and then came at me again.

I shoved him again, even harder this time. He seemed stunned by my ferociousness.

I stated with conviction, "I don't need a reason right now!"

I knew I could destroy him. He knew it, too.

His nephew ran off.

He said, "Look what you did. You scared my nephew."

I said, "You scared your nephew you fuckin' dumb ass. You started this shit up…I just lost my fucking job!"

I burst into tears again.

All of a sudden, a change came over him. I could see in his eyes that I had gone from being *other* to being *brother*. We had found a Point-of-Connection. He knew what it felt like to be fired. He could relate to that.

He said, "I'm sorry, man."

"Fucking Tribe fired me after eight years."

He empathetically questioned, "My Tribe?"

"Yeah." I nodded my head while looking him dead in the eyes.

I sniffed and turned to go. I took a step, and then did a one-eighty and walked directly back toward him.

He reached out his hand, which I took, and then he pulled me into his chest.

We hugged.

"I'm sorry."

"I'm sorry, too."

I thanked him, and then turned to go.

I could hear him blessing me.

When I got to the road, I turned and looked back.

He was pressing his open hand against his heart and nodding his head. I put my hand on my heart, smiled, and nodded back at him. He blessed me again. I kept my hand on my chest as I turned to head up the road.

I carefully traversed the next six miles of dark busy highway to town. It was good for me to have the time to process what had just transpired—*all of it*. I felt emotionally raw. I also felt apprehensive about telling my wife I'd just lost my job.

When I got into town, I walked straight to my favorite pizza place, ordered some focaccia and a glass of wine, and then sat and digested my thoughts.

I felt hurt, confused, angry, and betrayed; but I also felt a subtle, emerging sense of freedom.

First Day on the Rez

I arrived at the Tribal Center for my first day of work and asked the two women seated at the front desk where I should report for duty. They both gave me a puzzled look, but another woman standing nearby said she knew where I needed to go, the Eagle House down on Lower Rez. She offered to get in my car and show me the way. She said she needed a ride down there, anyway. I accepted her offer, and we walked out to my car.

She directed me down the rural highway that ran through the Reservation, to a turn down Reservation Road, and onto another turn that led down a side street into the woods. This side road led into a residential neighborhood—Tribal Housing. The homes were modest, unparticular. It seemed like any other low-income neighborhood, except for the trash. I was overwhelmed by the amount of garbage everywhere. It was in the streets, in people's yards, and all around their houses. There was fireworks debris lining the roads, and it was the middle of December.

We wound through the neighborhood, and then she directed me down a dead-end street where we entered the last drive. We passed a basketball court and parked in the lot out front of a house *turned* Youth Center, presumably the Eagle House.

"We're here", the lady said, and we got out. She walked me up to the building, and I followed her in. I saw my new boss Stan standing in the kitchen, which was the common area of the shared office. He quickly introduced me to a few people who were hanging out. There was a hip young Black guy, an older Indian woman, a younger heavyset Indian woman, and a young Indian man.

The older woman greeted me, while never looking into my eyes. She averted her gaze whether I spoke, or she did.

The young man welcomed me, reached out his hand, and said his name was Hawk. He gave me a look that said, *You sure about this, man?*

The Black guy looked at me like I was crazy, but also gave me a welcoming smile, shook my hand, and looked me directly in the eye. He seemed very cool and very smooth, like black silk.

The younger, heavyset woman looked me up and down, scrunched up her nose, and then gave me a look that came to be known to me simply as *The Look*. It said, *You disgust me. I fucking hate you.*

I met her look of disgust with a smile (something my Master Drummer from Ghana had taught me to do in situations like this), while I shrunk up inside.

Then Stan directed me to come with him so he could show me around Lower Rez. I had worked briefly with Stan at my last job where I was employed as a children's community mental health counselor. I'd been working at that agency for years, whereas he'd just come from working at another tribe. He said he'd been fired for some "fucked-up shit" (*FUS*), and he seemed traumatized and angry. He was partly angry because he was making half his former pay working as a counselor. He was mostly angry because he felt like he'd given them everything, and in the end, he got screwed.

As we drove around Lower Rez, I asked Stan about the Indian woman who gave me the look of disgust. He replied, "That's Piggy, she's our secretary, and a Tribal Member. Listen man, Tribal Members are the only ones who matter around here. You get that, and you may just last a minute. Also, some Indians hate White people, some Indians hate Black people, and some Indians hate both. She's all right with Black people."

He continued, "Look man, the only reason you got this job is because they don't have a Tribal Member who wants it. You gotta deal with some bullshit working at the tribes, but the Indians pay way better and work way less. They don't want to do Indian Child Welfare, so they bring in outsiders to do their dirty work. So, if you can weather the politics, there's some sense of job security, because no one wants to do this shit. On the other hand, because of the politics of our jobs, most everyone will want us fired, eventually."

Next Stan said, "As for social work on the Rez, man it's different here. Now listen, you're gonna remove some kid from his momma because she's on drugs, and she's off fuckin' the dude with the drugs, and she's been leaving the baby with different unsavory people, or unattended at home, right? Well, you're gonna remove this child and place him with his grandma or auntie on Monday, and on Tuesday you'll see him riding around the Rez with his momma again."

Now I must admit, I was pretty much in shock by this point. I'd done direct care and counseling with children and families for many years, including lots of work with at-risk youth. I had considered my former jobs to be a type of social work, but I didn't realize that for my new gig I'd be taking people's babies away or having influence on whether or not they could see their children. I really had no idea what actual social work entailed. I'd only heard about CPS coming out to investigate people for beating their kids. I was naïve when it came to issues of neglect resulting from drug abuse. I was definitely aware of addiction and drug abuse, but the idea of someone being so drugged-out that they couldn't parent their children was foreign to me. I had certainly never taken away anyone's child, let alone an Indian person's child, which felt incredibly loaded given the horrible history between Indian and White people. I had no clue what I'd gotten myself into.

Stan saw the look of terror and confusion in my eyes. He said, "Don't worry buddy, you got a great bedside manner. You'll do just fine. Besides, when they don't have a use for you anymore, you'll be gone anyway. They don't even need a reason. They've already got one—*you're White!*"

We drove around the Rez for quite a while that day while Stan continued discussing the fundamentals of doing social work in Indian Country. He showed me where many of our clients and their extended family members lived. He also identified the homes of local drug dealers and pedophiles, most of whom were Tribal Members.

He reminded me of a seasoned war veteran confidently discussing how to survive on the front line. He definitely seemed traumatized and a bit calloused, but he also still had passion for working with Indian children and their families. He knew we were fighting a war, but not against any visible enemy. We were fighting against drug abuse, depression, hopelessness, and apathy. This community was struggling to overcome the effects of attempted genocide, and we were assigned to man the trenches on a front line where we were not welcome—at least, not yet.

Jeez, talk about Denzel's *Training Day*, or Fulghum's book *All I Really Need to Know I Learned in Kindergarten*...I learned most of it that first day.

Most everything Stan told me that first day would eventually come true. Now, his statement about custodial grandparents letting the parents take the kids when they weren't supposed to was actually an exception to the rule. The truth is it's the grandmothers and aunties who raise most of the children on the Reservation—definitely the majority of the children in ICW—and the majority of these sweet, dear women are doing everything they possibly can to keep their children safe.

However, there were a few families I'd end up working with for years, who had grandparents and extended family members who not only did drugs with the kids and harbored them when they ran away from their placements or treatment programs, but also enabled their "relationships" with pedophiles and drug dealers. Don't take my word for it. Just ask the kids. If you take the time to get to know them, they'll tell you *everything*.

Day 2—My People Will Judge You

On my second day of work Stan told me, "I need you to transport a male teenager from our program. He's from another tribe, but our department has taken jurisdiction of his case. It's a long story with lots of political bullshit. Anyway, just take him shopping wherever he needs to go."

"He's got his own money," he said. "He gets a *percap* from his tribe. Just make sure you get receipts."

That was the first time I heard the word *percap*. It was also the first time I heard about a Tribal kid having his own money from casino profits.

I drove to where Stan said to pick him up out in front of Hawk's house. I saw a pretty big Indian teen watching me roll up in Shiva my '94 Legend coupe. He was checking out me, and my car. I pulled up beside him, asked if he were Rupert, and then introduced myself as Scott, Stan's new worker. He looked into my car and checked the back seat (kind of like a cop would), and then opened the door and got in. He settled into the passenger seat, looked me up and down, and then told me to head to the drug store.

He asked if he could change the radio station. I always allowed the kids to choose the music when they rode in my car, at least at first. I made sure to get my turn playing music I wanted to hear, and music I thought they should be exposed to.

Rupert asked, "Why you workin' on the Rez?"

"I needed a new job."

"Why with Indians?"

"I used to work with Stan, and I guess I'm interested in learning about your people's culture."

He looked at me like an innocent little lamb. Then he smiled as he peered down the road and said, "My people will judge you. When they get to know you, they'll take it back."

I'll never forget those words. The greatest single piece of wisdom I heard while working at the Tribe came from this young man.

Although, I wish he'd said, "*If* they get to know me."

I took Rupert up to the pharmacy, and then to run a few other errands before taking him back to the Rez. I dropped him off at Hawk's house, and then I headed back to the office. I felt good about my interactions with him. It seemed like we'd laid some good groundwork.

When I was getting out of my car at the office, I noticed a plastic bag on the floor behind the passenger seat. I grabbed the bag and looked inside to see if Rupert had forgotten something. He had. *Damn*, I thought. He'd left his purchase from the pharmacy—a pill cutter. I thought *Damn* because I knew I was about to ruin my initial progress at building a relationship with this young man. I knew because he was going to be pissed when I reported it to Stan, as it was my duty.

Funny thing, when I told Stan about it, he seemed more disappointed with me for reporting it than he was with Rupert for buying it. I guess he also knew I'd just blown any chance of connecting with him, because now Stan would have to address it, and Rupert wouldn't be happy with me. Sure enough, he barely acknowledged me during our next encounter. I'd certainly lost ground, and I didn't get another chance with him after that. Not so much because he was unwilling, but more because he just landed himself into one kind of trouble after another. Eventually, he got himself locked up for a very long time.

It was a good reminder about the importance of building the relationship first. You can't address issues with people or try to hold them accountable for their behaviors if you don't have a relationship with them. Or rather, you won't be successful in your intervention, and you'll sabotage any chances of building a deeper relationship. Had Rupert and I been through it a bit, had I been there to support him more often than to hold him accountable, our relationship would've had a chance. But starting out on that foot, it was doomed. Had I to do it over again, I would've addressed the issue with him myself, and then asked him how he wanted to handle it with Stan. That would've given him an opportunity to take ownership for his decision. It also would've taken me out of the position of reporting his behavior. Our relationship would've had a chance.

Day 3—Meeting the ICW Committee

On my third day I met Stan at the office first thing in the morning. He gave me a list with about twenty children's names on it. He told me this was my new caseload, and the children were my clients. Although a great deal of our work was with their parents, the cases were identified in court by the children's names. I'd come to find that in many cases we rarely saw the parents even though we were consistently making *active efforts* to engage them. Many of them were basically AWOL, off drugging—living the lifestyle that lured them away from being parents. Most of the children on our caseloads were being raised by their aunties and grandmothers, just as their parents had been raised.

Stan told me we'd be staffing cases with the ICW Committee that afternoon. The Committee was made up of adult Tribal Members from the community, mostly Elders, as well as a representative from Tribal Council. He said that we met with them once or twice a month to report our progress on our cases, gain the Committee's approval for child placements, and see if they had any recommendations for services for the parents or the children. He said I should just observe because he was already having challenges working with them.

What struck me most about that meeting was the behavior of the representative from Tribal Council. I didn't know much about TC, just that they were the governing body of the Tribe and that they were made up of elected Tribal Members. I assumed that as an official representative from the Council, she would represent herself and Tribal Council, well, professionally.

I watched in dismay as this woman spoke horribly about Stan, as though he wasn't even present, and she was sitting right next to him. She never once looked at him, so I wondered if she even knew he was the "Stan Brinks" she was going on about. It was kind of weird. With a condescending tone, she said, "Well, if Stan Brinks would do what he's supposed to do to properly run the ICW program, we wouldn't be having these problems. If Stan Brinks had any clue about the needs of this community and our children, then he'd make better decisions regarding the welfare of our vulnerable children. If Stan Brinks..." She continued to degrade him.

He just sat quietly. No one else at the meeting even seemed fazed by her behavior, but I was completely stunned. I found it extremely odd that she would talk so disrespectfully about Stan with him sitting right next to her, and yet behave as though she didn't know it was him. I wondered if it was cultural or just this woman's behavior. I wanted so badly to tap her on the shoulder and say, "Hey, you know that's Stan sitting right next to you?" Yeah, she knew.

That meeting was also the first time I heard Tribal Members talking about *culture*. They used the term very specifically to talk about the *old ways* of Tribal people. It was clear from their dialogue that they only considered culture to include traditional activities and behaviors such as hunting, fishing, and making regalia. As an anthropology student, I'd learned a different definition of culture. I was taught that culture was everything about a people, including the way we speak, dress, eat, think, express ourselves, etc. I really wanted to interject in the conversation and attempt to broaden the definition. For instance, I would have suggested that Indian men driving pick-ups with bumper stickers that say, "Indian Truck" is also part of Indian culture, but Stan had made it clear, *just observe*.

At the end of the meeting, Stan introduced me to the woman from Tribal Council, Nancy Waters, aka "Councilman Auntie". She didn't give me The Look, but she did look at me as though she questioned my motives. I tried to make small talk with her, exude enthusiasm about working at the Tribe, and show as much respect as possible. She seemed interested in talking to me about my reasons for taking a job as an ICW social worker. Since she also seemed to really hate Stan, he stepped away and gave us some space to talk. I told her I'd worked as a counselor and caregiver for children for the last eight or nine years and my path had led me to work with her Tribe. She talked briefly about how important it was for me to understand what had been done to generations of Indian children, and how important it was for me not to contribute to those problems, but to be a solution.

I enthusiastically asked her, "What's your role on Tribal Council?" She seemed guarded about it. An awkward silence ensued. I tried to acknowledge her role as a leader in the community, and then I asked her, "Who do you admire in the community? Who do think are the great leaders at the Tribe?"

She scrunched up her brow and made an innocuous comment generalizing about all the leaders in the community, and then she walked away. To me it seemed like a simple and appropriate question to ask a government leader. She seemed defensive and even a little perturbed. "*O-K*", I said to myself, not really sure what had just happened.

Stan came over and got me and introduced me to the other members of the ICW Committee. Three of them were Elder women who all looked at me with disappointment. One woman around my age was friendly and encouraging. She seemed to understand me from that first meeting. She knew I had a good heart, and I was there to help if I could. She could feel it. I could feel it in her, too. She was there for the children and no other agenda. Over time we'd forge a great working relationship. Her name was Flower.

The next day Stan called me into his office and said he'd received a call from Councilman Waters. Apparently, she had told him, "Tribal staff have no business asking personal questions of Tribal Council Members."

I had praised her and given her an opportunity to talk about someone that inspired her. I was genuinely interested in learning about the leaders in the community from one of their own. I had assumed that she'd love to answer this question, because it was a question I'd love to expound upon. It turned out to be another good lesson for me. In fact, it would become part of The Code: #2. *Don't name names, even in praise.*

Trash Day

As I drove in each day, it was hard for me to see all the trash around the neighborhood. I wondered how long it would take for me to get used to it. I made a comment to Black Silk about it, and he responded, "You think the yards and streets are bad—wait until you see the inside of some of the homes."

I knew that part of my job was going to involve doing child welfare investigations. I'd never done any investigations before, and I was feeling anxious about the prospect of having to evaluate the condition of people's homes. Now don't get me wrong, not everyone's yards were trashed. There were some properties that were completely immaculate. And then there were others that had garbage strewn everywhere. However, for the record, the nastiest houses I've ever been in belonged to White people—some of them my good friends.

One of the houses I passed everyday had a large mound of garbage bags piled up outside the kitchen window. I imagined they must just open the window and throw the bags out as they filled up. I guess you could say it was convenient—who wants to take the trash out, anyway? What I didn't realize yet is that several times throughout the year, the Tribe provided huge dumpsters at various locations throughout the neighborhoods, and people would load 'em up. From that perspective, it made a little more sense. I mean, why pay for garbage service or fees at the dump when you knew the Tribe would pay for it eventually?

It wasn't the mountain of garbage bags I found unnerving; it was the household trash in the streets and yards that drew my attention as I drove by each day. It looked like a pack of wild dogs had ransacked the neighborhood, knocking over garbage cans and dragging debris everywhere. Ever see a Rez dog? That hypothesis was probably not that far from the truth. Ok, but it looked like they'd struck months ago, and, yet, there never seemed to be a cleanup effort. Well, not for a while, anyway. Eventually, the streets and many of the yards did get cleaned up, but not until many years after I started.

Well, I say you can be part of the solution or part of the problem. I chose to try and be part of the solution. I had visions of recruiting some of the youth from our program to lead a community cleanup project, but I knew I wouldn't have a chance until I'd built relationships with them, and even then, it seemed unlikely. So, those fourth and fifth days I spent about two to three hours each morning picking up trash around our office. On the second morning I had filled a small dumpster just from trash around the yard. I was sure people thought I was crazy, or worse. I imagined people thinking stuff like, *Who does he think he is? Does he think he's gonna come and clean up the Rez?* Honestly, I didn't care. I couldn't stand the sight of all the trash, so I was, at least, going to clean up an area I felt somewhat responsible for.

Once I cleaned up the yard, I started delving into the edge of the woods around the property. It was even worse. I had barely scratched the surface with the yard. I found old wheels and tires, broken electronics, household garbage, an exercise bike—all kinds of rubbish was lurking in the shadows. I started to feel grossed-out by it. I was also starting to worry about picking up dirty needles or finding a dead body or something. Maybe that sounds a little paranoid, but when they discovered human remains buried on the Rez years later, my concerns were affirmed. I'm just glad I wasn't the one who found those bones.

When Stan arrived to work during the late morning on my second day of cleanup, he had a big grin on his face. He pulled me aside and said, "Hey man, you're not hear to change things. Don't get any grandiose ideas about making this place into what you want. It's not about what you want—it's about what they want. You'll see once you start doing investigations. You can't compare this community to your standard. You have to let them set the standard. You may have to lower your bar a bit on some things, but just remember, we're here to make sure the kids are safe. That's the most important thing. Well, keeping them safe, and keeping them with the Tribe if at all possible. The last thing we want to do is place an Indian child in a White home. Even if we pursue all other avenues, and there's no alternative options, we'll still have hell to pay if we place any of our kids with White folks."

He continued, "We wear several hats here. One hat is investigator. It's the toughest part of our job—having to remove a child from his parents or extended family members. It'll make you sick until your skin gets a little thicker. You just have to know deep down that the only time we do it, we do it for the safety of the child. It doesn't matter what anyone here thinks about us. I sleep good at night knowing I rescued a child from a situation of severe neglect. By the time we get the call, the extended family has pretty much tried everything to get the parents to stop using drugs. We're their last resort. Everyone in the community will know there's a problem before anyone ever calls us, so no one's surprised when we do show up.

"Another hat we wear is that of social worker. Investigation and placement are just the beginning of a case. Then we have to ensure that all of that child's needs are being met by their placement custodian, while simultaneously working to engage the parents in the court-ordered plan. You'll be good at this part because you're already good at working with kids and families. The goal of every plan is family reunification.

"Now, there are a lot of people who can do social work, and do it well, but as I already told you, doing social work in Indian Country is different. You have to not only become a great social worker, but you also have to become an even better diplomat, really, a politician. Because doing social work on the Rez means managing and surviving tribal politics, and that's some seriously fucked-up shit.

"Just imagine what happens when you remove a newborn baby from his young meth-addicted parents, and one of them has an uncle or auntie on Tribal Council. What do you think is the first thing they're gonna do? That's right, they're gonna call Uncle, and the case will quickly become all about you. Even though everyone in the community will already know that this young couple has serious drug problems, that Tribal Council Member will be calling you out on the carpet, so you better have your ducks in a row.

"Now that leads me to the next skill you must be really good at. You gotta document everything. You wanna survive out here for a minute, you better cover yo' ass, because being an ICW worker means you've got a big target on your back; well, that's in addition to the target you already have for being White.

"All right man, that's enough for now. You go do what you're already good at: go meet some kids on your caseload and start developing some connections. It'll take time. They'll be way more cautious and reserved than what you're used to. You'll start meeting some of the players when we go to court next week.

That's when you'll learn about what's going on with the cases. For now, go spend some time getting to know the kids."

Stan certainly had a way about him. He was a tall man with a fatherly demeanor. He'd bend down and put his arm around you and make you feel like you really mattered. He was good at that. Unfortunately, when he was playing politics, which seemed to be a great deal of the time, he'd also tell you whatever he thought you wanted to hear at that moment. That is, he'd tell you whatever he thought you wanted to hear that would ultimately benefit *his* political agenda. That was not my way, nor would it ever become *my way*.

Eventually it would catch up with him (we reap what we sow), but even then, he'd laid enough, uh, political groundwork, that even while they were catching up with him, he had plenty of cards to play. The way I see it, when you tell people what they want to hear vs telling them—as India likes to say—the *microscopic truth*, it always raises unrealistic expectations. Expectation is the greatest source of frustration. Stan never seemed worried about the potential consequences of playing politics, of raising people's expectations, unrealistically. Quite the contrary, he always seemed acutely focused on the hustle.

As I drove into work the next morning, I pondered what Stan had said the day before, "...you're not here to change things." I passed through the roundabout casually eyeing the junkyard to my right. Then I headed down the street that led to our office, noticing that mound of garbage bags piled up in the driveway to my left. At the end of the street, I cringed at the site of fireworks debris and household garbage lining the road. And then I pulled into our driveway and immediately felt a sense of pleasure and accomplishment as I witnessed the results of my own hard labor from the previous couple days. My scenic drive through Tribal Housing wasn't any better, but I'd made an impact on the property surrounding our office. It was unmistakable—*someone* had clearly made a difference, even if only a small one. I felt inspired by my own efforts. I felt a sense of relief as I drove up to the office and witnessed a nice clean yard and driveway.

And then I saw it—a big fat bag of fast food garbage sitting right in the middle of the lawn in front of the Eagle House. I had a vision of someone tossing that bag from their driver's window as they drove through the property. I had a gut feeling they'd done it just for me—a message to the White Man who fancied cleaning up the Rez. I heard my own words echoing in my head, *Does he think he's gonna come and clean up the Rez?* It felt like a small slap in the face.

And then I realized, *Wait a minute, I shouldn't take this personally.* They probably weren't even thinking of me when they littered that garbage. They probably didn't even notice that I'd cleaned up the property around our office. They were probably just doing what they normally did—dinner was finished, so they simply tossed the trash out their window.

I left that bag sitting where it lay. It was still lying there months later along with all the other trash that accumulated around the yard.

Tony

When Stan arrived to work the next Monday morning, he told me to come outside so we could discuss a case while he had a smoke. "I want you to go out to Shiny Days Elementary and see Tony. He's one of the kids on your caseload. Tony, his brother Randy, and their sister Shannon are staying with their grandma Vera. I'm getting reports that their mom Terri is drinking and using again and staying at the house, too. She's not supposed to be at the house. Her behavior is erratic when she's drinking. We need to get her to engage in services and set up supervised visitation. Go to the school and interview Tony. If you find out from him that Terri's been staying at Vera's house, you gotta go by the house and see if she's there."

"What do I do if I find her there?"

"Just tell her I said she knows she's not supposed to be there, she needs to go up to Substance Abuse and make an appointment, and then she needs to come see us. If she needs more information than that, tell her I said I've been hearing things about her from her family." He gave me directions to the house and sent me on my way.

I was familiar with the school. I'd been there numerous times before in my previous position. I still had the direct line for Beth the school counselor, so I called ahead to announce myself. "Hi, it's Scott. I'm working for the Tribe now in their ICW program. I want to come out and see Tony Smith."

She responded with polite salutations, and then said, "The Tribe is lucky to have you. I hope you can last out there—I hear stories. We have several Tribal children here and, honestly, I don't understand many of the decisions the Tribe makes regarding their welfare."

"It's all new to me. Honestly, I don't know what to tell you. I have no basis to respond."

"Let's talk about it again in a few months. I look forward to hearing your insights. Otherwise, my office is always available for you, Scott. When you get to the school, you can have one of the front office staff call Tony's teacher, and she'll have him sent to my office. I still have that small kid-size table with games and paper and stuff. You can use anything you want. I'll be busy running groups in the library." I thanked her and then headed out to the school.

When I got to the school I went straight to the front office, reintroduced myself to the staff, and then asked them to have Tony sent down to Beth's office. I signed in and then headed down there myself. I entered the room and found a seat at the small table where I could sit facing the door.

Tony entered a few minutes later. He scanned the room and seemed disappointed with what he found. I imagine he thought he was coming to see Miss Beth. It's a little early in the story for a montage, but feel free to imagine dozens of my initial meetings with the children going something like this.

I offered him a seat at the table across from me. He sat down and lowered his eyes.

I said, "Hi, my name is Scott Strider. I'm a social worker from the Tribe."

He looked up when I said, "the Tribe", and then lowered his gaze again. I offered him a piece of paper and some crayons, and then I grabbed some for myself. It's always easier talking to kids if you are doing an activity like coloring, shooting hoops, or riding in the car. Some of my best counseling sessions with teenagers transpired while driving around and listening to music. It takes the focus off the discussion.

He took the paper and started casually drawing a few lines. I asked him, "Do you know what a social worker does?"

Without looking up, he half questioned, "ICW?"

"Yes, I'm from ICW. I work with Stan." He glanced up for a moment again when he heard Stan's name. I asked again, "Do you know what a social worker does?"

"Take people's kids away when they're on drugs."

I wasn't sure how to respond to that. I said, "It's my job to help make sure that the children from the Tribe are safe. I work for the Tribal Member children. I work with their parents and their family members, but I work *for* the children, well, and the Tribe, of course. I'm your new social worker." I gave him my card, and said, "You can call me anytime and leave a message if you need my help, or if you have any questions for me. If you lose my card, everyone at the Tribe knows how to contact me. Your teacher, Miss Beth, and your grandparents all know how to contact me, as well."

We colored for a little while in silence. Then I continued, "So how are things going at your grandma's?" He looked up with a bit of surprise, and then went back to coloring. I asked again, "How are things going at your grandma's house?"

"Fine," he answered.

"How are your brother and sister doing?"

"Fine."

"How's your grandma doing?"

"Fine."

"How's your mom doing?" He stopped coloring and looked up at me. I said, "I was just wondering about her. I heard she's not doing very well."

Tony casually responded, "She's doing all right."

"Have you seen her over the last few days?"

He seemed puzzled by my question. "I see her all the time...when I'm not in school."

"Oh, ok," I replied, and we went back to coloring again. I finished with, "Well, I just wanted to introduce myself, see how you and your family are doing, and let you know how to reach me."

"Can I leave now?"

"Yes," I responded.

Tony walked out without another word, leaving his drawing sitting on the table. I put away the paper and crayons, wrote a quick thank you note for Miss Beth on my picture, and then put both of our pictures on her desk. I signed-out at the front office, said goodbye to the front office ladies, and headed for Grandma Vera's house, which was about five miles down the road from the school.

I located the address easily with Stan's directions. When I arrived, I found an older, single-wide trailer in a wooded residential neighborhood. The only vehicle present was a broken-down Mustang in the driveway. All the windows in the trailer were covered by blankets.

I went up the stairs to the front door and knocked. Immediately, I heard someone exclaim, "God damn it!" After a moment, a woman stepped out the door and demanded, "What do you want?" She was a stocky woman, somewhat masculine, with broad shoulders and thick wrists. I could smell strong alcohol on her breath. It was just after 10:00 a.m.

"My name is Scott Strider. I'm from ICW. I work with Stan. Can you please tell me your name?"

She had a cordless phone in her hand. She put it up to her ear and said, "It's *ICW*. I'll call you back." She stated the three letters "ICW" with contempt. Over time I would get used to hearing people say it like that. ICW has a horrible reputation in Indian Country. She replied, "I'm Terri—not like it's any of your business. What do you want?"

"I'm your children's new social worker. Stan told me to come by your mom's house, and if I saw you to introduce myself and go over a few things with you."

"Oh yeah, like what?" She took a step towards me and glared into my eyes.

Dutifully, I said, "Stan said to tell you that you know you're not supposed to be here, you need to go up to Substance Abuse and make an appointment, and then you need to come see us."

She started turning bright red. She looked like she was about to boil over. She took the phone and threw it against the trailer wall, busting it into pieces. Then she turned to me and yelled, "You tell that fucking...[n-word] boss of yours that he can go fuck himself! I don't have a drug problem. He wants to fuck with me and take my kids...fuck him! We'll see what Council says." She entered the trailer and slammed the door behind her. I heard, "Those god damn mother fuckers! Who do they think they are?"

When I got back to the Eagle House, I went straight to Stan's office and told him what had happened. He stretched back in his chair and clasped his fingers behind his head. He contently stared at me while a satisfied grin spread across his face. Then he started laughing. "Man, I knew she was there. She'll still be there tomorrow, but at least she knows that we know, and that we'll be keeping closer tabs on the house."

He continued, "So, no shit, she busted the phone right up against the side of the house? You know that was Vera's phone, right? Man...well, maybe she'll get down and see Elk at Substance Abuse. She needs an assessment. She thinks because she's not on meth like most of our parents, that, by comparison, her drinkin's not a problem.

"Her drinkin's a bigger problem than a lot of people's meth addiction. As long as she can still be at the house and see her kids whenever she wants, she'll never get clean. We need to keep on her with active efforts—ICWA demands it. [Indian Child Welfare Act of 1978, pronounced ick-wah]. Keep checking in with Tony down at the school, and next time you go, introduce yourself to Randy and Shannon. I want you to keep some pressure on Terri. The kids will be sure to tell her every time you go down to the school. I want you to stop by the house from time to time as well, but I doubt she'll answer the door again now that she knows who you are. Hopefully, she'll get down to see Elk, but don't hold your breath."

Tribal Court

It was time to go to court. Stan told me I'd find the entrance to the court at the back corner of the gym in the Admin Building. I drove up there and parked outside the gym. When I entered the building, a familiar smell struck me immediately—formaldehyde. *How strange*, I thought, *why would their gym smell like my middle school science lab?* That smell was unmistakable. I had detested it the entire time we dissected frogs. I came to find out that they held Tribal Member funerals in the gym.

A couple children were running around the edge of the gym while a few men and boys played basketball. There was a conference table with office chairs set up on the stage at the back of the gym. A couple men were sitting up there as well.

I walked along the wall that led towards a single door at the back corner of the gym. I knew that the double doors at the opposite corner led to the front desk for the Tribal Administration offices where I had initially presented myself on my first day of work.

I opened the door and peered in. I saw a short hallway with two small offices across the hall and a larger room at the end of the hall that appeared to be the courtroom. A woman stepped out from one of the offices and asked, "Can I help you?"

"Hi. My name's Scott. I'm the new ICW worker, and I'm here for court."

"Please have a seat out on the stage, and someone will be with you shortly."

"Ok, thanks." I rounded the corner, headed up the stairs to the stage, and found a seat.

The two men were sitting up there talking. They both appeared to be Indian men, roughly in their thirties. One of them was heavyset with long hair pulled back in a ponytail. The other one was tall and thin with buzzed hair. They were sharing stories about their attempts to get through some kind of event or experience. I wasn't sure what they were talking about, but it sounded like a rite of passage or something. I wondered if they were talking about *Vision Quest* or *Sun Dance* or some other kind of traditional ceremony.

The bigger man said, "Yeah man, I just went for my third time."

The skinny one chuckled. "Third time's a charm." He continued, "Joe's there now. He's on his fifth."

The first said, "Shit, that's nothing. I've met guys who've been way more than that."

They continued sharing stories about themselves and people they knew from around the Rez. They sounded like they were comparing attempted conquests, like how many women they'd tried to sleep with, or how many times they failed at an important task. It was familiar and foreign to me at the same time.

Then the big guy said, "Yeah, I've been three times, but I've never made it through. I bailed on that shit every time."

The other man just nodded.

They both sat quietly for a few moments staring at the floor.

The skinny guy finally said, "I'm gonna go again—once we get through fishin' season. I can't afford to go now, but I'll go once fishin's over."

"Yeah," the first agreed. "I'll go again, too. Maybe when Hell freezes over." They both broke into laughter. I couldn't help but giggle a little myself, and I didn't even know what they were talking about.

And then it became obvious to me. I felt naïve for not initially recognizing what they were talking about...going to *treatment*. Of course, I'd heard about it from television and movies, but I'd never personally known anyone who had gone to drug treatment. For these two guys, it was rather ordinary.

White Man

Stan directed me to go to the River Tribe's Reservation to attend court for some children who might be coming into our program. The River Tribe's ICW program had requested our presence at the hearing because, although these children were living on their reservation, they were Tribal Members from our Tribe.

I donned a button-down shirt and a tie, the standard male social worker attire for court, and headed down for the hearing. The River Tribe also has a casino. You didn't have to see the casino to know it existed. It was evident by all the new construction on the Reservation. Pre-casino tribes hadn't experienced the multi-million dollar makeovers. This tribe had a brand-new health center, a beautiful new administration building, and other ongoing construction.

I found the court building, parked, and went in to check the docket for the location of the hearing. The front entrance and the waiting area were already packed with people. One of the court clerks came out and requested that most of us wait outside near the entrance since all the noise was distracting one of the judges. She said we'd be notified before each new hearing.

I went outside with a few dozen other people and waited to be alerted. I was just standing there, minding my own business when I heard a man behind me utter, "*White Man*." He spoke these words with the same contempt I'd felt from Piggy on my first day of work. His tone said, *I detest you. You don't belong here!*

I knew it was directed at me. I didn't have to look around to see if there was another White Man who may have been the intended target. Part of me wanted to turn around and stare him down. Part of me wondered if he would have said it if he'd known I was there to help Indian children. Part of me, once again, shrunk up inside. I felt intimidated and uncomfortable.

And yet, I imagined this man had probably been at the receiving end of such derogatory remarks (and far worse) more than I would ever know. I was being educated in that moment. This was the first time I'd heard these words spoken in this way towards me. Of course, I'd heard them said in movies before, with the same contempt, but never directed at me. Never personal. Until this point in my life, I'd been sheltered and protected from this type of hostility (for the most part).

I imagined how many millions of Black, Brown, and Native people endured similar experiences (and far worse) on a daily basis—infinite times throughout their lives. I went from feeling intimidated to feeling shame. I felt shame for what I represented in this community—shame for the feelings that my white skin elicited. Then I felt compassion for what minority people experience in this country throughout their lives. Most White people never have to experience this. Most White people don't understand what it feels like to be harshly judged simply for *what vs who* they are. The tides are turning though.

During my sixth-grade social studies class (early eighties), I remember thinking that eventually the entire world was going to hate White people. We were studying slavery and the Native American genocide. I remember my teacher reading about how Indians were given the smallpox blankets. I remember thinking how horrible it was that White people perpetrated this kind of behavior on indigenous peoples all over the world.

I felt the same way about what was done to Black people during slavery. It would be another decade before I realized that slavery mentality had continued beyond Emancipation. As a child I was aware of racism, but I had no idea of the depth of it in our society. I had no idea that Black people still couldn't own homes in "progressive" cities throughout the U.S. well into the Sixties. I had no idea that some Tribal people currently suffered discrimination in even worse ways than the days of cowboys and Indians. I was unaware that Black men had more to fear every time they left their homes (and even when they didn't) than any other man on this planet. I didn't know that a DWB (driving while Black) was a criminal offense in many towns and cities throughout the "United" States—an offense that can get them shot! Black people do deserve justice and equality.

One of the traditional dances I learned from my Ghanaian teacher C.K. was *Sowu*, the Dance of Life. This dance teaches children to respect the Earth and their elders. It teaches that if a community works together, it can accomplish any task. It also teaches that if you have goodness in your heart, you can travel throughout the land and people will receive you with goodness. C.K. used to say,

"If you have goodness inside you, you can travel throughout your community and people will receive you with love. You can travel to Japan, or Russia, or Mexico and people will welcome you."

I believe the truth to be closer to, *If you have goodness in your heart, and the people whose community you are traveling in have goodness in their hearts, then you will be received and welcomed with love.*

Conversely, *It doesn't matter if you have goodness in your heart if the people you meet are full of hate.*

I'm not saying that everyone I met on the Rez was full of hate towards White people. In fact, many Tribal people were open and accepting. I am saying that there was a significant contingent that was extremely resistant, evil hostile, and they had no problem showing it.

Hating me based solely on my genetic makeup is no different than hating a Black or Brown or Red person based solely on theirs. Racism is racism. When will the cycle stop? I hate you because you hate me because I hate you because you hate me…ad nauseam. We all know the saying, *An eye for an eye makes the whole world blind.* It won't stop until we stop it. No one is going to do it for us. It takes a community to accomplish any task.

Wanda

I was sitting at my desk one afternoon when I heard a knock at my door. I said, "Yes. It's open."

The door opened, and one of the women who worked with the youth program stepped in. "It's me, Wanda. I wondered if we could talk for a minute."

"Sure," I answered, "come in and have a seat."

She walked in and sat down at my co-worker's desk and turned so she was facing me. After a heavy sigh, she said, "I don't know what to do."

I asked, "What's going on?"

"My children are all angry at me for my drug past. They haven't forgiven me. They keep bringing up things I did years ago, and now their children—my grandchildren—are in ICW, just like my kids were when I was using drugs. They blame me for their problems. They blame me that their children are in ICW." She started crying and stated again in desperation, "*I don't know what to do.*"

I got up and handed her a box of tissues. Then I sat back down at my desk and waited to see if she had more to say. After a few minutes I asked her, "Have you forgiven yourself?" She stopped crying and looked up at me—dead in the eye. I said, "How can they forgive you, if you haven't forgiven yourself?"

"How can I forgive myself? I don't deserve to be forgiven. I chose meth over being a mother to my children, and they're still suffering for it."

"Whether they ever forgive you or not, I think it's important that you learn to forgive yourself. If we can learn to forgive ourselves, we can learn to forgive others, and then, hopefully, they can learn to forgive us, too."

"Why would they forgive us, just because we forgive them? How would we make them change?" she challenged.

"Well, we can't make them change, but we can inspire them to change."

"And how do we do that?"

"We live it and exemplify it. By it, I mean forgiveness. We start with ourselves. My teacher C.K. Ganyo taught me, 'Charity starts at home.' That means we must take care of ourselves before we can take care of anyone else. C.K. also used to say, 'The first thing we must learn to do if we want to be loved is to love ourselves.' It's the same principle. If you want your children's forgiveness, then you must first start with forgiving yourself. When you begin to embody it, they will see it and feel it in you. How can they not forgive someone who embodies forgiveness? Especially their own mother. Every child yearns to have a loving relationship with their mother. Once you learn to forgive yourself, then you can also learn to forgive others. Learning to forgive yourself is the hardest part."

She started crying again, but this time she was also gently smiling. She sat there lightly weeping for a minute, and then she got up, came over and gave me a hug. She said, "Your teacher C.K. sounds like a very wise man. Thank you so much for listening to me," and she left.

The next morning Stan called me into his office as soon as he arrived at work. I came in and sat down in front of his desk. He gave me a look of disappointment. Then he said, "I got a call from Council last night. You had a complaint."

I thought for a moment about what had transpired over the last day or two. I couldn't think of anything I did wrong that would warrant a complaint to Council. I simply responded, "What was the complaint?"

"Well," Stan replied, "apparently, you've been counseling Wanda. She went to Tribal Council to complain that her co-worker was trying to counsel her. Councilman Smith quoted some policy about staff respecting confidentiality, and that sort of thing, and then he said you shouldn't do it again."

At no point did Stan ask me what had happened. The only thing that seemed to matter was that he got a call from a Council Member, and he wasn't too pleased about it. He continued, "Listen man. I told you that half this job is dealing with politics. You'll get more complaints. If you're doing your job, you're gonna get complaints. The question is, do you have your ducks in a row? Do you have your paperwork in order? Do you know what's going on with your cases? Until you figure out some guidelines for how to survive out here, you're gonna deal with some bullshit. Hell, you'll be dealing with political bullshit as long as you stay here—just get used to it."

Todd Smoke

During my second week Stan told me we could authorize free gas for our ICW clients up at RezGas. We just had to meet them over there and sign for their purchase in a special white binder they kept at the register. I ran over there to meet parents from our program four or five times during the next week.

On my fifth visit to RezGas there was a big bear of a man standing behind the counter. I asked him for the binder. He said, "Why do you need it?"

"I'm from ICW," I told him, "and I need to sign the book for gas for one of my clients."

"You can't do that."

"What do mean, I can't do that? I've been doing it every day for the past week. Who are you, anyway?"

He leaned into the counter and bent down until he was towering over me. In an authoritative, grizzly bear tone he stated, "Todd Smoke—Tribal Member."

I felt compelled to salute, but I just stood there.

Then he leaned in a little closer, thrust out his big paw, and demanded, "Who are you?"

In a meek, mousy voice, I mumbled, "My name's Scott. I'm the new social worker for the Tribe," as I put my hand in his giant paw.

He grabbed my hand, gave me a firm handshake, looked me dead in the eye, and said, "Welcome to the Tribe, Scott." He held my hand and my gaze for a moment before he released his grip and lightened his demeanor. Then, in a matter-of-fact way, he said, "You can't get gas the way you're going about it. Let me show you the proper procedure so nobody gets into trouble."

I felt embarrassed for assuming I knew more about the procedure than a Tribal Member employee who worked at the store. I also knew that Todd had just reinforced the local hierarchy. His body language and tone gave the clear message, *You're in my territory, don't forget it*. I hoped this wouldn't warrant another complaint to Tribal Council. Todd smiled as he helped me out, and then he wished me well on my way.

The next time I went into RezGas Todd was friendly and helpful. I sensed that his posturing during my previous visit wasn't personal but territorial. He was a big bear in a small forest, and I was a newcomer—a small one at that—who didn't know the territory. His imposing presence certainly commanded my attention.

Todd and I had many conversations over the years. One time he invited me to sit and eat with him at a Community Dinner, and we talked as men. Eventually, I would become his daughter's social worker due to issues with her mother. As far as I could tell, Todd was a good man and a good father. I appreciated his counsel, and over the years I felt we developed a kind of friendship.

One time I showed up to the Harvest Festival at the Tribe's organic farm feeling stressed and anxious. Yep, they've got a 100-acre organic farm, too. I didn't feel comfortable going in, so I stood outside and made phone calls. I always had numerous calls to make. There were usually two to three social workers at the most, and once again, I was the only one in the department, so I had all the cases. None of my co-workers managed to keep their jobs. Doing social work anywhere is challenging. Doing social work in Indian Country is downright treacherous.

I didn't feel comfortable going into the dinner because I had two inherent strikes against me. I'm a White Man, and I was an ICW Worker. Most people on the Rez didn't want to see either one coming. Well, unless of course, they're coming to the casino.

So, I'm standing outside the harvest dinner, pacing around, making calls—feeling anxious about going in—and I feel this tug at my shirt. I look down and it's Todd Smoke's little girl, Elaina. She gave me a big smile, said, "Hi, Mr. Scott," and then grabbed my hand and told me, "come in to eat."

My heart melted.

She used to melt my heart on a regular basis. Sometimes by singing young Justin Bieber (we both loved *My World 2.0*) and other times by watching her make pictures for her mother while I visited with her at daycare. Mostly she melted my heart by simply accepting me and recognizing that I was there to help her. Of course, I'm sure her dad had a lot to do with that.

I followed her into the Long House. It was cool. They had a bunch of traditional dishes with squash and greens and fresh veggies. They even had Elk Soup. The veggie dishes were great. The soup tasted horrible.

I stayed for a few minutes, walked through the crowd, and then disappeared (4th rule of the Code—*Keep your head down; don't attract attention*).

That little girl made it all worthwhile. The kids always made it worthwhile. Well, the children, the aunties, and the grandmothers.

Lester

When I arrived to work one morning, a man was sitting in my office. I said, "Hi, good morning. Can I help you?"

He responded in a markedly slower cadence, "I talked to Stan yesterday, and he told me that you're my new worker. You're Scott aren't ya?"

"Oh, ok. Yes, I'm Scott. Scott Strider. What's your name?"

"I'm Lester. Stan told me to go see Elk at Substance Abuse, and then come see you. I saw Elk yesterday afternoon. I'm scheduled to go to treatment next week. I want to set up some visits with my son Kenny... the State took him from his momma. Stan said that you'd help me get his case transferred to Tribal Court."

"Ok," I replied, "I'm glad to hear you're going to treatment—assuming that's something you need. I'm happy to help you set up visits with your son. I've seen his name on my case list, but I don't know any details about your case yet. Are you required by the court to go to treatment, or is that just something you feel you need to do?"

"I'm not required to do anything by the court," Lester replied. "His momma is court-ordered to do stuff. I just need to get clean so I can be a good father to my son. She lost him to CPS, and I want to get him placed with me."

"Is substance abuse treatment the only thing Stan said you need to do?"

"Stan said I need a parenting class and some specialized training because Kenny has special needs. Stan said I could take parenting classes at my treatment program, and you'll bring Kenny down to see me every week while I'm there. He said that once I get out of treatment and get a place, then you'll set up the other services for me and Kenny."

"How long do you expect to be in treatment?"

"Elk said I need to go for three to six months 'cause of my current drug use. It depends on how I do in the program. I'm ready to do it so hopefully it won't take that long. Most people aren't ready for treatment. Most people go kickin' and screamin'. My son needs me. His momma failed him. She's not going to get him back—she has too many mental problems. I have my own problems, but I know I can do whatever you want so I can get my son."

"Ok. Well, it's not totally up to me. Certainly, I must monitor your progress and make recommendations to the court, but ultimately, it'll be up to the court. Well, really, it'll be up to you. You do what the court requires, and the ball is in, well, your court."

Lester gave me a confused look. "I just told you I'm not required to do anything for court. His crazy-ass momma lost him. Stan said if I do all the things you ask, then I can get my son. What do you mean the ball's in my court?"

"Have you been part of the court process at all?"

"I just told you that his *mother* lost him to CPS."

"So, to be clear, you may not be aware of any court requirements because you haven't been involved with the court process. Once you get involved, then you'll most likely have some requirements."

"That's not what Stan said. He said I just need to do what you tell me, and I can get Kenny placed with me!"

"Lester, just hang with me for a minute. You have my commitment to help you. I just need to know what I'm getting into. I'll talk to Stan about how to help you transfer your case to Tribal Court, and I'll clarify with Stan if you're going to have court requirements once that happens. If you haven't been involved with the court process until now, the court may see you as an absent father."

"I'm *not* an absent father!"

"I'm not saying that you are, but the court may see it that way. You'll have to make your intentions of getting your son known to the court, and they may have requirements for you. Until I see the court order, I won't know for sure. Either way, I'll help you to the best of my ability.

"Let's assume the court will want you to do some things, like go to substance abuse treatment. When I say, 'the ball is in your court', I just mean it'll be up to you to complete any requirements. No one else can do it for you."

"Oh," Lester replied, "that part makes sense."

I continued, "So, if Stan said you can get your case transferred to Tribal Court, then you may also have to do some things the ICW Committee recommends."

"I have to do what the ICW Committee says, too? Dang, they're going to make this really hard."

"Well, my understanding is that they have influence over your case. If they think something is important, then most likely the court will adopt their recommendations as part of your plan."

Lester scowled. "Wait a minute. Who said anything about adoption? Maybe you don't know this yet, but we don't do adoptions here at the Tribe."

"No, no…I didn't mean to imply that your son would be adopted. I just meant that the court would make the ICW Committee's recommendations part of your court plan. The court will adopt their recommendations, so to speak."

"Oh, well don't talk about adoptions. That's what they do in State court. We don't do that in Indian Country. I'm not losing my rights to my son–*no matter what!*"

"I'm sorry, Lester, if I misspoke. I didn't mean to imply anything like that. I'll try not to use that word again with you. I see how that kind of language can be confusing."

"So, when can I see Kenny?"

"I just need to review your file and discuss your case with Stan, and then we should be able to set up some visits."

Lester stood up, clenched his jaw, and stared down at me. With a raised voice, he said, "What do you mean you need to discuss my case with Stan? I already told you I talked to Stan, and he said I could get visits once I met with Substance Abuse."

"I'm just trying to cover my bases. Again, I apologize if I'm making this more confusing than it needs to be. Frankly, a lot of this is new to me, and I want to make sure I'm doing everything I'm supposed to do. I'm here to help you, but I want to be sure I don't make promises I can't keep. If we end up working together for very long, you will see that I'm careful not to make guarantees or promises about such serious life issues."

"Life issues? What are you talking about? I just want to get clean so I can have my son."

"Lester, I can be a bit wordy. I'll try to simplify. Let's take this one step at a time. You said you're going to treatment next week."

"Yes," Lester replied.

"You want visits with your son before you go?"

He nodded.

"You need me to set it up. Is that correct?"

"Yes."

"Ok," I said. "I still need to learn some details about your case. I haven't met your son yet. I don't even know where he's placed. As you probably know, I'm new here. I just want to make sure I'm doing my job correctly."

Lester regained his composure. "Everyone knows you're the new ICW worker, Scott. Kenny's placed with his auntie. Stan has her number."

"Ok," I replied.

He sat back down. "I just need you to go pick him up so we can have a visit."

"I got it."

Then he leaned in. "Let me ask you this: why are you here? I mean, why did you come work for the Tribe?"

"Do you want the long or short answer?"

Lester shook his head. "Just give me the short answer."

"I needed a new job."

He chuckled. "Ok, fine Scott, give me the long answer."

I was starting to feel like I should wrap up this meeting before I said something else to piss him off. Lester was a little intimidating. He was a big guy with muscular arms, and he had a look in his eye kind of like a veteran who'd seen too much. I could tell from our dialogue that I needed to be careful what I said. My usual style of communication wasn't working with him. Against my better judgement, I went into the longer answer to his question.

"Well, you see Lester, you may not know if from looking at me—I mean my buzzed haircut and office clothes—but I'm really kind of a hippie."

Lester gave me a confused, but curious look.

"You see, I think everything in life happens for a reason. I believe we're faced with each other right now for a reason. I have something to learn from you, and hopefully, you have something to learn from me. I don't think it's mere coincidence that I'm your new social worker, or that you're my new client. I take my work very seriously—my role as a social worker and child advocate. I believe I'm here because it's in my highest good for my spiritual development. I believe the same about you and Kenny. I believe that we are in one another's lives so that we can learn from each other and help each other to grow. I obviously don't know what you think about hippies, but I claim that label with pride." I paused to get a read on him—to see how he was reacting to my statements.

"Pride, huh? Go on."

"Well, the stereotype of a hippie is a tree-hugging, weed-smoking, liberal. I admit that I do love trees, and I've certainly smoked my share of weed, but that's not what being a hippie is about to me. To me, hippies recognize the deep connection of all life. Generally speaking, hippies are not racist, sexist, or consumed with greed. To me, being a hippie means recognizing the value of all people. It means respecting the Earth and one another. It means recognizing that we're here for a purpose."

"What kind of purpose?"

"I suppose that depends on the individual. My purpose is to provide for my family, manifest my visions, and hopefully help inspire others to do the same."

"Those are all worthy goals, but, damn dude, I've got enough work to do on myself. I'm not trying to inspire anyone else to do anything. Good luck with that."

"You might be surprised by your ability to inspire others."

"Who am I to think that I can inspire other people or help them with their problems? I have enough problems of mine own."

"We all have problems, Lester. That's part of my point. It's important that we recognize it and focus on improving ourselves. When you focus on working on yourself, you naturally begin to follow your passion and start making positive changes in your life. People can't help but be inspired by your example. Even if it's not your intention. Passion is infectious. People are inspired by those who live their passion. Frankly, humanity needs more people like that. People with purpose."

"I'm definitely not thinking about helping all of humanity or anything like that. Besides, the world's pretty fucked-up. I think it's beyond helping. But you seem to think that mankind has a chance."

"This world is a fucked-up place, no question there. We're plagued with problems, hate, and polarization. The world needs more people with love in their hearts, compassion for others, and an awareness that we're all in this together. I think humanity does have a chance. I think that mankind can evolve if people start focusing on the well-being of others as well as themselves."

"Yeah, most people are just looking out for themselves."

"People think that their actions don't affect others. Or they don't care. What we do affects us personally at the deepest levels, and it also affects others the whole world over. Hippies recognize this. They recognize that we're all connected, and our behaviors and choices can have global consequences. Hippies also understand that we all have work to do in order to evolve our consciousness. So, yes, I do believe that mankind can evolve because I know that the right catalyst can trigger global change."

Lester was smiling. "Well, I wouldn't call myself a hippie, not by any means, but what you describe sounds like Tribal people. I am Tribal, and proud of it. I can relate to most of what you said, especially respecting the Earth, but I don't know what you mean by polarization."

"Lester, the whole world is sick with polarization. Black vs White. Liberal vs Conservative. Christian vs Muslim—opposite ends of the pole, or so they want us to believe."

"Who wants us to believe?"

"The Powers that Be…*The Evil Ones*…well, really, the Scaredy Cats—the people running the world."

"What?"

"Yep. The bankers and oil tycoons and big corporations—or the beings controlling them—that ultimately make all the real decisions affecting our lives. I call them the Scaredy Cats because they're terrified of us learning the truth. They know that if we really understood their agenda, we'd organize and stop them."

"It sounds like you're talking about some kind of New World Order or something?"

"Maybe."

"So, what's their agenda supposed to be?"

"Control. They want to keep us ignorant. They want us polarized. They don't want harmony on this planet. The inmates are easier to control when they're fighting—when they're focused on rebelling against each other vs rebelling against the dominant paradigm, or better yet, creating a new one."

"What *inmates* are you talking about?"

"We're the inmates. I say it's better that we create a new paradigm than rebel against the existing one. What we resist persists."

Lester laughed. "This is the first time I've ever heard a White person talk like this. You sound like you're including yourself with the minorities, the Brown and Red people of the world. What's a dominine paradant?"

"Dominant paradigm. That is the structure of life that is propagated, uh, promoted by the Powers that Be. It's the story we've all been fed. We've all been manipulated to believe that the way the world is now is the only way it can be, or, at least, the way it should be. Of course, you know as a Native person that it hasn't always been like this. People used to be in harmony with the Earth. People used to be aligned with their true purpose. Lester, contrary to what *They* want us to believe, we're all in this together. They want us fighting. They want us consumed with fear. They want us at opposite poles on everything. We are easier to control—to manipulate—when we're, well, polarized. If we are fighting with each other, then we aren't paying attention to their evil deeds. Divided we fall."

Lester scoffed, "That sounds like conspiracy theory."

"Exactly!" I proclaimed. "That's exactly what they want us to think: froofy, New Age, conspiracy-theory ideology. That's all part of their programming. It's easier to dismiss our thoughts when we are labeled as conspiracy nuts. There's intense social pressure regarding just that. Think about how people respond when anyone starts talking about aliens or government cover-ups. They immediately label the person a conspiracy nut. Really, it's quite brilliant. They have us so well-trained, that if anyone attempts to promote free thought or question authority, then they're labeled a nut, or even worse, a terrorist."

Lester gave a big, deep belly laugh. "Scott, you crack me up. I've never heard a White Man talk like this. Don't get me wrong. Indians know we can't trust the government. That's been proven again and again. But to hear a White person talking like this...well, really it's kind of strange and refreshing all at the same time."

"Well," I said, "to be honest, I learned a lot about the topic of polarization from my wife India."

"Really, is she into this stuff?"

"Well, I wouldn't necessarily say that she's into conspiracy stuff, but she knows a lot about spiritual development."

"That's cool."

"Yeah, it is cool. Really, India's been my greatest teacher when it comes to spiritual stuff. I've learned all my most profound teachings from her. She reminds me almost daily that we create our reality. She taught me the most powerful breathwork exercise I know. She was one of my first yoga teachers, *and* she's been an incredible, honest, and beautiful mirror all these years. Sometimes, *painfully* honest."

"You're lucky to have her in your life. It's good she's so honest with you. We all need someone to help hold us accountable." He chuckled. "I probably would've got in a lot less trouble over the years if I had someone like her in my life. Where did she learn all that stuff, anyway?"

"Man, she's studied all kinds of holistic disciplines from Ayurveda to Thai massage, naturopathic medicine, developing the brain, you name it. She has teachers of her own to credit. Maybe you can ask her about them someday."

"Maybe I will. She sounds pretty awesome."

"She is awesome. One of our greatest points-of-connection is through West African drum and dance. We spent years studying and performing with my Master C.K. Ganyo in his West African drum and dance troupe. India is a beautiful dancer. C.K. used to say that it was a marriage between the drum and the dance. When you see India and I drum and dance together, you will understand."

"Where's C.K. from?"

"He was from Ghana. He passed a few years ago."

"May Creator bless him. So, he taught you guys tribal drumming and dancing from Africa, huh?"

"Yeah, he taught us all kinds of stuff. You know, lessons about life, rhythms, songs, and traditional dances. He taught us that the knowledge and history of his people was in their music, specifically their songs, drumming, and dance. He even used to say that the true *Trinity* is drumming, song, and dance. All people everywhere share in *this* Trinity."

"Tribal people sure do, that's the truth. We know the power of the Spirit Drum, and we know that our sacred songs are healing. We also know our history through our traditional dances and regalia. White Man didn't take everything from us. I agree with C.K. that all people share in drumming, song, and dance. At least, Tribal people. He sounds like he was a very wise man. Although, I don't agree with his definition of the Trinity."

I smiled. "Maybe you will in time. Thank you for your kind words about Uncle C.K. He *was* a great man.

"So anyway, when India and I first got together over a decade ago, she taught me that there's love, and there's fear. We are always operating from one place or the other—there's no gray area. She taught me that we must always discern which place we are acting from, and self-correct if possible. Polarization is all about fear—fearing other people…fearing other ways of thinking and doing things…fear of the unknown."

"And them fearing us, too," Lester commented. "Fearing our ways of thinking and doing things."

"Yep. Both sides fearing each other. So, consider this. If our focus creates reality, or to be more specific, if our thoughts are manifested from our consciousness and driven by our will…"

"Kind of like Green Lantern's creations," Lester interjected.

"Yes, like Green Lantern's creations. If we focus on fear, then that's what we'll create. If we focus on abundance, then *that* it what we'll create. The Evil Ones know this truth, and they use it against us."

"What do you mean, 'they use it against us'?"

"Just think about the news. It's full of fear, and hate, and lack. It's the same with television advertisements. You watch them for very long, and the pharmaceutical companies will have you believing—*fearing*—that you have all kinds of different diseases and disorders. Of course, they've got the solution, or so they want us to believe. We've all gotten so used to it that we barely even question it."

"I have to admit," Lester reflected, "I usually feel pretty depressed after watching the news."

"We must be able to separate ourselves from all of it, stand back, and take a look with a fresh perspective as the *Observer*. When you become the Observer and stand back and watch it all from an unembedded perspective, the manipulation and brainwashing are all too obvious. Woops, there's another buzz word, *brainwashing*. We're so well-programmed, that when we hear that term, we also think *conspiracy nut…paranoid…delusional*."

Lester asked, "Have you ever thought about how they call television shows 'programming'? It's like they are telling us right to our faces that we're being manipulated."

"Ah, now you're catching on. Really, programming is a better term, anyway. If you simply think of our brains as computers—well, they are—then it's easy to see how programmable we really are."

"You mean like a processor and memory and stuff?"

"Yes, sir. And just like a computer, our brains run on default programs and factory settings that have been *installed* by a very effective socialization paradigm dictated by the Powers that Be."

"In English."

"Basically, they've manipulated us to think as they want us to, and they have built-in, firewall-like protection that prevents us from even questioning our programming—from thinking outside the parameters that they set up. Until we wipe these default programs clean and reprogram ourselves with new code—*conscious code*—then, frankly, we don't have a chance. We'll just continue to be automatons for the dominant paradigm—cogs in wheels that they designed."

Lester retorted, "That sounds pretty depressing, Scott. To think that we've all been manipulated into thinking a certain way, believing in certain things that *They* want us to believe…what hope is there in the world you describe? I'm sorry to say it, but it really does sound like conspiracy theory."

"Everything's on a continuum, Lester, like love and fear. Actually, let me correct myself, at least, philosophically speaking. We put everything on a continuum. Really, everything just exists; we're the ones who apply value to it. So, on our self-made continuum, we have love at one extreme, and fear at the other.

"Conspiracy theory's no different. There are theories that aren't that extreme, and then there are others that cut deep into the heart of our core beliefs. And you're right. It is depressing. Years ago, I did quite a bit of research into conspiracy theories. Some of it was easy to swallow."

"And some of that stuff sounds crazy as hell," Lester interjected. "I've heard those stories about reptilians controlling the world with their blue-blood Illuminati and their pedophile sex rings. That shit made me sick to even think about."

"Yeah, some of that stuff is sickening. I reached a point in my research where I became kind of depressed. I started to see evidence of corruption, lies, and deceit everywhere I looked. I had to stop focusing on it."

"It does make you sick when you look beneath the surface at all the horrible things the government has done, and probably continues to do. It's hard to trust that anything they do is really in people's best interest. Especially when you look at what they've done to my people."

"Frankly," I said, "I had to stop reading about aliens and secret societies, and cover-up after cover-up, and put my focus on things I actually have some control over, like my attitude. I still delve into the conspiracy stuff occasionally, like the alleged faked moon landing or *9/11* being an inside job, but mostly I choose to focus on myself. That is, I focus, as Gandhi said, on being the change—being a solution."

"Faked moon landing! *9/11* an inside job? Scott, your rabbit hole *is* deep."

"That's not even the deep stuff," I chided. "Haven't you heard any of the theories about *9/11*—about the trillions of dollars that went missing from the Defense Department the day before the attacks? Or how about the evidence of explosive residues that were found at the foundations of the Towers?"

"Yeah, I've heard about the explosives, and how the collisions alone wouldn't have collapsed the buildings."

"And what about the implementation of the *Patriot Act* right after *9/11*? They had that thing locked and loaded—ready to take away more of our rights and freedoms. Do you remember what also happened that same year?"

"It seems like there was a bunch of shit that went down during that time. What are you talking about?"

"Jr. Bush was put into office by the Electoral College even though Gore won the majority of the popular vote. That was still an ongoing controversy prior to *9/11*. After *9/11*, we never heard another word about it in the mainstream media. The American people came together to support their president against our common foe—just as expected. Give people a common enemy, and you can align them. Make people afraid, and they'll eagerly give up their rights. We lost a bunch of rights with the implementation of the Patriot Act, but it aligned us all right. Again, I say, we're so easy to manipulate."

"Man, I haven't thought about that election in a long time. Are you saying that it was a fraud?"

"Now Lester," I joked, "you know that's an entirely different tangent."

"But is that what you're implying?"

"Frankly, I think every presidential election is a fraud. Have you ever heard of the idea of covert vs overt control?"

Lester cocked his head and squinted at me. "No. What's that about?"

"Keep in mind, our whole line of conversation has been regarding how easy we are to control. I think I got this theory from David Icke, the *master* of extreme conspiracy theories. He's the one who writes about the reptilian agenda. Now, what do you think would be easier to control, a population run by a dictator, or a population that thinks they are a democracy?"

"I'm not sure what you mean. What are overt and covert controls?"

"A dictator is an example of overt control. It's obvious who's in control. It's obvious who to rebel against if there, was indeed, any kind of rebellion. With covert control, such as a democracy, the Powers that Be allow the people to think that they have a choice in their leadership by allowing them to cast their vote in a *supposed* democratic election. When, in actuality, they chose both the candidates."

Lester got it. "So, with a dictatorship, people would be more likely to rebel because they're being forced to comply, and they have a figurehead or government to rebel against. But in a covertly controlled democracy, they think they have a choice, so they're less likely to rebel."

"You got it," I replied. "I think that America is not truly a democracy. I think that They led us to believe we have a choice in matters, so that we're less inclined to rebel against our supposed leaders."

Lester reflected, "So, if we've all been manipulated so badly, and we're stuck in some kind of default programming, how do we break free of it? How do we bring about change in the world?"

"How would you answer that question, Lester?"

"In my heart, the first thing I need is Christ, and the next thing I need is my culture. And, if I understand you correctly, you're saying that the most important thing is not that we change the world around us, but that we stop giving in to fear, and we change our own attitude."

"Yes, Lester. I think that change starts at home. By home, I mean inside of us. We have to be the change we want to see in the world."

"Like Gandhi said," Lester chimed in.

"Yes, like Gandhi said. The amazing thing is that change can be triggered by something as simple as a mantra or a focused breath."

"What's a mantra?"

"A tiny bit of conscious code we reprogram our brains with."

"Oh, I think I know what you mean. Like an affirmation we say to ourselves until we believe it."

I nodded. "Until we *are* it."

"*And*," Lester stated, "we have culture."

"Culture is the cure," I agreed.

"Lester, we all have a lot of work to do to change this planet—to evolve the consciousness of the masses. For now, let's focus on getting you some time with your boy before you go to treatment. I know we can accomplish that together. We can discuss how we're going to save the world once you get back from treatment. Of course, I have some radical thoughts about treatment too, but I'll save those for another time."

Lester stood up and reached out his hand. We both smiled and shook hands while looking each other directly in the eyes.

"You're a strange bird, Scott. But somehow you give me hope."

With that he wrote down his phone number, asked me to call him when I had scheduled a visit with his son, and he left.

White Bison

Early on during my time with the Tribe, I attended a local gathering where White Bison was the keynote speaker at the event.

White Bison's talk was educational and inspiring. I agreed with his perspective on personal responsibility and victimhood. He talked about the *Generational Trauma* that plagues Indian Country, trauma that's passed from the first generation of trauma survivors to their descendants and respective offspring. He talked about how all Indian people today are suffering from Generational Trauma. He also spoke at length about addiction and recovery. During his talk White Bison said, "Addiction and envy are tearing apart Native America."

That statement struck me. I was already aware that Tribal communities suffered from drug and alcohol addiction; it was his comment about envy that caught my attention. I found it both surprising and confusing.

I asked Lester about White Bison's statement a few days later during our drive to pick up Kenny.

He responded, "Rats in a barrel."

"Rats in a barrel?" I asked, "What do you mean?"

"No one on the Rez wants anyone else to succeed. Everyone's jealous of his neighbor. If someone starts climbing the Totem Pole, then someone else wants to pull them back down, just like rats in a barrel."

"Misery loves company," I said.

"Yes," he agreed, "misery wants everyone else to be miserable."

This concept reminded me of rule #2 of the code: *Don't name names, even in praise*. It's difficult to praise anyone in Indian Country without eliciting envy; it will likely make others jealous. I could better understand why Councilman Waters was so resistant to name people whom she thought were great leaders in the community.

"Well Lester, as we discussed recently, there's love and there's fear. Envy is obviously a form of fear—a form of lack. People feel envy when they're afraid there's not enough for them, or they can't have the experience themselves if someone else is already having it or *gets* to have it before them. They fear that if someone else succeeds, then they won't be able to succeed. Or maybe they just think they'll never succeed, and they're jealous of those who do."

Lester nodded. "You do understand, Mr. Strider."

"This is a universal phenomenon. People everywhere are suffering from lack. We've been conditioned to believe that our lives are limited. Really, our lives are limitless!"

"Try telling that to an Indian."

"Honestly, Lester, I'm not really sure how to respond to that statement. My spiritual beliefs are being challenged by your reality as an Indian man, and it's very well possible that you will not agree with my perspective. Shoot, I may not agree with it after considering your position. I just hope you're not offended. It's not my desire or intention to offend or belittle you."

Lester reassured me. "It takes quite a bit to offend me. I don't imagine you'll be calling me a *featherhead* or anything like that?"

"Not even close. In fact, that's the first time I've ever heard that term."

Lester chuckled. "Well, I've heard it enough for both of us—how 'bout that!"

I smiled and shook my head. "No comment."

Then I continued, "Ok, so here's the underlying premise of what we've been talking about so far...*our thoughts create reality*. What we focus on is what we will manifest. So, how does this relate to lack and limitation?"

Lester thought for a moment. "If we focus on what we don't have, or what we can't do, then we'll create a reality where we don't have enough, or we can't do what we want."

I nodded. "The only true limits (spiritually speaking) are the ones we place upon ourselves. We can believe that other people put them there, but really, if we accept limitation, then it's our own responsibility."

"That sounds a little too idealistic for me. I mean, you're talking to an Indian Man who's experienced the limitations of the White World firsthand. I don't think it's just because I *believe* the limitations are real that they affect me. I believe they affect me *regardless* of what I think about them.

"Consider what's been done to generations of my people. We've been stripped of our culture, our values...our very self-worth. Are you telling me that these horrible things happened to Indians because we accepted them? Millions of my people died fighting their White oppressors because they did not accept the limits that were placed upon them."

"I understand what you're saying Lester, well as much as a White Man *can* understand. Perhaps I am too idealistic. I do believe that if we truly focus on something, we can manifest it. I'm not saying there won't be challenges and hurdles along our path, but I am saying we must believe it's possible if we're to ever take that first step. If we cower to our perceived limitations, we'll give up before we even begin. As long as we accept limitations, we will be limited. As long as we accept that the only way to live is the way that we've been oppressed and manipulated into believing, then that is how we will live. I'm suggesting that we continue to question our limits, and preferably—without bringing harm to us or our loved-ones—we conquer those limits."

"You haven't lived in a Red Man's skin. You have ideas that are not realistic for Tribal people."

"You're correct. I haven't lived in a Red Man's skin—not that I remember, anyway. And I'm making a broad generalization regarding the nature of reality, namely, that we have some say in how it unfolds.

"It's very challenging to accept these ideas when you consider what has happened, and what continues to happen, to the oppressed peoples of the world. This perspective suggests that we're all responsible for what happens to us. It suggests that we're not victims. This concept is very controversial and difficult to comprehend, especially when you consider it in reference to slavery, and genocide, and child molestation."

Lester challenged, "Are you saying that it's Native people's fault that we've been persecuted and oppressed by the White World?"

"Lester, I believe in reincarnation. I believe that we've come to this world and others, literally thousands of times—maybe millions—inhabiting just as many bodies and experiences. When you look at life through this lens, it makes more sense of how seemingly horrible things can happen to good people. Who knows what we did in our past lives? Who knows what spiritual baggage we're carrying, and what issues we need to work out in this lifetime so that we don't have to keep repeating the same mistakes and reliving the same horrible sagas? Some people call it karma. I don't know about karma, in fact, I don't even really know if reincarnation exists, but I can say that this perspective resonates with me, and it makes so much more sense than any other spiritual philosophy."

Lester looked curious and angry at the same time. "You haven't really answered my question."

"I've answered it. I just don't think you like the way I've answered. I'm choosing not to single out an entire race of people as being guilty of anything, but rather to share a general spiritual hypothesis about all of us. Namely, that we all create our reality."

"So, you *are* saying that Native people are responsible."

"I'm saying that everyone is responsible for their creations. No exceptions. No discrimination."

"Whatever, dude. That's fucked-up."

"Lester, I'm not trying to push these ideas on you or anyone else. I'm simply sharing my perspective. I don't expect you to agree with it, nor do I intend to use this premise as a basis to judge an entire race of people. My point is less about reincarnation, and more about personal responsibility when it comes to our spiritual evolution."

"So, what is your point?"

"Bottom line, I know it's important that we question and challenge our core beliefs, as difficult as it may be. Shoot, who wants to find out a belief they've built their whole reality on is false? Think *Matrix*. How revolutionary was it for Neo to learn that his reality was manufactured, and he was actually plugged into some machine being, *yeah*, programmed with what to think and believe? Such an awakening could clearly shatter our whole sense of self. Wouldn't it be worth it though if everything we'd been taught to believe was a lie?"

"Scott, I get your point about people buying into a false story of reality. Who knows what truths the government is covering up? I do think that we are being brainwashed to some degree or another. But it's kind of fucked-up for you to imply that Native people are responsible for what has happened to them. I find it offensive for you to even suggest such an idea."

"I'm simply proposing that we're *all* responsible for what happens to us, and I realize how sobering and humbling, and, yes, potentially offensive this perspective is. It's also very empowering. It's humbling when things don't go our way, but very empowering when they do. It gives me hope to think that I have some say and responsibility in my evolution…that I may actually have some control over what happens to me, or what I manifest in my life."

"That's pretty deep, Scott, but I think you are minimizing Native people's struggle when you say, 'it's humbling when things don't go our way'. I think most people would agree that genocide is a little worse than *things just not going our way*."

"I apologize. I didn't mean for it to sound like that. I meant to say something like, 'It's humbling and even demoralizing when we suffer and struggle in our lives.'"

Lester stated with conviction, "Well, nothing's going to change if we don't challenge the status quo. The current paradigm, as you call it, it set up to hold minorities down."

"Lester, there are Indian and Black and Brown people who are challenging the limits of the dominant paradigm. There are White people doing it, too. They're challenging the oppression and hate that has proliferated on this planet for so long, and they're bringing about change. Change begins in our minds and our hearts. As long as we think change is impossible, it won't happen. As long as we blame others for our situation, it won't change. We become stuck in victim consciousness. When we embrace the possibility of change…when we're willing to question our core beliefs and take responsibility for our growth, then we open our reality to a new experience. We open to the ability to create change."

"I guess I understand what you're saying. It's hard not to feel a bit reactive and get emotional about it, but, deep down, it makes sense. It makes sense that we need to take more responsibility for our personal growth. We can't expect anyone else to do it for us. But, honestly, I wouldn't even know where to begin?"

"All creation begins with a thought, and it ends with doubt. Even the *Bible* says creation began with a word. What precedes a word, but a thought? We must believe that change is possible, or it will never manifest. If we doubt our ability to manifest a new paradigm, then we'll remain prisoners to this one."

"How are we supposed to do that, though? Create a new paradigm?"

"With our thoughts. But let's take it a step further. What precedes our thoughts? *Breath*. One of our most powerful tools to manifest change in our lives is breathwork. It's not only our main source of fuel, but it literally keeps the spirit in the body. Stop breathing for too long and where does the spirit go? Well, I don't know where it goes, but I know it doesn't stay in the body."

Lester expounded, "I don't know anything about breathwork, but I agree that my people have some great leaders who are beginning to bring about change. They're bringing change because they have a vision, a thought as you say. Some of them are really beginning to make a difference. The problem is that many of my people are so stuck in their fear that they're sabotaging the efforts of the people trying to help. I thought about what you said about polarization. There's polarization happening right here on the Reservation. It's happening between *Big Family* and *Little Family*."

"Big Family and Little Family?" I questioned. "Please explain."

"Big Family sits on Council. Big Family gets the best jobs and most of the funding that comes to the Tribe. Their companies are awarded the contracts for new construction projects. Big Family makes sure their family members remain in positions of power, while members of Little Family are looked down upon, and they're not able to get the best jobs or access to all the government grants the Tribe receives. There are Tribal Members here who are getting rich and powerful, and there are others, like my family, who never seem to get a chance. We don't have the same opportunities as the members of Big Family."

"Lester, I think your teaching about Big Family and Little Family will help me to better serve the Tribal families I work with. Although I'm surprised to hear your perspective, it helps me to understand some of the dynamics I've already witnessed at the Tribe. As for my perspectives on reality, I don't claim to have all the answers. And I do realize how offensive it may sound for me to imply that we're all responsible for what happens to us, especially given what's been done and continues to be done to the oppressed peoples of the world. I just know we need to be asking the right questions. More importantly, we need to be willing to consider the possibility that we're wrong about our core beliefs."

"What good will it do to question our core beliefs, but drive us crazy?"

"It's part of our healing to question our core beliefs—to free ourselves from some of those beliefs. We are our worst judges, and wardens. We imprison ourselves with some of our beliefs. We even imprison others.

"I met this hippie guy last summer at Heaven Hot Springs, and he gave me a teaching on this very topic. He asked me, 'What do you have to be good at to put the right sequence of letters together to form a word?' He assured me that it wasn't a trick question."

"What'd you answer?"

"What would you answer?"

"Spelling."

"Yep, casting spells."

Lester leaned back and scrunched his brow.

"And what do we form when we put together a complete set of words usually conveying a question, statement, or exclamation?"

"That's easy. A sentence."

"That's right. We make a sentence with our spells. Or, more precisely, we sentence ourselves and others with our spells."

"That's interesting. A sentence, like a curse or judgement."

"Language is powerful. Our thoughts are powerful. Our thoughts are greatly influenced by our beliefs. We sentence with our thoughts...our spells...our beliefs. It serves us (and others) to be more conscious and deliberate with our thoughts and our words, and more accountable for their effects."

"Some people are just unwilling to see things from another perspective. They don't care how their thoughts affect other people. They think they're right no matter what."

"I have my own definition of a fanatic," I said. "To me a fanatic is unwilling to consider the possibility that they're wrong. In my opinion, fanatics are very dangerous people."

"Fanatics from any religion are dangerous."

I agreed. "Fanatics from any group that push their agenda on others."

"So how do we know to ask the right questions?"

"We first have to be willing to hear the answers, or more importantly, we have to be willing to accept that the answers may be true. When we focus on evolving our minds, the questions will come to us. *Focus creates reality.* If we focus on our evolution and quit running the factory-installed programs, then we can at least clear some drive space and start asking some new questions."

"The things you're saying about people not being willing to consider the possibility that they're wrong—that makes sense. People have been wrong about all kinds of things over the ages, like the Crusades and the Witch Trials. My people have literally been massacred because of the White Man's beliefs. We do need to challenge our thinking, not only for ourselves, but when it affects the lives of other people, too."

"Lester, I wish more people were open-minded like you. One of my favorite Metallica lyrics is 'Open Mind for a Different View' from 'Nothing Else Matters'. The reality is that much of the world in stuck at one end of the pole—it doesn't even matter which end—and they're unwilling to get unstuck, to open their minds."

I continued, "It doesn't matter if the Moon Landing was faked or if *9/11* was an inside job. It doesn't matter who's running the world or what their agenda is. As long as we don't evolve our Collective Consciousness, and move along the path of *Collective Enlightenment,* then we're doomed. We don't have a chance of making it as a society if we don't learn to get along and accept/embrace that we're all in this together. The 1% isn't even 1%. The people running the world are so small in numbers compared to the masses of individuals whom they've built this false paradigm upon. They're terrified of us learning the truth and evolving our consciousness. Their façade completely depends on us believing in it."

"You really believe that just by changing our thinking, we can change our reality? I mean, the reality of the dominant paradigm?"

"It's only real because we believe/accept that it's real. Think about Queen Mab from Sam Neill's *Merlin*. Stop empowering her, and she ceases to exist. Consider currency. A dollar bill has value because we agree on it, certainly not because it's actually backed by anything of value (not anymore). It's no different than board games where we're doled out pieces of paper with numbers on them representing value, and we agree that it's worth something. What happens in those games when the money runs out?"

"What do you mean? You just reuse it."

"Yep. You either recirculate the same pieces of paper, or you get something else to represent the money, which represents the value, when all along, it's just a piece of paper. If you could, you'd just print more money. What do you think they do? They're the only ones who possess the true value (resources), while we use the *thing* that represents the value, and then we pay them interest for the right to do it. They create money out of nothing, lend it to us, and then we're indebted to them for life. All based on an agreement that's founded on a false belief."

"I've heard how money used to be backed by gold and silver, but that there isn't enough gold to back all the currency circulating around the world. I've also heard some stories about the Federal Reserve and the World Bank, and how they have systematic plans for crippling and indebting developing countries."

"Yeah, I've read about some that stuff too, but that's a whole other tangent. My point here is about how limiting our beliefs can be, and how we can create something out of nothing (like money or debt) with a belief. My drumming buddy Dave once told me a story about working with a shaman down in the Southwest. He watched this man put his hand inside of a boulder. Then he watched the man pass his arm through a cactus. They weren't doing any special medicine. A woman in the group objected, 'You can't do that! That's not possible!'

"The medicine man told her, 'You can't put your hand in the rock because you *believe* that you can't put your hand in the rock. In my world, I *know* that I can put my hand in the rock, so I do.'"

"I've heard some stories from the Elders that you wouldn't believe."

"I might surprise you. I think anything's possible. However, I don't just believe in everything."

"What do you believe in?"

"Well, I believe in things that I can experience with my senses. I also believe in things that I can both feel in my core and make sense of with my rational mind."

Lester responded, "I can agree with that."

"That said, I also think it's possible that what I perceive as my senses may just be bits of code running in some grand simulation. In other words, I'm open to the possibility that what we call reality is just another version of virtual reality."

"You mean like we're all plugged into some game, but we don't know it."

"You said it. Belief is a dangerous thing, especially when unfounded. That's why it's so important for us to be willing to question our core beliefs. We must *know* what's right for us, not just believe it. Truth is subjective. Everyone has their own truth, and many believe that their truth is the only one. *Fanaticism?* C.K. used to say, 'There are many paths to the mountain top, but they all go to the same place.' Many groups think they corner the market on truth. *They* are the chosen ones, which I guess gives them exclusive rights."

Lester questioned, "But how do we know when we're acting based on belief vs knowing?"

"Discernment is about knowing. When you truly know something, there's no room for doubt. Wisdom is about knowing. Wisdom is knowledge experienced. Love is knowing. Do you doubt your love, or do you feel it in your core? I imagine that you know you love Kenny, without question."

"Of course, I do. I never doubt my love for my son."

"Learning to differentiate between believing and knowing is all part of our work. When you practice disciplines to foster your growth, you tap into your essential core self, the part of you that doesn't doubt, it only knows…the part of you that is God. Do you think God thinks or doubts anything? Or does God simply know everything? *To know God is to know.*"

"Amen to that," Lester responded.

"*And*, maybe what we perceive as love is just chemical manipulation of our hormones to make us believe we're feeling love. Honestly, the simulation hypothesis makes more and more sense to me. Our emotions might just be part of an advanced virtual game. I mean, just consider that our reality might be a completely internal experience, and we're literally plugged-in somewhere. Shit, maybe we don't even have bodies."

"It's official. You're crazy."

"Like yourself, I'm convicted."

"Well, just don't make a religion out it." Lester chuckled.

"I'm not a fanatic, Lester. I'm open to all possibilities…and none."

"Well, sir, I'm pretty much a fanatic. I realize it may sound silly to you, but I don't have any doubts about Jesus."

"I admire your conviction, and I agree with you that you're fanatical about Jesus, but, to me, being fanatical isn't about the absence of doubt."

"So, tell me again, how you define a fanatic?"

"Someone who's unwilling to consider the possibility that they're wrong."

"Well, that includes millions of people."

"Billions."

"Scott, I told you before. The world's a fucked-up place. You're not going to change billions of people."

"Not by myself."

"I see. So, you're recruiting, then, like a pyramid scheme."

"I'd never compare my mission to an MLM, but many of those people certainly qualify as fanatics."

"Is that your mission, then? You're going to change one fanatic at a time?" Lester giggled.

"That sounds like misery."

"Multi-level marketing or changing the minds of fanatics?" Lester questioned.

"What's the difference?" I said. "I once posted my definition of a fanatic online to a group of old high school friends. I challenged if they were willing to consider the possibility that they may be wrong about their core beliefs."

"Did anyone reply?"

"One friend responded."

"What did he say?"

"*She* said, 'I'll never change my mind, and I'll never admit that I'm wrong.'"

Lester laughed.

I continued, "That kind of thinking scares the hell out of me. What can you do with that? There's no room for conversation or speculation—no room for growth. She's not just entrenched at her end of the pole, she cemented herself to it, with her beliefs, I might add."

"Wow! Yeah, that kind of thinking doesn't really provide any room for other possibilities. That's really kind of sad."

"I do have compassion for her," I said. "I imagine it can be terrifying to question beliefs you've held as fundamental truths for your entire life. Just think about how you felt when you learned for certain that Santa Claus wasn't real. That simple truth may not have shattered your sense of self, but for me it was certainly discouraging to realize that something so sacred was a complete and utter lie. There are some great Jesus and Santa parallels, but we're just about to arrive. We can continue this another time, if you please."

"Jesus and Santa, huh? Like I said, you're a strange bird, Scott. Yeah, let's talk about this stuff more later. I'm also still curious to hear your 'radical' thoughts about treatment."

We picked up Kenny and went to a park so they could visit. It was cool seeing them together. As I watched Lester interacting with Kenny, I couldn't help but think about our conversation in the car. I wondered if human beings really had a chance.

Monotone Sue

I was on the job for a couple weeks before I finally met the other social worker in our program, my co-worker Monotone Sue. Now usually having flat affect and being incredibly monotone were traits that would make someone uninteresting and forgettable. Quite the contrary, these defining traits made her incredibly unique. Most people couldn't come off sounding so monotone and flat if they tried. Seasoned actors couldn't do it. She was as genuine as could be. Every word this woman spoke was so dry and drab that I found it kind of interesting.

We shared an office together. *That* was challenging. Ok, so I have this deep-seated sense of fairness. I'm a younger sibling which may have something to do with it, too—I always want my fair share.

So, initially we shared the office with one of our assistants, not Piggy, but another woman from the Tribe. This woman was really sweet and polite and messy. Ok, so maybe I'm a little OCD, but I like things a certain way. My friend Denni refers to this, uh, trait, as being very particular. Call it a euphemism. Anyway, this woman liked to eat sunflower seeds, and she showered the shells all over the floor around her desk, which was about a foot from mine. The carpet was peppered with sunflower seeds, staples, little pieces of paper…all kinds of stuff. I crunched my way around our office each morning. It amazed me that she didn't seem to notice. Granted, it was her office, first. Who was I to challenge the status quo? So, I didn't. I just waited until after she left each day before I'd come in and vacuum. Well, I waited until everyone left the office, and then I vacuumed the entire first floor. Now don't get me wrong, I kind of wish I didn't have this trait of being, uh, overly particular. In fact, it would be kind of nice to be able to sit in a room and not have the debris on the floor or the arrangement of the desks drive me nuts, but it does.

Well, she moved out into her own office shortly after I arrived, and I was left to share the room with Monotone Sue. I still kept vacuuming her office though. I like vacuuming. It pleases my desire for neatness and a sense of order.

I got a kick out of listening to Monotone Sue talk on the phone. I mean, really, she was so freaking monotone. I found it more and more amazing as time went on.

And then I came in one day to find her desk, which was previously flush against the wall, sticking out into the middle of the room, taking up well more than her fair share of the office. Trust me, *I measured it*. Ok, so it wasn't just that she was taking up more than her fair share of the room. Her choice of positioning was totally *un-feng shui*. It bothered me, and I couldn't let it go. I know, they say, pick and choose your battles, and this one was probably kind of pointless, but I did bring it up to her. She looked at me like I was crazy. Maybe I am. I can own that, too. Although, *crazy doesn't know crazy*. The fact that I can own that I might be crazy actually implies that I'm not. Have you ever tried pointing out crazy to someone who is truly bonkers? They don't get it! That's part of the art of doing social work—pointing out and addressing issues with people who didn't think they had any, particularly the mentally ill clients.

Well, Sue didn't seem to think too much of me after I confronted her about fairness and feng shui in our office, but, ultimately, it didn't matter. She got fired a few weeks later. She borrowed Stan's GSA and managed to forget to return the gas card, which was attached to the key chain. Yeah, it was actually attached. At least, that's what Stan said. He also said they tracked subsequent gas purchases that were made with that card over the next few weeks, and they were all completed within a one-mile radius of her home. Go figure, one down. Yep, she was the first of many of my co-workers to get fired. That was also par for the course.

Chain of Command

Shortly after Monotone Sue was fired, Stan and Director Lucky hired two more middle-aged, Native women. They were both educated and competent. One of the women was a bit of a space cadet, but likable and well-meaning. The other one was grounded, professional, and attractive. They were both good people, and they had the skills to perform effectively as ICW social workers. I figured my days were numbered since Stan had told me several times, "As soon as they find some Natives that can do this job, they'll get rid of you."

With Sue I never feared for my job. Her tone wasn't the only thing that fell flat. She just didn't seem to connect with anyone—her clients or other professionals. These ladies, however, were getting their jobs done. I liked and respected both of them, and more importantly, so did their clients.

Well, this is a very short, albeit fascinating part of the story. These women found documentation that basically proved that one of our managers was committing tax fraud (among other things) by claiming kids from our program on his own personal taxes. It appeared that he and the children's grandmother were in cahoots. This would not be the only accusation made regarding their inappropriate behaviors. My new co-workers took the evidence directly to the Tribe's legal department.

Ready for the interesting turn of events? They were both fired. Yep, you read that correctly. What's all the FUS about tribal politics? Two employees find evidence that one of their managers is committing tax fraud. They take it directly to the legal department, and *they* get fired, while he keeps his job. He was a politician. They were doing what was right. Watch for a pattern, and you may see a trend.

The Tribe took this as an opportunity to set a precedent with all their employees. Word quickly got around the Rez, *Violate Chain of Command for any reason, and you will be fired!*

This is an important part of the story. I'm also setting a precedent. Oh yeah, two more down.

Rookie Mistake

After my second and third co-workers were fired, Stan was promoted to Assistant Director. To my surprise, I was promoted to ICW Supervisor. I think Stan was attempting to recognize the fact that I had all the cases again (I got them all after Monotone Sue was fired, too) and reward my work with a nice pay raise. The title didn't mean much to me since everything was coming my way regardless, but I definitely appreciated the raise.

Director Lucky had a reputation for never being around. He could be reached, but he was rarely seen. He always had a State meeting or something to attend, or so he said. He had set the example for leadership in our department. Stan followed suit. It became more and more difficult to track him down or get a response from him on pressing matters. I tried numerous times to get direction from him on several different issues heating up with my cases. I could see trouble brewing, and I wanted input from Stan.

I called him multiple times about my concerns, and he would always blow me off. Well, to be fair, at first, he gave me the impression he was going to make time to meet with me to discuss my concerns (he was a politician), and then he just stopped responding. When I tried to corner him at the office or out in the community, he always had somewhere else to be, or something more important to attend to, or so he said.

I started sending him detailed emails addressing my concerns. I had numerous situations that needed his direction. I became more and more fearful of the potential backlash if our clients started going to Council to try to get their needs met. *They did.*

I was sitting in my office one morning, and I could hear Stan on the phone talking to Lucky about those very situations. Apparently, Council was getting on Lucky for "problems with the ICW Department". I heard Stan blame all of it on me. I was pissed. I'd been trying to get his help on those specific issues for weeks, and now he was blaming me for not handling them.

I decided to forward those emails to Lucky—the ones where I had detailed my concerns and asked for Stan's help. I even cc'd Stan…I wasn't hiding anything. He knew right away I had complained to his boss about him.

I was immediately demoted. At least I wasn't fired (but you already knew that because there's much more to this story).

Stan told me, "Look man, shit rolls downhill. If your boss wants to blame some shit on you, then you let him. That's all part of the game."

He continued, "We had to teach you a lesson. You can't call out your boss to his boss. You're lucky we didn't fire you, but you're a good worker, and it was a rookie mistake. If you try to complain to the Tribe, we'll just fire you anyway, so don't waste your time.

"Listen buddy, I already told you…you complain about your boss or any Tribal Member, and you might as well say good-bye. Doesn't matter if you're right, you're White, so in their eyes, you'll always be wrong. Even though they need you to do this work, they'll never admit it, and the second there's a barely qualified Tribal Member who wants your job, you're gone. Well, once *you* train them. You just gotta play the game. Keep using that good bedside manner and building relationships with the Tribal Members, but keep your opinions to yourself.

"This time you'll keep your job, but if there's a *next time,* you might as well pack your shit."

I told him, "I'm not playing any games. I just want to do good work and take care of my family." And then I took a deep breath and calmly questioned, "What about integrity, Stan? What about doing what's right?"

His response, "*Integrity doesn't pay the bills.*"

"It pays my bills," I said. At least, it did.

I reviewed my file at Human Resources a few months later. It said that I was demoted; it just didn't say why. In the end, that rookie mistake cost me almost a year's pay.

Of course, I still held most of the cases for the entire time I worked at the Tribe. In fact, even when we had three other social workers and two assistants, I still did all the investigations; carried most of the cases; trained each new co-worker, including a few supervisors; *and* held down the fort after each of them ultimately got fired. I really didn't mind the workload. Things actually went better in the department when it was just me. During those times, ICW had way less complaints to Council and way less drama in our department.

My only real complaint was about the money. Not only did Stan demote me, but he'd also told me I'd receive a step raise every year on the job, and I didn't. I wish he'd never told me that. It raised my expectations. I was promised a few raises over the years that I never received.

Accepting Reality

Fred was a father I worked with for years. I call him Fred because he reminded me of Fred Flintstone. He was about my height, but square and stocky with jet black hair and a big personality. I tried to reach him numerous times to discuss his children's cases before he finally called me back to arrange a meeting. We met at his girlfriend's mother's house. As far as I knew, we were the only ones there. He didn't invite me in, so we sat out on the front steps while we talked.

I asked him, "So, how you doin', man?"

"How am I doing? How do you think I'm doing? Fucking bastards at ICW took my kids."

"I realize that you're angry at ICW, and, well, I'm from ICW, but let's focus on what we can do to help you reunite with your children."

"ICW's gonna help? Right. It's not just ICW. Xena's pissed at me. For that matter, her whole family's pissed at me. I've got no friends other than the assholes I do drugs with. I sit in that garage all day staring at the wall and sucking on that glass dick. No one comes to see me and check in on me. Nobody really cares how I'm doing."

"Well," I responded, "I know we're just meeting, and you have no reason to trust me or believe me, but I can honestly say I care about how you're doing."

"Yeah, why would you care?"

"Well, for one thing, I've met your children, *and* I've talked with both their grandmothers."

"You talked to my mom?"

"Yes. I also talked to Xena's mom. They both feel that your children are really struggling not having you in their lives. So, if nothing else, I care about how you are doing because I think your children deserve to have their dad back."

"Like you can do anything about it."

"Fred, I take my work very seriously. It's my duty to help you get your kids back, and I have every intention of doing just that."

"Shit, ICW's gonna help me get my kids back? It's ICW that took my kids! If it weren't for ICW, I wouldn't be in this situation in the first place. It's fucking ICW's fault I lost my kids."

Fred escalated. "None of this shit ever should've happened. I shouldn't even be in this situation…I bet your gonna tell me I need to go do a drug test or go to treatment or something before I can even see my kids!"

"Now Fred, I didn't say any of that. Please try and take it down a level so we can talk. Getting upset is not going to help you get your kids back."

"Talk about what?"

"Well, we can keep it simple and talk about your court requirements and visitation and stuff, or we can go deep and take a look at what's holding you back in the first place. I hate to jump in deep right away, I mean, we just met and all, but some of the things you're saying inspire me to share some of my personal perspectives—if that's all right with you."

"Personal perspectives about what?"

"About the situation you're in. Some of the things I have to say, or, at least, ask, will probably be difficult to hear. I didn't come here to piss you off or get into it with you. Again, it's my intention to help you get your kids back."

"Yeah, well get on with it, what have you got to say that I haven't already heard?"

"Well, first off, would it be fair to say that you blame ICW for losing custody of your children?"

"I already told you that."

"Why did ICW take your kids?"

"Come on man, you *are* ICW. You know why we lost 'em."

"I have a good idea why, but the truth is I don't have all the facts. I also know there's *always* more to the story. I've heard Stan's side of things. I haven't heard your side."

"You know, man, Xena and I've been using, but we weren't beating our kids or anything. We're still taking care of 'em."

"So, then why did ICW show up?"

"Probably cuz of Xena's sister. She's pissed at us for hocking her Xbox."

Feigning naivety, I asked, "Xena's sister caused ICW to show up?"

"Well, she's probably the one who called you guys."

"Called us and said what? That you hocked her gaming system?"

"No, come on man, you know what I mean."

"Do I? I can't say that I do. I assume you mean that she accused you of stealing her Xbox, and then taking it to the pawn shop."

"Yeah, you got it."

"Ok, but what's that got to do with ICW?"

"She accused us of hocking it so we could get drugs."

"I got that part, but ICW's not the police. So why would she call us?"

"She probably thinks we weren't taking good care of the kids."

"Hmm. Is it possible there's any truth to her assertion?"

"To her what?"

"Is it possible there's any truth in what she's saying about you neglecting your children?"

"We didn't neglect them. We leave them with Xena's mom or sister when we go out partying."

"Do you come back to get them when you say you'll be back?"

"Um, we don't usually give an exact time when we'll be back, but they are in good hands with their grandma and their auntie."

"Correct me if I'm wrong Fred—I'm new here—but doesn't Xena's sister also have drug issues?" Fred just looked at me. "Also, you said you don't usually give an exact time. What do you tell Grandma or Auntie when you leave the kids with them?"

"We just tell them that we'll be back."

"So, is it fair to say that when you leave the kids with their grandma or auntie, that there's no specific plan in place as to when you'll return to get them?"

"I guess so, but we always come back."

"What's the longest you've been gone?"

"I don't know—maybe three or four days."

"What do you tell the children when you leave like that? Do they expect you to be right back, or do they know it could be a few days or more?"

"We don't really tell them anything?"

"Do you give their grandma or auntie money for food and stuff when you are gone?"

"We don't have any money. Their grandma usually has enough food for them."

"You don't have money to leave for the kids' food, but you have money to go partying?"

"Well, not really." Fred half chuckled. "That's why we took the Xbox."

"Do you blame their auntie for being angry?"

"She didn't have to turn us in to ICW."

"To be clear, Fred, I never said she did turn you in to ICW—you did. Frankly, I don't know who turned you guys in, but I do know that you were reported for neglecting your children due to your ongoing drug use."

"It was probably her."

"Does it matter who it was?"

"Hell yeah, it does. Whoever did it's responsible for us losing our kids."

"Ok, so help me out here. Is it ICW's fault or is it the fault of the person who turned you in?"

"*None of this should have even happened.* It doesn't matter now. Fuckin' ICW's gonna make us go to treatment."

"I didn't know that ICW could make you do anything."

"Well, if we want to get our kids back, that's what we have to do."

"How do you know that? As far as I know, this is your first contact with those *bastards at ICW*." I looked him directly in the eye with a slight grin and waited for his response.

Fred laughed. "Yeah, those fuckin' bastards."

"So Fred, I've heard you say a couple times now that this shouldn't have happened. Don't get me wrong, but I bet little Freddie and his sister are probably feeling the same way. Who do you think they blame? Do you think they also blame ICW, or do they blame their auntie?"

"No, I don't think they know enough to blame anyone."

"Is blaming other people for this situation making it any better? I mean, is it helping to motivate you to do what you need to do to get your kids back?"

"I already told you. I haven't been doing anything but sucking on that pipe."

"Don't you miss your kids?"

"Of course, I do. I think about them all the time. I just can't seem to stop sitting in that fuckin' garage getting high."

"High on what?"

"What the hell do you think? It ain't weed that got us into this."

"Honestly, I'm not sure what to think. What got you into this?"

"Meth, man. Fuckin' meth."

"That *shit* is poison," I stated with conviction.

"Sweet poison that makes all your troubles go away." Fred squinted his eyes and stared off into the horizon while a smirk formed on his face.

Again, feigning naivety, I questioned, "It makes your troubles go away?"

"Well, it does when you're high," Fred proclaimed.

"And then what?"

"And then you come down and that shit is right there staring you in the face again. So, you get high, *again*."

"So, Fred, can I share one of my perspectives with you about making positive changes in your life?"

Somewhat reluctantly, he responded, "What is it?"

"Well, think about it this way. We've all heard about the monk or spiritual teacher who sits in a cave up on top of a mountain meditating all day, right?"

"Yeah, I guess so."

"Well, one of the things those spiritual teachers talk about is human suffering. They say that one of human beings' greatest sources of suffering is not accepting reality."

"What do you mean?"

"Well, some of the indicators that a person is not accepting reality are when they say things like 'it shouldn't be this way' or 'that never should have happened', or perhaps they put all their focus on blaming other people for their situation. Sometimes they make 'poor-me' statements and operate from a place I call *Victim Consciousness*. Those are telltale signs that they're not accepting reality as it is. They're putting their focus into coming up with reasons why things shouldn't be the way they are vs focusing on accepting what *is* and identifying what needs to be done in order to move forward."

"That makes sense."

"Some of the things you're saying sound like you haven't accepted the reality of your situation. You said you sit in that garage getting high all day. That may serve as some kind of escape from your current emotional pain—your troubles—but it doesn't solve anything. In fact, I would venture to say that it makes things worse."

"I can't argue with you there; but it's not easy getting off the pipe."

"If it were easy, we wouldn't have so many drug addicts."

"So, what are you suggesting?"

"I'm suggesting you stop blaming ICW and Xena's family for this situation. I'm suggesting you take an honest account of yourself—your role in all of this—and you start taking responsibility for your part. I'm suggesting you begin working on accepting reality as it is. Once you do that, I have no doubt you'll be able to move forward with a plan to get your kids back. I'm not saying it will be easy, but at the core, it's really quite simple."

"That all sounds good," Fred chided, "but *reality's* another story."

"If you say so. I say it's all about priorities. Is it more important for you to sit in the garage getting high, or is it more important to be the dad who your kids deserve—the dad who deep down you really want to be?"

Fred didn't respond. He sat staring at the sky for a few moments. I shared the silence with him.

"So, what am I supposed to do? You want me to go to treatment?"

"Right now, I'd really like to hear what *you* think you should do. Do you think you need treatment?"

"Aw fuck, I knew you were going to want to talk about treatment."

"Fred, I didn't bring up treatment. You did."

"Everybody in ICW has to go to treatment."

"Has to?"

"If they want to see their kids."

"Unless you're currently high or an active threat to your children, I would never get in the way of you seeing them. Quite the contrary, I think you should see them. I'm sure they miss you. I also think it would help motivate you to make some positive changes if you were seeing your children regularly. It would be harder for you to hide from, well, *reality*."

"You're probably right. It would help me if I could see them. So, what else can I do, you know, to make positive changes in my life like you said? I feel really stuck."

"Well, honestly, you seem really depressed to me. It that a fair assessment?"

"Yeah. You'd be depressed too if you lost your kids."

"I hate to even imagine such a thought. Well, it would help if you developed some self-care practices."

"What kind of self-care?"

"Really, that's up to you. Things that work for others might not work for you. It's your job to identify things that will help you to feel happier and better about yourself. I imagine you probably aren't feeling very good about yourself these days." Fred just shook his head. "I can share some of the things that I do to take care of myself, so at least you have some examples to think about. From there I'm sure you can come up with some things on your own, but I'm also willing to help you."

"What do you do? Exercise and stuff?"

"Exercise is a great start. I bet you probably haven't done much physical activity lately. It's always good to get our blood flowing, get outside and get some fresh air, you know, fill our lungs with oxygen."

"I used to lift weights."

"I used to lift too back when I was younger. We used to spend hours in the gym. I found a practice that's more sustainable, though."

"Oh yeah, what's that?"

"I do yoga."

"Yoga huh, I hear that's really good for you."

"I feel way better when I do it, not just physically, but emotionally, well, spiritually, too."

"No shit?"

"Yeah man, I feel more energized, more grounded, more intuitive…it has *many* benefits. I incorporate breathing exercises into my yoga practice as well. Really, breathwork is the core of my practice. It's a very powerful tool in and of itself."

"Breathwork huh? What do you do?"

"There are many different techniques. I can show you some if you are interested. Ultimately, they all flood the body with oxygen. They calm and focus the mind. And as you may already know, focusing on the breath is at the core of many meditation practices."

"I didn't know that."

"Breathing is so automatic that we take it for granted, and yet, it's one of our most powerful tools, if not *the* most powerful one. It's our main source of fuel. Think about it, how long can you go without food?"

"I don't know, a few weeks, maybe a month."

"And how about water?"

"Days, maybe a week or two at the most—if you aren't in the desert, anyway."

"And what about air?"

"Well, that's a no-brainer. A few minutes at the most."

"Unless you are David Blaine or some kind of yoga master. Those guys can go longer, but, yes, the average person can only make it a few minutes. Shoot, the brain begins to die after about six minutes without oxygen. Oxygen literally keeps the spirit in the body."

"That's an interesting way to think about it."

"So anyway, I encourage you to think about practices you have utilized throughout your life that have made you feel calmer and more energized and bring them back into the fold. Again, none of this stuff is necessarily easy—habits can be hell to change—but at the core, it's very simple."

"I've heard that before... *simple not easy*."

"Yep!"

"So, what else have you got to share with me?"

"How deep do you want to go?"

Fred laughed. "Well, how about some practical tips to help me stay clean."

"Hmm, let's see. Well, I learned some great rules for manifesting one's visions from a sacred manuscript I came across during my anthropological studies. This manuscript was allegedly hidden from society by an ancient, secret order of monks."

"Really, that sounds mysterious."

"No man, I'm just messin' with you. Well, I was an anthropology student, and I did study the culture of wealth consciousness and manifesting one's greatest desires, but there wasn't any secret order of monks—not that I know of, anyway."

"You're a real comedian, Scott."

"So anyway, during my studies, I identified five key concepts that very successful people have in common. Well, I don't know if concepts is the right word, but basically there are five things these people had in common while manifesting their visions, and I believe whole-heartedly in all of them."

"So, what are they?"

"#1 They had a burning desire. They woke up with their vision in their mind, and it was the last thing they thought about before they went to sleep. It was their number one priority. Their lives would not be complete unless they manifested their vision. I think of James Hetfield sitting in his car writing lyrics during his work breaks, or Kirk Hammett riding his bike way across town to get guitar lessons with Joe Satriani when James and Kirk were both just teenagers. Those guys were focused. They definitely had a burning desire to manifest their visions."

"You talkin' bout Metallica?"

"No other. Do you envision yourself getting your children back?"

"Sometimes."

"#2 They believed they could do it. Creation begins with a thought. They believed in themselves. They overcame their doubts. If you 'sometimes' envision getting your kids, then it's likely that you also 'sometimes' don't envision getting them. We need to stoke your flames of belief in yourself, so that you believe it the majority of the time."

"Yeah man, I certainly have my doubts."

"Fred, we all do. I think it's a fundamental component of the human experience. When we doubt ourselves, we don't succeed."

I continued, "#3 They believed the sacrifice was worth it. Sacrifice comes in many forms, from the actual work it takes to accomplish a task, to the opportunity cost of missed-out experiences. They believed that no matter how hard they had to work, or what sacrifices they had to endure, the success would be worth it.

"You seem concerned that you may need to go to treatment. Treatment may just be a sacrifice you must endure if your ultimate goal is reuniting your family."

Fred nodded his head.

"#4 They surrounded themselves with successful or like-minded people. It's hard enough to battle our own doubts, let alone battle the doubts of others. These incredibly successful people made sure to surround themselves with others who supported their vision. I imagine James and Lars meeting for the first time and sharing their respective visions. They certainly magnified the power of those visions when they combined them to form Metallica. And what about Robert Plant and Jimmy Page? Or Eddie Van Halen and the boys? On his own Eddie is an amazing virtuoso guitarist. With Van Halen he's a rock god. Shit, he set the standard for cool, 80's rock guitar riffs. He did that by combining his vision with other like-minded people. There're so many great examples of bands whose members had the perfect chemistry to catapult them to stardom *because* they worked together. The power of their individual visions grew exponentially when they combined them. Winning Coach always said, 'Together everyone achieves more!'"

Fred grinned. "Ha, ha, I've heard that one before."

"And finally, #5, They took action."

"That sounds pretty simple," Fred responded.

"Yes," I replied, "simple, but not easy. So, if we apply these concepts to your life, the first question I would ask is 'Do you have a burning desire to get your children back?'"

Fred just stared at the ground.

"It may feel like you don't have that burning desire just yet, but I wouldn't be surprised if it lives deep down inside of you, and it's just covered up by all the drugs and disappointment."

He perked up a bit hearing those words.

"Whether or not I have a burning desire, I don't believe in myself, and I don't have successful people around me."

"I said, 'Successful or like-minded'. I also said, 'People who supported their vision'. I bet that you have people in your life who support your vision of getting your kids back."

"My mom supports it."

"*So be it.* Who else can you identify?"

"Xena supports it. She's a badass and all, but she's not a bad mom. She loves our kids. She just got caught up with the drugs and all. But she wants our kids back."

"I bet you could probably think of all kinds of people who support you and your family."

"Yeah, I guess so."

"But who do you surround yourself with?"

"Drug addicts."

"Fred, it looks like you have some things to think about. How about we check back in with each other in a couple days and see where you're at with all of this. Please consider identifying some self-care practices and think about some of the ideas I've shared with you regarding personal responsibility and goal accomplishment. Be honest with yourself about what you really want, even if you think you can't accomplish it. In the meantime, I'll let Xena's mom know it's ok to allow supervised visits with the kids as long as you two meet the conditions I already described."

"That sounds good. You've given me a lot to think about."

I wished him well, and we parted. I could transition into an extensive montage here. I worked with Fred and Xena for years, and it was definitely a rollercoaster ride. They did eventually go to treatment, a few times, and they did get their children back.

Fast forward from this first meeting with Fred to a Sobriety Dinner I attended at the Tribe years later. I'd come with my drummer buddy Bret to perform a few pieces of music on the *Dununba* drums. After our performance, several members from the community took turns getting up to share stories about their sobriety. Fred was the last person to speak into the mic that evening. He had quite a bit say about what it took for him to manifest his vision of sobering up and reuniting his family. He talked about believing in yourself and taking action to accomplish your goals. He talked about surrounding yourself with people who will support your dreams. The last thing he said was, "I'd like to thank the people at ICW who pushed me so hard to do what I needed to do to be successful. They never gave up on me, even when I was ready to give up on myself." He looked at me and grinned as he spoke those last words.

Sasha

Sasha was one of my first cases. She was only four when she was *taken by ICW*, as people in the community would say. Sasha was abandoned at the gas station on the Rez, allegedly by people whom her mother had left her with while she was off on a binge. Both of her parents had a long history of drug addiction and were rumored to be deep in their use. Members from the community were up in arms. "How could you abandon a helpless little child at a gas station? What kind of person would do such a thing to an innocent child?" I kept hearing those types of questions from the ICW Committee Members and other professionals involved in her case. Initially, I shared these perspectives. Over time I came to realize that it was one of the safest places in the community to abandon a child. The staff at RezGas would notice her immediately and call nearby Tribal Law Enforcement (aka *Tribal*), and an officer would contact ICW.

That's exactly what happened. Tribal got involved, placed this child with her fictive grandmother, and then notified ICW. That was the first time I heard the word fictive in relation to a relative. Fictive is non-blood. So, she was placed with an Elder who was grandmother to some of her cousins but not her. For placement purposes, she was *like* family. It was also the first time I learned that Tribal Police could take a child into custody without a court order, but ICW could not. If the court wasn't open or a Judge wasn't available, we were dependent on the police to place a child into protective custody.

When Stan briefed me on Sasha's case, he said "Her caregiver's a Tribal Elder, and her brother's on Tribal Council, so don't make any waves. We don't need TC breathing down our backs any more than they already are." He continued, "This little girl's mother has several other children that she's not raising, and none of the fathers are doing anything to comply with the court, so basically your focus will be on maintaining the stability of the placement with her fictive relative, Granny Kristine. You can ask around about the parents, but until they go to treatment, we're not going to be able to engage them.

"We really have no idea what this little girl has gone through or how long she's been bouncing around among them strangers. Trust me, it was strangers that dropped her off at RezGas. No Tribal Member would've done that—they'd be too worried about being spotted. You gotta manage the politics on this one cause who she's placed with, but you make that little girl the center of your decision making. She's going to need some counseling, and her caregiver may need some help from the Tribe. Call Granny Kristine and set up a time to go out to the house. She lives on Upper Rez."

I called her caregiver, fictive grandmother Kristine, and set up a time to come out to her home and meet her and little Sasha. She sounded bothered when I called her to set the appointment, and then she appeared even more annoyed when I arrived on her doorstep. I reminded myself of my duty to serve the children. I wasn't there to get Elder Kristine to like me. I was there to make sure little Sasha was safe and all her needs were being met. I stood on her doorstep with resolve, smiled, and said, "Hi, my name is Scott. I'm Stan's new work—"

She interrupted, "I know who you are."

"Of course," I replied, "I'm just trying to be courteous. You must be Miss Kristine. How are you today?"

She just stared at me.

"I wondered if I could ask you a few questions about Sasha before I see her." She opened the door, stepped onto the deck, and continued to stare at me without saying a word.

"How is Sasha doing in your home?"

"She's fine."

"Are all of her needs being met? Is there anything ICW can assist with?"

She looked me up and down, and then in a condescending tone she said, "ICW's never been much good for anything. ICW isn't getting the parents to treatment. Her mother's a drug addict, and she's not from here. What are you doing to help her father who *is* from here? Are you going to get him into treatment?"

"I'm sorry, but I was just assigned her case. I haven't met with either of her parents yet. Stan directed me to come out to your house to see Sasha and offer you any help we can."

She flatly stated, "Her dad ain't gonna do nothin'. He never has, and he never will. Her momma ain't gonna do nothin' either. We'll be raising her. Yeah, her needs are being met; she's with me, isn't she? You want to see her; you'll have to come back. She's with her cousins."

"Oh, I thought she was going to be here."

"Why would I keep her home just to meet you?"

"My apologies," I said, "I wasn't aware that she wouldn't be here. It's my duty to see her in person and report on her welfare. Can we schedule another time that I can come over to see her?"

She stared at me for a moment, huffed, and then gruffly stated, "Come back tomorrow."

I didn't dare ask what time. I returned the next day at the same time, knocked, and no one answered. I noticed the vehicle that was parked in the driveway the day before was gone, so I just assumed Granny Kristine was out. It took three more phone calls and two drive-bys before I caught her at home again.

When I did finally catch up with her, Granny Kristine answered the door, and then, again, exuding reluctance, opened the screen door and stepped onto the porch with Sasha trailing behind. I just smiled at her. I decided that this time I'd resist my inclination for small talk and instead focus on accomplishing my face-to-face visit with Sasha, and then be on my way. I'd learn over time that engaging in small talk with certain people was a setup for trouble. It often gave them a target to focus their unhappiness on. Or it gave them ammunition for future politics. The more you tell people about yourself, the more they have to use against you. It was Rule #5 of the Code, *Treat it like court. Be professional and only answer what is asked* (no more). Do not volunteer unnecessary information.

I could see Sasha standing meekly behind Granny Kristine. Granny Kristine noticed me looking down at Sasha behind her, and she stepped aside and grumbled, "This is your ICW worker."

Sasha peered up at me with her pretty doe eyes. She didn't say a word. She was a beautiful little girl with big brown eyes that reminded me of a Japanese anime' character. She had a distant look in her eyes, kind of like she was lost in another world, yet she still had a sense of innocence about her. She seemed shy towards me and submissive towards Granny. I figured that was a normal reaction to meeting yet another new adult, and, as for Granny Kristine, shoot, I found myself being a bit submissive around her, too.

Over the years, Sasha and I ended up spending quite a bit of time together. Sometimes, it was during our monthly face-to-face visits, others while taking her to various appointments, and sadly–all too often–moving her to new placements.

During one of our outings, I had my first experience witnessing the intoxicating effects of sugar on a child. I'd taken Sasha to our local fair-trade café for ice cream after one of her counseling appointments. Prior to indulging in some ice cream, she was quiet, calm, and collected. It was amazing to see how buzzed she got literally moments after ingesting a single scoop cone. She was bordering delirious. If you had witnessed this same abrupt behavior change in an adult, you'd likely contribute the effects to meth or cocaine–some kind of serious upper. I'd heard about the effects of sugar on young children, but I'd never observed the drastic transformation for myself, not like that. She became giddy with laughter and then started spinning in circles and dizzily flailing around. She could barely contain herself. Although I did find her behavior to be somewhat amusing, it was also concerning. Another drug addict was born!

One day on the way to an appointment, I decided that I'd play a song for her from *10,000 Days*, Tool's newest album at the time. A couple days before, my good friend Foldy and I had been discussing our appreciation for "Jambi", the 2nd track on the album. There's a climactic moment in that song where the tension pulls and builds in *atypical* Tool fashion until all the instruments drop out and you hear this single, definitive bass slide. Little Sasha spontaneously burst into cheer when she heard that bass slide. She raised her arms in the air like she was riding the downhill on a roller coaster and shouted, "Yay!"

Another Tool fan was born!

Lester in Treatment

I didn't take Kenny the first time I went to see Lester in treatment. I wanted to check out the facility and see what kind of space they had for family visits, as well as make sure to identify any risk factors for Kenny. The facility was tucked away in the woods a few miles from the interstate. After I checked in at the reception desk, Lester's counselor came right out and introduced himself. He gave me a brief update on Lester's progress, showed me to a meeting room, and then said Lester would be in shortly.

Lester arrived a few minutes later *full* of energy. He seemed genuinely happy to see me. He sat down and started discussing his progress right away. He shared about participating in groups and doing his *steps*. He was jovial and light-hearted in a way I hadn't experienced him before. It was refreshing. I told him how Kenny was doing, and we also discussed the logistics and expectations for upcoming visits.

Lester listened to everything I had to say, and then he leaned in with a serious look and said, "So, come on, Scott. You told me you had some radical views about treatment. Here we are at treatment. Why don't you share some of your thoughts about it?"

"Well Lester, any discussion of my perspective on treatment involves some discussion of my perspective on life—really, Consciousness itself."

Lester had a gleam in his eye. He rubbed his hands in anticipation. "You mean spiritual stuff."

"Yes, spiritual stuff. Well, ok." I smiled. "Are you ready?"

"And waiting," Lester responded with a smile.

"Lester, what's the first thing you do at every sobriety meeting before you talk about how things are going or share your story?"

"Hmm," Lester pondered, "we introduce ourselves."

"And what else?"

"Um...oh, we say that we're an addict."

"And doesn't this treatment model encourage you to say and think that you'll always be an addict?"

"Yes, it does, but…"

"Hold on a minute. Isn't one of the major tenets of this model the principle that you are powerless over your addiction—in fact, it's a *disease*—and you must turn your will over to a power greater than yourself?"

"It does encourage us to ask God for help in conquering our addiction if that's what you mean. And, yes, it does teach us that we are powerless over our addictions without Him."

"And it teaches that addiction is a disease, correct?"

"One of the worst."

"Focus creates reality, Lester. Most spiritual teachers agree about this one concept; well, at least, the teachers I listen to. What kind of reality are you creating if you continually tell yourself you're an addict?"

"A reality where I'll always be an addict."

"And what kind of reality do you create if you keep telling yourself you're powerless over your addictions?"

"A reality where I'm powerless over them."

"Exactly. It's the same with *addiction is a disease* mentality. With that kind of thinking, we also create a reality (mind-set) where we're powerless over addiction. Now, to be clear, I'm using the laymen's definition of disease vs the medical definition. In other words, I'm not talking about how addictive behavior and thinking affect the brain, but rather referencing that most people commonly accept that a disease is something you have no power or control over.

"What reality do you create if you believe you need something greater than yourself to overcome your addictions?"

"Scott, I'm not sure where you're going with this, but I do believe in something greater than myself. I believe in God. I believe with God's Grace I *can* overcome my addictions. Don't you believe in a higher power? Don't you believe in God?"

"I do believe in God, but I'm pretty sure that my definition varies a bit from yours. Lester, I don't believe we're separate from God. There's an inherent implication with the Christian perspective, and, therefore, with the tenets of this treatment model, that God is something outside of us, that we're separate from God, and that without intervention from something outside of us—something greater than us—then we're powerless to overcome our addictions."

"I would agree with that. We *are* separate from God, and we do need Him to overcome our problems."

"Well, I did say that my thoughts were radical. I propose to you, my friend, that we're not separate from God, that God is inside each and every one of us, and that we came here with everything we need to conquer our addictions—our demons, if you will. Lester, I propose to you that we are God!"

"Come on Scott, are you just trying to get my goat? I know you can't really believe that."

"Nope, I'm not trying to get your goat at all, but I am encouraging you to look at life through a very different lens. I'll come back to this part about us being God; that's definitely a conversation in and of itself. Shoot, a whole book could be written just about *that* concept. For now, I have another question for you. What kind of reality do you create when you sit around with other addicts retelling the same stories about how fucked-up you got, and all the stupid shit you did?"

"I don't know. What kind of reality does that create?"

"One where that kind of behavior is normalized. One where stories like these are glorified and exemplified to such a degree that these acts begin to sound like rites of passage to the young people. How many times have you sat in community sobriety dinners and listened to men and women share their party stories while children run around the gym?"

"Tons," Lester answered.

"Is that behavior being normalized with the children? Do they begin to believe it's a normal rite of passage to go through the addiction cycle because *everybody* does it?"

"I see what you mean," Lester affirmed.

"I just heard a Native man speak about his work with Native youth, and he said the boys didn't believe him that he'd never been to jail. They told him, 'All Native men go to jail.' That was the only reality they'd experienced. He showed them another possibility. He showed them a reality where a Native man doesn't go to jail, and he becomes a positive influence on the youth, essentially, helping them to avoid that fate. He also shared stories about men who did go to jail, and still became great leaders in their communities."

Lester reflected, "I think I understand. You're saying that if we keep telling drug stories and focusing on being addicts, then we'll continue to create those experiences. We'll reinforce the idea within ourselves and with the people who hear our stories, that they're normal life experiences that everyone goes through."

"Yes, Lester. That's why it's so important we're aware of the messages we're programming our brains with as well as the messages we're promoting to others in our community. If we keep telling ourselves we're addicts, then that's precisely what we'll be. Unfortunately, the current reality is that we're *all* addicts to one degree or another. We've been programmed for that, too! Granted, not everyone suffers from meth or heroin addiction, like many of the ICW families, but we're all addicted to something, be it alcohol or weed, sugar, food, lust, anger, being right, being a victim, judging others, gaming, gambling, scrolling, texting, drama…there's certainly a litany of possibilities.

"Once again, I say, the Scaredy Cats benefit from our shared afflictions. The more addicted we are, the easier we are to control. Think about it. Take something as seemingly innocuous as marijuana. If you're more focused on satiating your desire to get high, to be comfortably numb, than you are on evolving your consciousness and changing your life, then what are the odds that you'll change?"

"The odds suggest that we'll put more focus and energy into being high, than on evolving."

"Consider the cycle of addiction. Don't most addicts spend a great deal of their time either being high on their chosen drugs or on carrying out the logistics to actually acquire them?"

Lester related, "It depends. For some people, it's easy to get drugs. Meth is cheap, and heroin is getting cheaper. They can be high all the time if they want. But I think that many addicts probably spend more time trying to get money for their drugs and connect with their dealers, than they do being high. Of course, they—*we*—spend a bunch of time recovering from our use as well."

"Recovery…more down time. More time where people are out of the game. Do you think it would be easier to control a population of addicts or a population where people take personal responsibility for their evolution and maintain a clear mind?"

"Well, that's a no-brainer!"

"Indeed, it is. Ok, now for the God part. Although I was baptized as a baby, I didn't go to church growing up, and I don't consider myself a Christian…big surprise, I know. As a very young child I remember thinking that religion was just an easy answer for everything we didn't understand. If we didn't know the answer, then God did it. It seemed like a big cop-out. We could avoid deep thoughts about the nature of our existence. We could avoid taking personal responsibility for our actions (aside from our presumed responsibility to choose Jesus). Shoot, we could avoid all kinds of things by simply accepting the *Universal Truth*—it's all God's plan."

Lester was nodding.

"I was six years old when *Star Wars* came out. It made a lot more sense to me from a spiritual perspective. The premise of the *Force* really resonated with me—the idea that there's a Universal Force connecting all living things, and that we have a responsibility to choose between a Light or Dark path (love or fear). And, of course, the idea that we can learn to harness this Force to become more spiritually advanced or evolved."

"Harness the Force?" Lester scoffed. "Are you saying we can be a Jedi or like Jesus or something?"

"Funny you should ask?" I jovially responded. "I do believe we can advance spiritually, kind of like a Jedi, but you're the one who just brought Jesus into it."

Lester retorted, "Moments ago you said you weren't a Christian, and then you said something about a presumed responsibility to choose Jesus. You brought *Him* into the conversation."

"Touché. Well then, since we're on the subject, I will say this. I do believe Jesus was here to teach us that God is in all of us, and the things he could do we can learn to do greater. Lester, God *Is* in us."

"But Scott, fantasizing about being a Jedi is one thing, you're not really saying we can be like Jesus, are you?"

I affirmed my position. "I believe human beings are capable of just about anything; so yes, I do believe we can be like Jesus. I believe that's precisely what he was here to teach us."

"You're crazy!" Lester exclaimed with a big belly laugh.

"By the way Lester, as much as Jesus might want us to get our shit together, he is not going to do it for us. I think, these days, he's probably more a 'watch from the sidelines' kind of god. I'm sure he's cheering for us; well, hopefully he is. Of course, if the stories are true, then he's omniscient, so ultimately, he knows what we're going to do anyway; he doesn't need to wait or watch or come back.

"Tell me this, do you think Jesus doesn't have anything better to do than wait for your life to unfold? Especially if he already knows what you're going to do. Why would he need to wait for you to change? Why would he need to leave and come back later just to see if we've evolved? What's the point?"

"Go on," Lester urged.

"Jesus' message was corrupted. They use his teachings against us."

Lester scrunched his brow and gave me a puzzled look.

"Think about it. Most conservative Christians not only agree with the concept of free will, but strongly argue for it. It's a cornerstone of the Christian faith; for that matter, it's the cornerstone of most religions."

"What do you mean?" Lester questioned.

"From their perspective, we have free will, just as long as the most important decision we ever make in our lives is to choose Jesus, otherwise we're damned to

Hell. How free is that? As long as we make the right choice on this one decision, then we're free. Otherwise, we're fucked!"

Lester nodded. "Pretty much."

"Free will implies personal responsibility. So why then would the most important decision we exercise with our free will be to give up all our power and responsibility to another entity outside of ourselves (a potentially imaginary one at that)? This line of thinking is incredibly contradictory and self-sabotaging."

I had Lester's full attention.

"Now consider this…if we truly are responsible for our own spiritual growth, what a brilliant way for The Powers That Be to control people. Convince us that the most important decision of our lives is to give up all our power to something outside of ourselves (Jesus, Jehovah, the Church, you choose). Give it up to Jesus, and he'll take care of everything. You don't have to do anything else…so you won't! You won't do the work to evolve because you are waiting for someone else—*something else*—to do it for you. Brilliant I say, *just brilliant*. In fact, you can commit murder, rape…hell, all the sins known to man…as long as you just ask Jesus for forgiveness, well, and you *start* following God's rules, then you're good, you're in!"

"I've never thought of it that way before".

"Jeez," I joked, "I've never thought of it that way either. Actually, that does sound pretty good. You mean, all I must do is accept Jesus into my heart and follow the rules, and then I don't have to do anything else? He'll take care of everything? You'd be a fool not to do it, right? Kind of like being a fool to be naughty when Santa knows everything, and he'll only reward you if you're not naughty and you do what you're *supposed* to do. Just follow Santa's rules, and at the end of the year you'll get your reward."

"Scott, you crack me up. I must admit, I've never thought about the similarities between Jesus' story and Santa's story—especially the part about Santa knowing everything we do, and we get rewarded at the end if we follow his rules."

I continued pontificating. "Santa's story is really a great reinforcement for the Jesus story. We only have to wait a year to get rewarded by Santa. And we get it every year as long as we follow his rules. Kind of makes the idea of waiting to die before we're rewarded with heaven a little easier to swallow. I mean, that's a long time to wait, to throw caution to the wind, and hope—*have faith*—that we're right. Shoot, you could waste your whole life being wrong before you ever find out."

Lester seemed to be pondering my sermon.

"That's ok," I said, "you'll have plenty more lifetimes to try to get it right." I became increasingly sarcastic. "Wait a minute? *Is* there some kind of parallel here? I mean a Jesus/Santa parallel?

"Lester, sadly, we're all way too fucking easy to manipulate. And they start programming us when we're so young and impressionable. They even convince our parents it's ok to lie to us. They convince us it's ok to lie to our children. And you don't think they're lying to us?

"Why would they want us to do that? Why would they want us to lie to our children? Why would they want to indoctrinate us into believing in imaginary beings from such an early age? Why would they want us to think there were some universal rules to follow, and if we don't follow them, then we'll be punished or damned? And when we do follow them, we're rewarded. But only at the end—only *after* we die."

"You have to have faith. You have to know that the Lord will take care of you. I have faith in Jesus. I have faith in His Grace."

"Keep telling yourself that. Keep believing that if it serves you. I'll say this though: what a great way to control people. So simple that it really is brilliant. And there's so much social pressure to conform and comply. What's wrong with *you* that you haven't accepted Jesus? Aren't you a good American? Don't you support our troops?

"Lester, we've all heard the axiom, *If it sounds too good to be true, then it probably is.* Doesn't the Jesus story sound just a little bit too good to be true? It's just like an MLM or a pyramid scheme. It all sounds great until the bottom falls out.

"And what about all the suffering we endure during our lives on Earth? I know Christians get tired of this question, but if Jesus gave his life so that we don't have to suffer, then why do we suffer so much while we wait to enter heaven? *I know, I know.* Follow the rules and be rewarded in the end."

Lester responded with conviction, "Christ is *my* Savior. Many Tribal people believe in Him."

"I'm sorry, but why would so many Native people adopt a religion from people who oppressed and tried to annihilate them in the name of that very religion—the same religion that was forced down their throats in the boarding schools? The same religion that taught them that being Native was bad…their culture was bad…their language was bad.

"Talk about programming. It would truly baffle my mind why so many people get bamboozled, and fall for this okey-doke, if it weren't so easy for me to see how successful our collective programming has been. In some ways, I feel like *Neo* looking down at many of you still plugged-in to the machine. I'm over here hollering—*cheerleading*—'Wake the fuck up!'"

Lester interjected, "Well, you see what happens when people don't comply. They literally either lose their lives, or they lose everything that is meaningful to them. It's no wonder that most people nowadays just go along with the flow."

"I know it's easier to just go with the flow in the short term. Familiar is comfortable. Change is scary as, well, *hell*. But what about the long game? We need to look at the big picture. We need to consider what our conformity will cost us in the end. Face it, we've all been brainwashed, and they've done a fabulous job doing it. Most people are afraid to even consider the possibility that what I'm saying is true. It would rock their worlds—wouldn't it—down to the core. I must be crazy. I *must* be a conspiracy nut. Don't get too close, you might get it on you."

Lester burst into laughter again. He sat back in his chair as his chest rumbled.

"We're easy to manipulate and control because they've bred generations of fanatics—people who are unwilling to consider the possibility that they're wrong. They've convinced billions of people to fear questioning their beliefs because the punishment is so severe if we don't comply. At the least, we're shunned and ostracized from our communities. At the worst, we're damned to

Hell for eternity. If there's a Hell, we're in it now. It's a *very* bad dream, and we need to wake up.

"They want us to give up all our power. They want us to hate each other. Divided we fall. Programmed we follow. Fearful, we cower."

"Damn, Scott. That was quite a soapbox speech. I must admit, though, that what you're saying makes more and more sense to me. To continue with your computer analogy, it's like we're all in sleep mode, and if we do attempt to wake up, then the operating system is already loaded and the programs, our collective programming, just kick in and start running. This could go on forever. Well, I guess until our hard drive fails. Scott, the things that you're saying about God aren't just radical; they're ludicrous! You actually believe that we're God?"

"Lester, I believe it; hell, I'd go as far as saying *I know it*. I know that God is everything. There's no separation. We do ourselves an injustice believing that we're separate from God and we need something outside of ourselves in order to evolve spiritually. Their whole paradigm is built on us believing that we need *them*…we need the church…we need a pastor or minister to help us to understand God…we need Jesus to have a relationship with God. If you can accept that we *are* God, you essentially cut out the middleman. Truth is, if you want to be clean…if you want to conquer your addictions…you only need to look within yourself. *There*, you will find God!"

Greasy Weasel

One morning during my second month at the Tribe, Stan called me into his office and said, "I need you to go meet up with Tribal Police at Greasy Weasel's house down on Lower Rez. He's a Tribal Member, and they're investigating him for drug activity. He's had a lot of traffic at his house during all hours of the night, and Tribal thinks there may be children in the home, so you need to go perform a child welfare check".

"I've never done a child welfare check. What do I do?" I humbly responded.

With a sly grin that I didn't understand at the moment, Stan replied, "Don't worry buddy, Officer Brown will tell you exactly what to do. Just do whatever he tells you." I had a feeling that Stan knew more than he was letting on.

I got the address and drove over to Greasy Weasel's house on the other side of the neighborhood. Two Tribal police rigs were already there. One was parked in the driveway and the other one was on the front lawn. Two officers were standing in the yard near the second vehicle.

I parked in the street and then walked up and introduced myself. One of the officers identified himself simply as "Brown" and then motioned for me to follow him over to the side entrance of the house. He said, "We have reason to believe there are children in this home who are at risk of being abused or neglected. We need ICW here to do a welfare check."

He walked up to the slightly-cracked, side door and then turned and stood on the landing looking at me. I wasn't sure what to do.

He said, "The door is open. You need to go in and do your welfare check."

I was confused. I didn't think I had the right to just walk into the house, but Stan had clearly directed me to do whatever Officer Brown had told me. I felt a little fearful walking into this unknown situation, but at least I had an officer at my back. *Shouldn't he be going in first*, I thought, *to secure the premises and all?*

I pushed the door open and stepped into a dimly-lit, laundry room that led to the kitchen. Once I was in the door, both officers pushed past me and proceeded to wonder throughout the house. I stepped into the kitchen and stood for a few moments while my eyes adjusted to the light. Both officers returned after a few minutes. Officer Brown said that no one was home. *He didn't seem surprised.* Neither officer said anything else about the children. The other officer said he would inform the Chief, and he left.

Officer Brown turned to me and asked, "Do you smell that?"

I could smell all kinds of funky odors, but I wasn't sure which offending scent he was referring to. He pointed toward the pantry closet and then told me to open the door, so I did. I saw smashed bits of cereal and crackers scattered over mostly empty shelves. I looked back at Officer Brown, and he said, "Look again. Second shelf from the top." I looked up above my head and noticed a water bong perched up on the shelf. Officer Brown reached in and grabbed it and then said, "Man, you couldn't smell that?"

At that moment, a man came walking into the house behind us and demanded, "What are you guys doing?"

Officer Brown held up the bong and asked, "What's this doing here?"

"Hey, that's not mine," the man responded, "somebody left it here."

Officer Brown replied, "GW, you know you shouldn't have any drug paraphernalia in your possession."

"There's nothing in it. You can't do anything about it. Hey, what are you guys doing in my house, anyway? You don't have a warrant."

The man looked to be in his mid-thirties. He was thick and tall and greasy. He wore stained, gray sweatpants and a faded, blue t-shirt that had the arms cut off. His hair was in a small, thin ponytail, and his face had scattered patches of beard.

Officer Brown looked over to me and said, "Scott here is from ICW. He has reason to believe there are children living in the home who may be at risk of abuse or neglect. He's here to perform a child welfare check." Officer Brown looked at me with the same sly grin that Stan had when he sent me over to the house.

Greasy Weasel got very defensive. "There's nothing going on here. My kids don't even live with me right now." He looked directly at me and stated, "ICW already did an investigation on me. I'm clean. ICW doesn't have shit on me! You can go up to the court and see for yourself. All that stuff got cleared up. They couldn't prove anything!"

Clearly, I had no idea what Mr. Weasel was talking about, but his behavior did raise some red flags. Experience had taught me that usually when people are overly defensive, there's something more going on, more to the story, so to speak. Of course, he did just come home to a social worker and a police officer in his kitchen—both uninvited—so he certainly had reason to be defensive.

He continued, "This better not be about Sasha coming over. She's only been here a few times when my mom goes to play her bingo. I told you I was already investigated. I'm clear. You guys have no business being here."

Well, needless to say, I was feeling pretty confused about my role in this situation. I wasn't aware of any reports of abuse or neglect regarding Greasy Weasel, and the police hadn't named any children. Greasy Weasel was talking like *we* had done something wrong, that we had violated his rights somehow, and I was starting to wonder about it myself.

He started to sound like a whiny teenager. "I didn't do anything wrong. I'm innocent. My uncle's on Council, and we'll see what he has to say about all this."

That statement got Officer Brown's attention. In fact, it was the only thing Greasy Weasel said that did.

"Settle down big guy, there's no need to get TC involved. We're just here checking out some community complaints about extra traffic at your house these last few nights. You know you shouldn't have this bong here. I'll let you off on a warning for now."

Officer Brown exited the home, and I followed him out to his car. After he got in, he looked up and said, "We'll let you know when we need you again," and then he left.

I turned back to see Greasy Weasel standing in the doorway glaring at me. As I walked to my car, I couldn't help but wonder what business he had with Sasha. I also couldn't help but feel like I'd just been used.

When I got back to the office I went straight in and explained everything to Stan. He said, "No shit, Greasy Weasel came in the side door while you two were standing there looking at his bong? Damn, I bet he was surprised." He sat back and laughed intermittently while repeating pieces of my story back to me. "The door was slightly cracked, huh? Ha, ha, ha...what are you guys doing in my house? Ha, ha, ha." He seemed generally amused by the whole situation.

Then Stan got a serious look on his face—the most serious I'd ever seen him. He looked angry. He leaned in and with a much quieter voice he said, "You know he's a pedophile, right? *Everyone* in the community knows he's a pedophile. That makes me very concerned to hear that Sasha's been over there. We gotta do somethin' 'bout *that*. Yeah, Greasy Weasel is Kristine's son—Granny Kristine—and if she's been dropping little Sasha with him so he could [he paused as a sick look formed on his face] uh babysit...ah man we gotta do somethin' 'bout this quick.

"So, here's the thing, Scott. We've got to protect this child, but we can't go after the grandmother, she's an Elder. We'll find another way to get Sasha moved. We'll say that it's to benefit Kristine because the girl has so many problems, or that an Elder shouldn't be in this position taking care of such a needy, young child. We'll come up with something, but we can't leave that little girl to those sick motherfuckers!"

He just sat looking kind of dazed, staring at the wall for a minute. Then he questioned, "What kind of sick person do you have to be to deliver a four-year-old girl to your grown-ass pedophile son?"

I questioned back, "What do you mean we can't hold Kristine accountable?"

"Scott, I told you buddy. Tribal Members are the only ones that matter around here. Elders are the most important. Greasy Weasel is a Tribal Member. His mother is a Tribal Elder. Shoot, his uncle's on Council. We can move Sasha, but we can't do anything with the rest of 'em. People have already lost their jobs trying. How you think I got my job? That's right, the ICW supervisor before me thought she'd been here long enough to take this family on. You see how that worked out.

"Child molestation happens everywhere, and this community is no exception. The problem is no one here's ready or willing to deal with it. If you try to take it on, you won't have a job. Shit man, they'll fire you just for putting somethin' like this in writing."

I was having difficulty understanding. I knew that Tribal people believed in respecting their elders. I think most people do, traditionally. I didn't know that Elders in Indian Country were also entitled to a sense of immunity. Now, I realized there was likely more to this story, and we would need to investigate if we had any chance of uncovering the truth, but Stan had made it clear—we wouldn't be investigating Grandma Kristine solely because she was a Tribal Elder. Well, *and* because she had a brother on Council. That was the first time I experienced *Elder Immunity* but certainly not the last.

He also made it clear that I wouldn't last a minute if I tried to confront child molestation in any of my cases. I couldn't help but wonder if this also had something to do with the Big Family/Little Family dynamic that Lester spoke about. I thought, *Greasy Weasel has an uncle on Council—he must be part of Big Family. But where does that put little Sasha?* I wondered. *She must be from Little Family.*

We did get Sasha moved quickly and set up with a counselor. Unfortunately, she was moved several more times again right after that. She was clearly suffering. She acted out everywhere she went, and no one seemed to be able to handle her behaviors long term. She lived with her auntie and brother for short periods in-between foster placements, so she did stay connected to her family, but she definitely had a hard road ahead of her.

A couple months later during a Review Hearing at Tribal Court, Sasha's caregiver informed the court that Sasha had disclosed sexual abuse to her counselor. It was the first I'd heard of it. The judge got all flustered. She seemed like she didn't know what to do with this information. She looked so confused. Everyone in the courtroom was looking to the judge for direction. Finally, she said, "Bring Sasha in, and I'll interview her myself. I'm calling a twenty-minute recess."

Her caregiver got Sasha from the gym, and Judge BS took her into her private chambers. They emerged about five minutes later. Judge BS said something to the court clerk, the clerk took Sasha over to her caregiver, and then the Judge went back into her chambers. Judge BS came out about twenty minutes later still looking as flustered as ever. She asked for Sasha to be taken back into the reception area, and then court was called back into session.

Judge BS said, "I interviewed Sasha, and I have reason to believe that she was coached. She said that Mr. Weasel put his penis in her butt, but I don't think that a four-year-old child would know to say *penis*. She clearly disclosed that something was done to her, but I think that her language was too mature for a four-year-old. I think that the ICW Case Worker led little Sasha to make this disclosure."

That last statement stunned me. The news of Sasha's disclosure was just as new to me as it was to the judge. Mind you, the counselor and caregiver should've called me immediately after Sasha made the disclosure, definitely prior to court, but that was another issue.

So, we had a Tribal Elder (allegedly) delivering her four-year-old, fictive granddaughter to her adult, pedophile son to be babysat, the child disclosed abuse at the hands of this man, and Judge BS was blaming me for coaching her to come up with this story. Since I already had a bit of experience with Judge BS, I wasn't completely shocked by her assertion. I didn't secretly call her "Judge Batshit Crazy" for nothing. *How did she come up with that one?* I thought. Really though, it was obvious to me. At least, part of it was obvious. Sex abuse hit a little too close to home for the judge. This wouldn't be the only case where I saw her become unnerved over child molestation allegations, and then, ultimately, do nothing.

A few months later in court, the clerk handed me a filed affidavit from a teen girl who also claimed that Greasy Weasel sexually abused her. In her disclosure she gave specific details of the rituals he would perform during her abuse, including how he would have her bathe and dress in new white tights that he'd cut the crotch open. She wrote about how he would comb her hair as part of the grooming process (deviant manipulation).

When Judge BS found out that the clerk had given me a copy of the affidavit, she became agitated and scolded the clerk for "…sharing evidence with an ICW caseworker". I learned later from the clerk that Judge BS refused to accept this young girl's testimony (a detailed written disclosure of abuse) as evidence. Apparently, she had decided—without doing a hearing or investigation—that the affidavit was fraudulent.

The girl's mother contacted me directly a few days later to express her outrage with the court. I felt helpless. I didn't even know what to say to her. She was exasperated. "Scott, I've been dealing with the Tribe and this court for years. I'm not surprised by what the judge did. I've already been trying to get copies of the records from Tribal Court for previous sex abuse investigations regarding my other children. The clerk told me they don't have any files regarding those matters. Scott, we had full-on hearings that went on for months, and you're going to tell me the court doesn't have any record of it? Can you please search the ICW files at your office and see if you can find anything?"

I did search our files, but I couldn't find any information on those children or Greasy Weasel. I couldn't help but wonder if there'd been a cover-up. Greasy Weasel was right. He was clear. We had nothing on him. Nothing, but a four-year-old's word.

Don't Worry Honey, It Happens to All of Us

I went to numerous gatherings, trainings, and conferences during my time in ICW. At one of the Native-organized conferences, I saw a video where a young Indian girl was attempting to get help from her auntie because she was being molested. It was clear that it had taken a lot of courage for this young girl to approach her auntie, disclose her abuse, and ask for her help. She obviously trusted this woman greatly.

Her auntie put her arm around her, gave her a comforting hug, and then told her, "Don't worry honey, it happens to all of us." She went on to reference her own abuse at the hands of numerous male family members. She also talked about how her sister (the girl's mother) and numerous other family members had also been molested. Then she minimized and normalized every bit of it. She gave that vulnerable, little girl the impression that it was just something she had to go through—some kind of demented rite of passage.

One of my Tribal Member clients told me about the *Rape Shack*. He said, "It's basically one of those temporary buildings like the ones we use to sell fireworks. Guys construct 'em out in the woods around the Rez so they can take young girls there, drug 'em, and gang bang 'em. Tribal [Tribal Police] tears them down when they find 'em, but then the Rape Shack just pops up somewhere else out in the woods. This has been going on for years. Everyone knows about 'em. *Indians are doing it to Indians*. No one is stopping it from happening. We've been taught to hate the White Man, but it's our own people who are now raping our children."

This kind of behavior is by no means limited to Native communities. It happens everywhere. The world is plagued with pedophiles and rapists.

My first job in social services was working in a couple group homes in North Phoenix in the early '90s. Both homes housed 13 to 17-year-old boys. One was filled with gang members. The other was comprised of juvenile sex-offenders. The sex-offenders all had a single trait in common: they had all been molested when they were young.

When I first started working in those group homes, and I would tell people about the work I was doing, many people—men and women—disclosed to me that they'd been molested when they were young...some by uncles, some by aunties; some by a brother, others by a cousin; many by "trusted" community members including teachers, coaches, and babysitters.

Child molestation is a learned behavior. People don't come into the world that way (well, at least, *most* people). Some people become abusers after being abused. They create more victims and continue the cycle. Their recidivism rates are deplorable.

To be clear, I'm not saying that all victims of child molestation become warped and turn into child molesters. Most victims remain healthy and honorable people. I *am* saying that most child molesters were once molested themselves.

I told C.K. about my work with this population in the group homes. He said, "We have a solution for that in the village. We tie a rock to their backs and dump them into the ocean."

I'm not suggesting that we simply execute all the child molesters. We do have a justice system, right? Innocent until proven guilty. I honestly don't know what the solution is, but I do know that as long as people cover it up and pretend it doesn't happen in their community, then this sickness will continue to proliferate.

Another one of my clients, Still Waters, once told me, "Everyone is afraid to call out the pedophiles in the community and hold them accountable because everyone has at least one pedophile in their family. If you call out the child molester in my family, then I'll call out the one in yours. So, most people turn a blind eye and pretend it doesn't happen. They fool themselves into believing that it only happens in other families, when deep down they know the truth. Truth is, it happens to many of us on the Rez—boys and girls."

I empathized with him, "Sadly, it happens to millions of boys and girls all over the world. It's not just happening on the Rez."

Beyond Judgement

When I arrived at Lester's treatment program for our regular check-in, I found him in a less than joyful mood. He immediately started in about how frustrated he was with one of the residents in the program, a guy named Jeff.

"He takes up so much space. Every time someone else is talking he has to interrupt and tell some story about helping the homeless, or some other do-gooder deed. Enough about the homeless, already. Most of them are drug addicts just like the rest of us here."

"It sounds like he's got you really frustrated," I baited him.

"I'm not the only one who gets frustrated with him. I've talked to the other residents, and no one likes him."

"Well, it's unanimous," I said, "he must be a horrible person."

"Well, I'm not saying that he's horrible, but he is a real problem, and the worst part of it is that he just doesn't get it."

"He doesn't get what?"

"He doesn't get how much I want to punch him in the face." Lester smiled.

I shook my head and grinned. "When did he arrive to the program?"

"A couple days ago, but it already feels like a couple weeks."

"What is it specifically that's driving you nuts about this guy? I mean, what makes him such a problem?"

"He just takes up so much space. He talks loud. He doesn't pick up on social cues. Man, there could be six of us glaring at him, and he's going on happy as a clam about how he was called by Jesus to serve the homeless. It's a little too much for me. You know I serve Christ, Scott, it's not about that. It's just being around this guy really pushes my buttons."

"What else?"

"What do you mean?"

"What else bothers you about him?"

"When you try to talk to him, it's like talking to a wall."

"In what way?"

"Man, I'll be so frustrated with him, and he's trying to be my buddy, saying we've got work to do, you know, the Lord's work. He just doesn't get it."

"Maybe he'd rather have you as a friend than an enemy."

"When I'm pissed at some junky, I don't need them trying to be my friend."

"You'd rather they be your enemy?"

Lester took a moment before responding. "Well, when you say it like that. We don't need to be enemies or friends. I'd rather have nothing to do with him."

"Lester, I have some advice for you."

"I'm not in the mood for one of your big spiritual discussions."

"Sorry, dude, but at the end of the day, it's *all* spiritual."

"Whatever. What've you got to say? *It's my fault?*"

"I'm not saying anything is your fault. I'm just trying to understand the situation. First of all, no one else can get us frustrated. We can become frustrated based on how we react to their behaviors, but they're not responsible for our actions. When we make them responsible, we give up our power to them. Never give up your power to anyone or anything. Take responsibility for your emotions and your behaviors."

"As much as I want to tell you to ef-off, I hear you. I know what you're saying is true."

"So, does this man Jeff have any redeeming qualities? I mean, if you had to come up with something positive to say about him, what would you say?"

"He loves the Lord."

"That's one Point-of-Connection for the two of you."

"A big one, but..."

"Hold on," I interrupted. "What else?"

"He's working on his recovery."

"Another POC."

"Huh?"

"POC. Point-of-Connection. Something you have in common. Something you can both relate to."

"Yeah, I guess so."

"What else?"

"Come on, Scott. Give it a break."

"Come on, Lester. Give me one more!"

Lester let out a deep sigh. "He has a positive attitude."

"Do you really mean it, or are you just saying something to shut me up?"

"No, I mean it. He's annoying and all, but he really is pretty positive. In fact, it's one of the things that's so annoying about him. Every time someone in group complains, he always tries to put a positive spin on it."

"The guy doesn't sound so bad to me. I agree, though, sometimes you just want to be in a funky mood without someone trying to cheer you up. Is he going to be here for a while?"

"Unfortunately, it looks like we'll both be here for a while. My counselor thinks I need more clean time under my belt before going back to the Rez."

"Do you agree with your counselor?"

"Yeah, probably. I've been thinking about using, and some of the people here are really triggering me. Jeff's not the only one."

"So, you have a choice. You can continue to focus on the things that bother you about Jeff, and the other residents—and give up your power—or you can focus on their positive attributes."

"That's not going to be easy."

"I know. It's easy to judge. It's another thing to focus on people's positive qualities. Well, especially when we're already convinced we don't like them."

"We talk about judgement a lot in group. People in recovery are often afraid of being judged by their family and friends."

"We don't have any control over other people's judgements, but we do have control over our own; that is, if we choose to exercise it. Learning not to judge is a very powerful spiritual discipline in and off itself. Most spiritual teachers speak about the benefits of letting go of our judgments."

"That all sounds good. I've heard it before but doing it's another thing."

"Are you willing to try?"

"Scott, you know I'm game for anything, but I've tried letting go of my judgements before, you know, walking in Christ's path."

"I respect that."

"Yeah, but then some dumb ass always fucks it up for me." Lester giggled.

"Someone else messes it up, huh?"

"You know I'm just messing around. But it's not easy to let go of judgement. Not at all."

"You're right. It's not easy. But it can be simple. Can I help you?"

Conceding, Lester said, "What you got?"

"I have a simple practice I do that will help you grow beyond your judgements. The first step, of course, is being willing to work on it. Most people aren't even willing to take this first step. Thankfully, Lester, you have an open mind, one of the things I most appreciate about you."

Lester joked, "I have a witness! Thank you, kind sir."

"I see you. You are indeed, witnessed. Be clear, my friend, I'm not saying that I've grown beyond my judgments, but I am making measurable progress. That said, the next step is having the discipline to learn to recognize when you're judging. It could be something as simple as thinking someone is stupid because of the outfit they wore. Or it could be thinking racist or sexist thoughts.

"Once you've identified and owned that you're judging (and I mean judging, not observing or discerning, but having a specific derogatory opinion about that person based on superficial criteria), then you must identify exactly what is it you're judging about the person. Are they being stupid? Maybe you think they're mean. Maybe you think they're lazy. Maybe you think they're an asshole. Be specific; it's important."

"When you say it like that, I guess my judgment of Jeff is that he's not aware of how his behavior affects people around him."

"So, are you judging him for being oblivious?"

"I guess I'm judging him for being stupid. Too stupid to realize that he's annoying the hell out of the rest of us." Lester chuckled.

"Great. That's the first two steps in this process. Now here's the twist. It requires that you be transparently honest with yourself. You now ask yourself, 'Where am I behaving this way in my life?'

"I promise if you ask yourself that question with humility and grace, and a genuine desire to grow, to evolve your consciousness, then the answer will come from within you. You'll know exactly where you've been exhibiting the same behavior in your life that you're now judging in Jeff, or anyone else for that matter, which is why it's being reflected back at you in the first place. We're all mirrors for one another. Everything we see, good and bad, is a reflection of us. Once you identify your specific judgement, then you can work on that part of yourself, if you choose."

"I don't know about that, Scott. You're saying that whenever I see bad behavior that it's really part of me I'm seeing in someone else? Sorry, man, but that doesn't make sense to me. If I see some toddler throwing a fit at the mall, how's that a reflection of me?"

"In that case I don't think you'd be judging, but just observing. However, as for this child's behavior being a reflection of you, can you relate to the frustration this child was experiencing?"

"Yes."

"Can you relate to the feeling of innocence of this child?"

"I've been corrupted for a long time."

"But you still know what it means to be innocent. It's something you still have inside of you."

"I'm not so sure, but if you say so."

"So, are you judging this alleged temper tantrum throwing toddler, or are you simply observing and recognizing their behavior, even identifying with it?"

"Oh, well, no I'm not judging them, they're just a kid. I guess I'm just observing them, and maybe relating to what they're going through."

"So, I'm specifically talking about using this practice in situations where you're judging other people."

"Like the situation with Jeff."

"Exactly."

"Ok, so you're saying that I'm focused on this behavior in him because I also have it in me?"

"Yes. *And*, I'm saying that once you recognize this behavior in yourself, not only will you have more compassion for Jeff or anyone else exhibiting the same behavior, but, more importantly, you can work on it for yourself."

"I can do that," Lester stated with confidence.

"If you can open yourself to this process, I promise you'll grow."

"The Lord knows I need it, that's for sure."

"We all do, Lester. Lead the way."

"More like, *get out of the way*."

"As long as you're on the path, and you're making progress…that's what counts."

"Well, I've said it before, Scott. I'm following Jesus. I'm on His path."

"Some say that you can't actually see your path, until you look behind you and retrace your steps. The path before you hasn't been laid, yet. Every time you make a decision, and take another step forward, you further define your path."

"I can see that. My path has taken many turns that I didn't expect. I suppose all of them were my doing. I'm the one who made the decision to go down that path and suffer those consequences. So, here I am in treatment, once again. Everyone here pretends like it's the last time, but many of us can't wait to get out of here so we can get high. If it weren't for Kenny, I wouldn't have stayed this long."

"Well, thank Jesus, you now have the responsibility of being a parent! If stepping up as a dad is a motivator for you, first of all, I respect that more than you can imagine, and secondly, I'll support you with getting your son in every way I can." And I did. For the next seven years. In the end, Lester got his boy.

Good Will Prevail

For as long as I can remember, I've had this deeply-instilled belief that good will prevail—that at the end of the story, justice is served. In almost all of the great stories, good prevails in the end. It's the most common story arc in modern fiction: *All is Lost* ¾ of the way into the story, and then success and accomplishment at the end. Even if the end was only thirty minutes later like on *Super Friends* or an hour later with *Voyagers*—as long as the *Omni* was green and the good of history prevailed—then our heroes could go on with their stories. The stories couldn't continue, however, until good was done. Good always won out.

Empire Strikes Back was the first movie I remember as a kid where evil prevailed. As an adult *Crouching Tiger Hidden Dragon* was the first movie I remember with a truly tragic ending. Of course, now *Game of Thrones* throws out all of our Hollywood expectations for any character's mortality.

Like Phineas Bogg from *Voyagers*, I have my own Omni, only mine is internal. It's based on my own moral compass and intuition, and it served me, and the families I worked with, well over the years. Whenever I found myself stuck in a case—red light on the Omni—and not sure how to proceed, I would meditate and focus on the best interest of the child and ask for guidance from my Higher Power. For me mediation is more powerful than prayer. Prayer is talking to God. Meditation is listening. I know that intuition and inspiration are Divinely directed, and I depend on this internal guidance in all of my work. I took my role as social worker very seriously. I believed it was my duty and spiritual mission to do my best to serve all the families I worked with to *their* highest good. My role in any case or situation was not resolved until I'd achieved a green light—then, and only then, could I move on.

It's why I'm writing this book—my Omni's still red. I don't expect it to turn green simply by me sharing these stories, but I do hope this book will help inspire change at a global level that will help right our course on this planet, and ultimately, give us all a green light so we can move forward with the next episodes in our collective journeys.

Elder Dorothy

The first few times I called Dorothy she was rather reserved. I called her regarding her great niece who was placed with her by ICW. She always seemed surprised and even a little put off that I was calling.

In the beginning most people I called seemed surprised to hear from me. It didn't matter if they were a family member or a professional contact. I gathered that most people were not used to hearing from an ICW caseworker, other than when ICW called to ask them to be a placement. Once the child was placed, however, they rarely heard from the worker. Again, not my way.

Over the years I had numerous contacts with her, and I grew quite fond of her. Years after my initial contact regarding her great niece, I contacted her regarding being a placement for her granddaughters. Par for the course, their parents were drug addicts, and they were not following through with court recommendations for treatment. Their father was a Tribal Member who had a difficult time not drinking at work. He kind of reminded me of Droopy Dog. His movements were slow and lethargic, and he spoke in monotone. He seemed so defeated, and yet, he clearly loved his children. I got the sense he knew he was not able to meet his children's needs, and he recognized they'd be better off with another family member. I always encouraged him the best I could. I also always shared my appreciation for working with his family.

Their mother was a piece of work. In every conversation I ever had with her she brought up sex. It didn't matter what we were talking about, she would manage to sexualize the conversation. Shoot, we could be discussing her children's school curriculum, and she'd find a way to interject inappropriate sexual comments.

One time she was talking to me about why a particular treatment program was not appropriate for her. She said it was because the group facilitator didn't wear any panties under her short skirts, and she was constantly flashing her wares to the participants in the program. "How am I supposed to focus on my sobriety when this lady keeps flashing me her hoo-hoo?" Given my experience with this woman, I kind of wondered who was flashing whom. I'm not exaggerating. Every single conversation I had with her would go *there*. At first, I thought maybe she was testing the waters with me, until I witnessed the same behavior with her in front of her children. For her, everything was about sex. It creeped me out, and it made me worry about what she'd exposed her children to. I assumed that she had her own sexual abuse history. I hoped she hadn't inflicted any harm on her children. All things considered, the kids were pretty well-adjusted. At that time, they weren't getting into any trouble, and they were always respectful to me, especially the eldest girl.

Dorothy did end up being a placement for her granddaughters. As time went on, she became more and more open and accepting of my help. She also became one of my very favorite grandmothers on the Rez. We worked well together as a team, and I felt appreciated and respected by her.

Eventually she became seriously ill and ended up in a local nursing home. I visited her a couple times before she passed. During my last visit I brought my *bansuri* flute to play for her. I had recently had it custom made by a master craftsman from India. I thought it would be a nice gesture to play for her and show her how much I really cared. Really, *it was a gift from her*. As I played, I was able to become vulnerable and genuinely express my love for her. She received me completely. I felt totally accepted by Dorothy, even loved, and that was one of the greatest gifts I received during my time in Indian Country. For me, being accepted is a form of love. Fear = rejection. Love = acceptance.

Stan

When I started working at the Tribe, Stan had already been there for a year and a half. He said when he started, there were over 70 cases, no files—just stacks and stacks of papers—and they didn't even know where half the kids were placed. For as much flak as he got from the community, Stan made a lot of progress with the program, and he definitely knew Indian Child Welfare. He tracked down all the children, dismissed numerous cases, moved many of the children to more appropriate relative placements, *and* started to build a team of professional social workers.

In all my years working in ICW, Stan was the only person who really understood how to do social work in Indian Country. He knew we had to confront tribal politics in order to carry out the duties of our positions. He believed that this required both the skills of a social worker and a politician. He was both: a State-trained social worker *and* an East Coast hustler.

He was also a good teacher. With Black Silk's guidance and support, Stan was able to train a few of us to be very effective ICW social workers. One such worker named Jah Lion became a good friend. I call him Jah Lion because he had a beautiful mane of long powerful locks when I first met him. He also exhibited great enthusiasm and integrity. Whenever we ran into each other throughout our workday, we'd enthusiastically proclaim, "Everything is Awesome!" It was our way of sharing a little levity and supporting each other in dealing with all the stress and FUS of our jobs.

Jah Lion used to pound his chest with his open palm and say, "I'm a professional. I know no other way to be." He would pontificate about social justice and human rights. He often proclaimed, "Being right is not justice. Being effective is just right." I always found truth in his sermon. He was a light and an inspiration in our often stressful and depressing work.

Now Stan was a whole 'nutha story. I often didn't agree with Stan's politics, or, at least, what I thought I knew of them, but I could see that he knew how to do social work in Indian Country, and ultimately, that meant we were helping more Indian children. I could stand behind that.

I never could tell if Stan really liked playing politics. I assumed he probably liked it no more than a soldier likes going to battle.

He'd say, "Man, you know we're always gonna be at the center of the drama doing this job. This shit can get real crazy in a minute. You'll think you just did a great job connecting with a family and helping them to see their kids, and the next thing you know you've got Council breathing down your back. Just keep your focus on the kids as much as possible. No one around here really understands what we do. They think they do. They think we just take babies and make people go to treatment. If only it were that easy. If they had any clue of the shit we go through to do this job—to protect *their* children—then maybe we'd earn some respect."

He'd laugh. "Well, they know enough to hire us to do it. Ain't no Tribal Member wants to do this shit. Trust me, if we get a Tribal Member working in ICW, they're here for another agenda—either to spy on us or to try and influence the outcome of a case. Why you think half those women are on the ICW Committee? They're already convinced that we're doing something wrong. They're there to try to tell us what to do, and not one of them has a formal education."

Everything Stan taught me proved to be at least partially true, and everything he ever said would happen, eventually did. I often resisted his lessons, but in the end, I realized what a master of Tribal ICW he'd become.

Black Silk

In all my years at the Tribe, I never met anyone with more passion and dedication for serving the Tribal Youth than Black Silk. He ran the Youth Program, he had a vision for how amazing it could be, and he had the determination and resourcefulness to make it a reality. More importantly, the kids liked and respected him.

All organizations rise or fall on leadership. Black Silk is a great leader. He surrounded himself with good people. His passion and vision were contagious, and most of his staff caught it. I sometimes envied his position. It seemed like he was able to focus on creating positive experiences for the youth, whereas ICW was so steeped in dysfunction by the very nature of our work. Most of the families we worked with possessed the *deadly cocktail*, as a fellow social worker coined it: drug addiction, domestic violence, and mental illness. We were constantly faced with these afflictions, and we had to be skilled at confronting each of them head-on. Black Silk and his staff certainly had to deal with these maladies, but he was focused on creating and offering solutions vs holding people accountable for their problems.

Of course, every summer when I saw him in the midst of running the Summer Youth program, I certainly didn't envy him. I witnessed him working harder than anyone else on the Reservation. Passion can be insurmountable, and he had plenty. Unfortunately, this often made him a target of dirty politics. He made things happen, and he got attention for doing it. Many people on the Rez were at odds with this. They didn't like the attention he was getting. They didn't like that he was creating change, even if positive. It took me years to understand why people would be angry with someone who was doing so much to benefit their community, but eventually I'd experience it for myself. Rocking the boat violates rule #4 of the Code: *Keep your head down; don't attract attention.* Black Silk taught me that rule.

I never would have lasted as long as I did without Black Silk's guidance. Several of my rules for The Code came directly from him. For instance, Black Silk would tell me, "Know your job. Do your job." (Rule #3 of The Code). It sounds simple, right, and yet it's so easy to get distracted from our purpose and our duties. Focus creates reality. When you have a focus—a mission—and you know what you need to do, you are way less likely to get off track. Trouble often came when people lost focus from their duties. Even when they had good intentions—trying to be helpful or trying to do the right thing. If it wasn't their job, they were setting themselves up for trouble.

One of the dance movements C.K. taught from *Sowu*, the Dance of Life, instructed, *be very precise with your footsteps*. He used to say, "If you are on your way to school, don't stop at Circle-K." Or he would say, "If you have set out to accomplish a specific task, don't stop and get down in the bush [striking curious animal poses]." This movement in the dance stressed how important it was for us to maintain our focus in our work and our creations. Trouble would come if we left our intended path—if we lost our focus.

Black Silk was a politician in the good sense of the word. He didn't play politics, but he did manage them. He held his vision for a Youth and Community Center that would benefit everyone on the Reservation. He planted seeds wherever he could, and he lobbied Council as well as other Tribal leaders and directors. It took years of tacit determination and dedication to this focus, this vision. Eventually, others were inspired to believe in his vision, and the Tribe built a multi-million dollar Youth and Community Center. Of course, Black Silk never got *any* recognition for it. The Tribe certainly rose under his leadership.

Earth Tribe

I love to be with *My People*, as India likes to describe them. By My People, I don't mean White people—I mean hippies. Granted, most of the (American) hippie community is White, but everyone is accepted regardless of how they appear. Really, what I prefer to call this community is the *Earth Tribe*.

About six months before I started working for the Tribe, I went on a two-week vacation from my previous job. I needed it. I was burnt-out from the duties of my position as well as the politics. My agency had recently been absorbed by the older, larger mental health agency in town. They said it was a merger. They also said that nothing would change for us. It felt more like a takeover, and, of course, everything changed, but that's another story.

India's childhood friend was in town for a couple weeks, so she planned to stay home to spend time with her. That meant I had my entire vacation to myself. I could follow my fancies and basically go wherever and do whatever I wanted. I love road trips, so I loaded up Shiva with all my camping gear and drums as well as other road trip necessities, and, well, I hit the road.

My first destination was Heaven Hot Springs somewhere outside of San Francisco. I had a dear friend Lovely who had worked and lived there before, and she was back at it again. She always beamed when talking about her experiences at Heaven. I already loved going to Sanctuary Springs in Oregon—one of my favorite places to be—so I was eager to experience another hot spring resort where I could camp, hike, soak, and indulge in tasty vegetarian cuisine.

I'd recently purchased Audioslave's album *Out of Exile*, and I was waiting to listen to it until I had an optimal listening experience—just me and Shiva and the open road. I couldn't wait to escape the pressures of my job. I longed to focus on myself, my music, and having a good time.

I vividly remember winding down the rural Northern California highway past rolling, wine-country hills and random, roadside fruit stands. Although my official road trip had begun almost twelve hours earlier, it was at this point that I felt my vacation actually began. I pulled out my new Audioslave cd to christen my journey. [I'm *Down on the Upside* without Chris.]

You know how some songs you just like instantly (kind of like people)? I mean, within a few notes of the song starting, you already love it. I felt that way about the title track of *Out of Exile*, the second song on the album. I was listening to that song when I arrived at Heaven. The synergy of that moment was sublime.

Heaven had many similarities to Sanctuary, but some very significant distinctions. They both have hiking trails, natural mineral hot springs, and wonderful staff, but Heaven was much bigger, and it had a bit of a meat market vibe. Now, keep in mind, most of these natural hot spring resorts (there are others) are clothing optional around the pools. If you've never been naked in public, or simply around a bunch of naked people, it can initially be quite unnerving. Although, after assimilating to this kind of environment, it can actually feel quite natural and relaxing, depending on the community that surrounds you. If you hang out with hippies long enough, you'll eventually find yourself in situations with public nudity, especially if you're gathered around a backcountry swimmin' hole.

That aspect of Heaven didn't feel so natural to me. In fact, it was the first time I had the experience of feeling like an objectified piece of meat. I don't know if it's because Heaven is so close to San Francisco, but apparently it attracts a lot of gay men. The way that some of the men looked at me was quite flattering. However, there were a few others whose looks made me feel extremely uncomfortable, even violated. That experience helped me to understand what many women must endure when they are objectified by men (objectified period)—very creepy and disconcerting to say the least.

Regardless, I committed myself to being comfortable in my birthday suit in public, which included not sucking in my belly or being afraid to be seen emerging from the cold pool. In fact, I pushed my belly out a little further and laughed in the face of cold-induced retraction.

I saw more penises, butts, and boobs during my stay at Heaven than I ever care to see again. For what it's worth, the penises and butts all started to look kind of the same, respectively. Occasionally you'd see a really big one, a penis that is, and occasionally, you'd see a really small one. Otherwise, they all looked very much alike. I found this quite reassuring.

Occasionally, you'd see a really nice rear end, but otherwise, most of the butts looked like they shouldn't have been seen at all. For that matter, I found that most people looked better with their clothes on. Funny, but they say that we reveal ourselves when we put our clothes *on*. Think about it; clothes reveal a lot about a person.

Now the boobies, *they* were interesting. I've never seen so much diversity in my life. Sorry, but I'm going to deprive you of *those* details.

Overall, it was a beautiful experience. I connected with my friend Lovely, and she helped me to relax and release some of the pent-up emotional stress I was carrying. I also ran into an old college friend from Arizona State who we used to call "Crazy Cathy". She wasn't crazy by any means; she was just incredibly expressive without any apparent concern for what anyone else thought of her—really, a very admirable quality. I totally enjoyed seeing her as well.

Meat market or not, Heaven is definitely a healing environment. Historically, Native people were known to have traveled great distances to soak in those salubrious springs. (I know.) It didn't take long before I started to feel the beneficial effects of Heaven. Of course, the healing process is not always comfortable or easy. At one point I started to feel anxious and restless. I could feel intense emotions surfacing, and I wasn't sure what to do. I was standing on a tall wooden deck that overlooked the trees and some of the offices. Instinct compelled me to reach out over the railing and grab a small tree that shot up past the platform. As soon as I held the tree, I could feel some of my anxiety drain right out of my body, presumably down the tree into the Earth, like a lightning rod grounding current. I still felt somewhat emotional, though, like I needed my momma. Intuition then led me straight down to Lovely's office where as soon as I walked through the door, she embraced me in a mother bear hug. I started to cry. Yep, more tears. Lovely continued holding me while those tears turned into sobs. I felt safe with her. I felt loved. My heart swelled.

When I was done, we released our embrace, and Lovely said with a big smile, "I told you Heaven was a healing place. It really is sacred land." I couldn't argue with her. Thank you, Lovely. Thank you, Heaven.

There was an event one night where many of us gathered to dance to the groovy tunes of a local hippie band as well as dance and play to our own music. I had my djembe with me, so I brought it out and joined in a spontaneous jam with numerous other musicians. Several people responded positively to my drumming–it was rather affirming. After we played and danced for a while, there was a guy who recited long sections of Kahlil Gibran's *The Prophet* by rote. He'd allegedly memorized the entire book! I say, "allegedly", but really, I have no reason to doubt his claim given his stellar performance.

I met many wonderful people that night, one of whom gave me a recommendation that would be life-changing. He told me about an upcoming festival on the Yuba River called Divine Independence. It was a consciously-focused alternative gathering to the typical 4th of July celebrations. He told me that a gifted young devotional singer named White Light would be performing there, among other artists and musicians. It sounded intriguing to me, so I decided that would be my next destination when I left Heaven.

India first turned me on to devotional music through artists such as Krishna Das and David Stringer. They both perform/facilitate a style of devotional music called *Kirtan* or *Bhajan*. Krishna Das' music had already become a staple long before I discovered White Light. I still sing along to his album *Live on Earth* weekly.

Thanks to the Beatles, you're probably more familiar with this style of music/devotion than you realize. Think "Hare Krishna" or "Om Namah Shivaya". Of course, I'm sure you remember "My Sweet Lord" by George Harrison. Good stuff, Maynard!

Essentially, names of deities–manifestations of the *One*–are chanted in Sanskrit in call-and-response fashion. My chanting yoga-teacher friend Caleb once said, "All the chants basically mean, 'You love God, God loves you, and so forth.'" As you can probably guess, I'm also not a Hindu. I claim no labels when it comes to spirituality, well, other than hippie. I do love to sing though, and it feels wonderful to sing these chants. They say you don't even have to know the meaning of the Sanskrit words—you'll be affected by their vibration, regardless. Makes sense to me; we *are* vibration. Why wouldn't we be affected by the vibration of a word? Why do you think it's so powerful to chant with other people? Stronger vibes, man.

Communal singing/chanting is a very effective tool for supporting our inward journey as well as our outward community journey. It feels great to sing alone but singing with other people is Divine. Additionally, these chants are usually accompanied by the harmonium, a little keyboard with a bellows. You play with one hand and pump with the other. The harmonium resonates beautifully with the human voice.

After a few days of soaking up the vibes at Heaven, I hit the road again and headed for my next scheduled gathering with My People. It was a much longer drive than I expected. I got turned around in a few places along the way, and ultimately ended up driving through most of the night. When I finally found the place, it seemed too late (or early) to enter, so I parked my car on the side of a backcountry dirt road and tried to get some sleep, unsuccessfully. I was exhausted by the time I finally arrived on the property that morning.

The owner of the property, California Joe, had recently sold his business and used the profits to buy up almost a mile of waterfront on the Yuba River. You couldn't see the river from the main house. Getting to it required a somewhat treacherous hike down a steep, washed-out road with many switchbacks. After my grueling drive, I didn't really have the energy for the hike, and California Joe wouldn't be transporting people down in his truck until later in the day. For the most part, the property seemed pretty dry and dusty and not particularly alluring. It certainly didn't give me a great first impression. I even kind of wondered if I'd made a mistake in coming. It was such a stark contrast from the lush pools of Heaven. There was a pond on the upper part of the property though, so I took a quick dip (yes, with other naked hippies) which helped to invigorate my spirits, and then I decided to pitch in where I could and help with the setup for the event.

Joe asked that I carry a table down to the front gate where one of the volunteers was stationed to greet visitors. It was one of those heavy, old conference tables with a set of thick, pipe-like, retractable legs on each end. I balanced it on my head and started down to the front gate. While I was walking, the rhythm of my stride caused one of those heavy sets to come loose, and it crashed down right into the bridge of my nose. I felt kind of woozy and disoriented. I also felt that familiar wet and warm sensation you sometimes get after receiving a blow. I lowered the table down by my side and reached up to feel my nose. It wasn't gushing, but there was a fair amount of blood oozing from the fresh gash. For the second time I felt like I'd made a mistake in coming to this event. I kind of felt like crying, not because of the pain, but more from my physical and emotional exhaustion. Yeah, even though I'd had a bit of a catharsis at Heaven, I hadn't yet realized just how drained I was from my work in community mental health.

I do realize that I've now told you about three other times in this story where I did cry (in "The Last Day on the Rez" and just above), but really, I don't usually cry so easily. In fact, like most boys growing up, I learned how not to cry in most situations where I would have benefited from letting loose a few tears. I've learned over the years that it takes a stronger man to cry than it does to hold back those tender emotions. I can honestly say that sometimes I long to have a good cry. Unfortunately, I spent so many years learning how to hold back my tears, that they often elude me, even when they're most welcome.

When I got down to the gate, I introduced myself to the welcome lady, Shanti. She was very appreciative of me bringing the table down to her. Apparently, she'd been waiting for it for hours. I complained about my little incident on the way down and told her that I was thinking about leaving. She attempted to encourage me. "Hey, we're all on some kind of retreat, right? It's so beautiful here, just look around you. Have you *even* been down to the river yet?"

I resisted. "It's hot and dry and it took forever for me to get here."

"Hang out with me for a little while before you return to camp. I'm happy to be here, and my happiness is infectious."

She offered to smoke a joint with me. "It will help you to feel better."

I declined.

India and I were focused on having a baby. I wanted to be as clean and clear as possible while sharing my seed with my Beloved and focusing on inviting this little being into our lives. At this point I was in the middle of a fifteen-month stretch of daily yoga and clean living.

Shanti proceeded.

We sat in the shade under a small tree and chatted for a little while before I headed back to camp. I liked her, but I wasn't allowing her happiness to infect me. I kept resisting. I planned to leave when I got back.

I'd paid quite a bit up front for the three-day festival weekend, so I approached Joe when I got back to camp to see if he would refund any of the money before I left.

He wouldn't.

I told him about my incident with the table.

With a smile he exclaimed, "Good deal. You just worked off some karma!"

I frowned.

He *also* asked, "Have you even been down to the river yet?"

"No," I replied. "I think that I should just head back to Heaven or find another destination for my trip."

"Listen," Joe says, "Heaven has its hot springs—that's what makes it magical. The Yuba is what makes this place magical. I promise if you go down and take a dip in the river, you won't want to leave."

As much as I wanted to give up on that place, I acquiesced and agreed to stay, at least, until I experienced the Yuba.

"If you're not up for the hike, just stick around camp for another hour or so, and I'll take a group of people down in my truck. I can't say you'll regret it if you don't, because, frankly, you won't know what you're missing. But I do know you won't regret staying once you get down there. Besides, we've got some really great food and music on the way. Shoot man, the festival hasn't even started yet. We're just getting prepped."

On that note, one of his crew interrupted inquiring about logistics for the event, and Joe was off. He hollered back at me as he was leaving, "You're going to love the Yuba."

I decided I'd walk down to Shiva and gather up a few of my things. When I got back to the parking area, I felt like I was getting strange looks from people. I found it surprising and even a little odd. I was so looking forward to feeling welcome and comfortable among My People. I didn't understand it. I assumed that maybe it was because I didn't look like the average hippie—my hair was buzzed, I wasn't donning the latest hippie fashion, and I drove a cool black car with chrome wheels as opposed to an old VW with *Powered by vegetable oil* on the bumper sticker.

Looking back, I realize that really it had everything to do with my internal consciousness. Even though I loved to be part of this community, a part of me feared they would judge or reject me as not being "hippie enough". One of my favorite personal quotes applies here. Well, frankly, it applies to all situations. *Our perception of the external world is a direct reflection of our internal consciousness.* If we feel ugly inside, or we look for ugly in the world, that's what we'll see. Conversely, if we feel beautiful inside, and we look for beauty in the world, we'll find it. I feared rejection, so I looked for evidence to support my theory. And I found it!

I gathered up my gear and went looking for a good spot to set up camp. I continued to feel like I was getting strange looks from people. I also continued to feel like it was a bad idea to come to this event. There were numerous campsites located in a wooded area not far from the pond, so I ventured over there and meandered around looking for the perfect spot. Joe had constructed various wooden platforms to use as bases for tents, and he also built some pretty cool little wooden structures that people could sleep in.

While I was walking around, I came across a woman and her newborn baby hanging out on the deck of one of those platforms. She smiled when we made eye contact, so I walked over to greet her. She was sitting in lotus position with her baby cuddled up on a blanket next to her—a feminine manifestation of the Buddha. She and baby both had brown skin, soft round features, and deep dark eyes. They both looked completely blissed-out. When I gazed into their eyes, I witnessed eternity. This baby was fresh from the *Void*—the Mind of God—and she was exuding this Divine vibration. Her momma was resonating with the same potent magical energy. I fell in love with both of them instantly. My heart glowed.

After wishing them well, I found a great spot, set up camp, and then headed down to the river. I maneuvered my way down the steep, winding road, which emptied into a small, high-desert canyon with gorgeous, clear rushing waters. The Yuba! Where to begin. It truly is magical. Those clear, vibrant waters immediately washed away more of the remaining gloom I'd been feeling. I swam out to a big rock in the middle of the river, laid my naked body across the hot stone, and melted into nothingness. I could feel accumulated stress draining out of me. I sang part of an *Orisha* song I knew—my way to honor the Yuba. I had truly arrived, and I was grateful.

Several other festival goers gradually gathered down at the river, and before long, a pretty happenin' scene developed. There were people swimming and climbing the rocks around the river. Others were sunbathing, eating, or playing music. You could hear laughter and acoustic guitar echoing off the canyon walls. People were genuinely having an ecstatic experience.

I felt drawn to an Earth Tribe brother who was standing talking to a couple beautiful, young Earth Tribe sisters. They were just wrapping up their conversation when I approached, so I walked up and greeted him. He received me with a huge smile and radiant eyes. I immediately felt welcome. We just stood and looked around the scene for a few moments, while sharing the space and our smiles.

He had beautiful dark skin. He was a little taller than me, a little thinner, and he was gifted *within* measure. Holy God was he gifted! We created quite a contrast; you know, our skin tones and proportions. Interestingly, I found that I wasn't intimidated standing next to him. Normally, I wouldn't have even considered standing naked next to a man of his magnitude. But alas, I could see the beauty in each of us. I didn't feel lesser with him by my side. In fact, in some ways I felt more beautiful and comfortable in his presence. I was able to appreciate our distinguishing characteristics.

We shared some POCs regarding our love for sacred music and writing. I told him about my first book I started writing which chronicles my experiences with Uncle C.K. I felt an immediate connection with him. I call him *Asantehene*, the name for the Ashanti King.

I'd experienced quite a transition from the state I was in when I arrived. Between Shanti, Buddha Momma and her baby, the magical Yuba, and then my meeting with Asantehene, I was feeling accepted, and I was on my way to being rejuvenated.

I decided to head back up to my campsite and get some sleep before the evening performances began. Unfortunately, I tweaked my lower back during the hike up from the river. By the time I got up to the camping area, muscles in my sacrum had completely spasmed. I found it increasingly difficult to walk. Before heading into my tent, I decided to stop at the Yoga Yurt and stretch out for a bit. There was a woman lying down with blinders on. I quietly rolled out a mat and started to do some *asana* (yoga poses and deep breathing), but it was too painful, so I just laid down in *shavasana* (corpse pose).

After a few minutes, the woman approached me and said, "I was just over there meditating, and I'm getting a strong feeling that you could use some help. Would you mind if I placed my hands on your neck?"

Wow, I thought, *how's that for intuition?* Of course, I welcomed her assistance. Not only could I use the help, but I was totally intrigued by her awareness. She told me to lie still while she crouched behind my head and cradled my neck. Almost immediately, I could feel a tingling sensation running down my legs, kind of like when your leg falls asleep, but with no discomfort. That tingling feeling intensified until I could literally feel energy surging down my legs and out the bottom of my feet. I'd never experienced such a sensation, and I found it a little overwhelming. After about ten minutes, I felt the urge to go outside and plant my feet on the ground. I shared my desire, and she encouraged me on. I exited the yurt and went down in the grass where I stood in my bare feet. That tingling sensation magnified. I could feel energy flowing out the bottom of my feet into the ground.

When I returned to the Yoga Yurt, the woman was putting her shoes on to go. I was a little disappointed to find that our session was over, but she gave me a big smile and stated, "Mission accomplished."

"What did you do to me?" I asked. "I mean, that was amazing. I've never experienced anything like it."

"I performed some cranial sacral massage on you. It helps regulate the flow of cerebrospinal fluid. My spirit sensed that your spirit was in need, so I heeded your call."

"Ok," I said, having no reason to doubt her testimony. "Thank you so much. I'm grateful for your help. I'm *grateful* that you're aligned enough with your intuition to sense what I needed."

"Pass it on," she said with a smile, and then she left. I went to my tent and passed-out.

It was dark when I awoke to the sounds of familiar groovy music. It was the band I'd heard at Heaven playing their song, "I Want to be Naked". Like I said before, *hippie band*...My People. To be clear though, I think that you're all *My People* whether you realize it yet or not.

So, what is it that I love about hippies–about Earth Tribe people? Well, to be clear, I'm using my definition of hippies–people who choose to focus on evolving their consciousness and developing sustainable practices to foster this transformation. With that definition in mind, we can expand the group to include all kinds of people who meet these criteria. Really, everyone is welcome and encouraged to participate. There are certainly other groups of people in the world that embody these perspectives, and I'm here to tell you, they're *all* hippies. For instance, those yogis up in the mountains of Tibet and Nepal...hippies! Shamans and medicine men from around the world...yep, hippies. Sufi Devotional singers from Pakistan...you guessed it, they're hippies, too, just like many other people all over the world. You should know by now that I hold that term in the highest regard.

So, a few different unmemorable artists performed, and then White Light came out. I was hooked by his first few notes. Apparently, the theme for the weekend was *Magical* because when White Light started playing, I was enchanted. His music flipped a switch in me, and my heart burst open! I felt immense joy just sitting in his audience.

He sang in numerous languages including Spanish, Hebrew, and Sanskrit. His music pulled me right in. I found myself singing along to every one of his songs.

His real gift wasn't his performance, as talented as he is: it was the healing power of his music. White Light is a healer in the truest sense of the word. After I heard him play, I went back to bed. I was completely satiated. I felt transformed, however fleeting, or impermanent.

The next morning when I awoke, it felt like the muscles in my lower back had cemented together. The bumpy ground beneath my mat was no help. My spirits, however, were soaring. I felt elated. With a combination of effort and pain, I packed up my camp and headed down to my car.

I saw White Light in the parking area. He was loading his car a few spots over from mine. I went up to greet him and praise him for his remarkable performance. He casually looked deeply into my eyes, smiled, and gently responded, "Oh thanks, brother. I'm glad you enjoyed my performance."

When he looked at me, I felt like he really saw, *me*.

I purchased the only cd he had left on him. It was his first album he made as a teenager. He plays like eight different instruments on it. I listened to that album throughout the rest of my journey. I sang along to every song. I've been singing along to his music ever since.

Over the years I've purchased most of White Light's albums and listened to them hundreds of times. I've listened to his live, acoustic, solo album the most, but many of them have gotten their due attention. His music would eventually help ground me and prepare me to face the Rez each day with an open heart and an optimistic mind. I was confronted with such dysfunction on a daily basis that I came to depend on White Light's music and the music of other devotional musicians. I listened to him during the morning while I did yoga. I'd sing along with him on my way to work, and then I'd sing along again at night as I held my son in my arms and bounced him to sleep on our yoga ball. I always feel calmer, more aligned, and more loving after listening to—and singing along with—White Light.

It wasn't just the devotional musicians who got me through my years on the Rez. Their music only took me so far. It was kind of a strange dichotomy, but after a few hours on the job, I could no longer listen to this genre of music I'd embraced just earlier that morning. I came to realize that I became more hardened as the day went on. The more intense my interaction with one of the tweaking parents, the harder I became. Then I needed some music with an edge to help break up that heavy energy. At that point I would turn to Tool, Audioslave, and Metallica. They'd help me to let out some of that pent-up aggression, and they'd also recharge me for another round. Thanks fellas. All of you!

Indian Child Welfare

Being an effective ICW social worker is all about the relationships you build—the relationship with the child as well as your relationships with the parents, the grandparents, the aunties and uncles, representatives from Tribal Council, the court, the ICW Committee, law enforcement, education, mental health, medical and dental, substance abuse, domestic violence, supervisors and directors, the community...really, the Tribe as a whole. A good ICW social worker will balance all these relationships and more for the benefit of the child. A great social worker will always remain *child focused*. That means building the case around the child and always doing what's in the child's best interest.

ICW is about preserving Indian homes, families, and traditional culture. The *Indian Child Welfare Act* (ICWA) returned the power to the tribes to decide the fate of Indian children who were unsafe or at risk of being abused or neglected. ICWA gave the tribes jurisdiction over their own Tribal Member children *and* over Native children from other tribes who were domiciled on the tribe's reservation. In 1978 the tribes went from having zero power over their own children to having ultimate power over their own and, in many cases, other people's children—Tribal and non-Tribal.

Although the letter and spirit of the Indian Child Welfare Act are pretty clear, everyone seemed to interpret the Tribe's ICW code differently, or perhaps they "interpreted it" to their advantage, depending on the situation and whose family was involved. For instance, interpretation often depended on whether the children were members of Big Family or Little Family. Yes, more tribal politics, more FUS.

The part of ICWA that was most abused and manipulated was the determination of jurisdiction, which quite simply involved determining who has authority over a child, including the right to award custody. Our department and Tribal Court were notoriously inconsistent when it came to matters of jurisdiction, even though it was the first thing the court did in every initial hearing called the *Preliminary Inquiry*. In fact, it was one of the main purposes of the Preliminary Inquiry. The second purpose was to determine if the child was considered to be *A Child in Need of Protection*, as defined by the Tribe's ICW Code. Two questions are answered in the Preliminary Inquiry: Does the Tribe have jurisdiction? Is the child a Child in Need of Protection?

The Tribe's ICW code clearly stated that the Tribe had jurisdiction over any child who was (1) the biological child of an enrolled Tribal Member *and* (2) either already enrolled in the Tribe or eligible for enrollment in the Tribe; *or* (3) the Tribe had jurisdiction over any child who was an enrolled member of another tribe (or eligible for enrollment) and currently domiciled on the Tribe's Reservation.

Descendancy was not enough! Our department referred numerous cases to the State over the years involving children who were descendants of the Tribe, but who either did not have an enrolled biological parent (1), or the child themselves was not eligible for enrollment in any tribe (2&3). As you will see, the Tribe was sure to include a big loophole in the code regarding jurisdiction.

I witnessed many *abuses of power* by the Tribe, but the worst was with the Indian Child Welfare Act—the power to take away anyone's child, as they see fit. The Tribe's own code stated that in matters where jurisdiction was in question, the Tribe had the authority to determine if they wanted to take jurisdiction (the first of the loopholes). In other words, *they will take it if they want to*. As you will see in the next chapter, even in matters where jurisdiction wasn't in question, and the Tribe clearly had no right to take jurisdiction, they did. They eventually came up with another jurisdictional loophole—*The Adoption List*. All in good time.

I called the State regarding jurisdiction in dozens of cases. It didn't matter who I talked to from frontline social workers up to managers and directors; if I said the Tribe wanted jurisdiction in the case, they instantly capitulated. In fact, they always seemed relieved they didn't have to handle it. Well, they are state social workers; they're more overworked than public school teachers. In all situations, they never required proof that the child was an enrolled Tribal Member or eligible for enrollment in any tribe. Let that one sink in. In all cases the State *never* required proof that a child was truly a Native! They just took our word for it.

Because Grandma Wanted It

My leadership at the Tribe had made it exceedingly clear: we were to do no involuntary terminations of parental rights and no adoptions! By this point in time, Tribal Court had only terminated parental rights in one case, and that parent had initiated the process himself—he wanted his rights terminated. It was my case, and I was well aware of the fact that this was an exception to the rule and to our practice.

Around my fifth year with the Tribe, I watched in dismay as our department removed a non-Native child from a non-Native teen mother whose parents were also non-Native, and she and her child did not live on the Reservation. The girl's grandmother was a Tribal Member, but this young mother and the rest of her aforementioned family members were not eligible for enrollment in any tribe. As I mentioned previously, descendancy was not enough—not by the code, by precedence, or by our practice. The Tribe's ICW code stated that the Tribe had ultimate jurisdiction in any municipality, as long as the child was either already enrolled in the Tribe, or, at least, eligible for membership in the Tribe. This child was neither.

I knew the Tribe had no jurisdiction over this child by their own ICW code (loopholes notwithstanding), and therefore, no right to open a case. What made this situation even more appalling was that Stan told this young mother that her baby would be adopted.

I watched from the sidelines as Stan directed one of my co-workers to not only file in Tribal Court to have this child removed from her mother's custody, but to also keep telling her that her parental rights would be terminated, and she would have to give her baby up for adoption. These actions went against everything I had been taught about Tribal jurisdiction and best social work practice. I felt so sorry for this young mother. She had no idea what her rights were, and no one from our department or the Tribe seemed willing to tell her. The case was staffed in court and with the ICW Committee numerous times. Everyone sat back and watched this baby get taken from her mother and given to a Member of the Tribe. This is exactly the kind of story that gives social workers a bad reputation for stealing babies.

Even in State social work, in most cases parents could be in noncompliance with court orders for about a year before the court would even begin to entertain the possibility of terminating the parent's rights, and it would take even longer for a child to be adopted. I really couldn't understand why this mother had been told from day one that her rights would be terminated, and her child would be adopted. *It stunk to high hell.*

About a year into this case, my supervisor who was handling it was fired (for some unbelievable FUS), and it became my case.

Fuck! I thought. *This goes against everything I've been taught about Indian Child Welfare.* I knew in my heart I should make it right. I also knew that making it right would shift the focus to me (violating Rule #4 of The Code—*Keep your head down...*), and I would likely make some enemies doing it. No doubt, someone with power was behind it.

One day I asked our ICW assistant who had been closely involved, "What the hell is going on with this case? Why did the Tribe take this child? Why did Stan tell the mother that she had to give her baby up for adoption?"

"It's very simple," she replied. "Grandma wanted it done, so Stan did it."

Her grandmother was the Court Director.

This made a lot more sense given the dynamics of the case. The baby was placed with a Tribal Member who was directly related to the Court Director. Also, I knew from experience that the only hearings the Court Director sat in on were for cases that were either highly politicized or involved her family members. This case was both. The Court Director sat in on all of the hearings for this case. She knew exactly what was going on.

It was politicized in the sense that many high-level directors knew about it, they knew it was bad business for the Tribe, and yet no one was saying a word on behalf of the mother or the child. They were all turning a blind eye to dirty politics.

I kept thinking about this poor little girl who would grow up wondering why her mother had abandoned her to the Tribe. It would be years, but I knew at some point she would have questions regarding her past in ICW. I knew because some of my teen clients used to ask me those very questions. "Why did my mom give me up?" "Why didn't she want me?" "Why didn't she fight for me?" "*What's wrong with me?*"

The first time I met with the mother, I educated her about her rights. I told her the Tribe's ICW department had no right taking her daughter. She seemed to believe me, but she also seemed totally afraid. She said, "What can I do against the Tribe? With all their money and power, what chance could I possibly have against them?"

I told her, "I'm not suggesting you fight the Tribe. I'm telling you that you don't have to have your parental rights terminated and give your daughter up for adoption as my predecessors have convinced you. You can complete the court-ordered services, get Elisa back in your custody, and get your case dismissed. And then, if you decide you want to fight them for any wrongdoing, that's your business."

I guided her throughout the reunification process. I encouraged her the best I could every time we spoke. She was so discouraged in the beginning.

She was consistent with her visits, her appointments, and her schooling. Over time she gained confidence in herself and trust in me. Together, we helped her get her daughter back and get her case dismissed.

Before I got that case, the Court Director had always been really friendly and supportive of me. She would invite me into her office, share food with me, and let me use her computer. We even shared our disdain for Judge Batshit Crazy. The Director was friendly like that with me for years—we never had an issue.

Then out of nowhere, she accused me of sexual harassment (hitting on her). Now keep in mind this lady was literally almost 80 years old. I guess that was the best she could come up with. That's really saying something since I'd been presenting ICW cases in her court for years. Apparently, she couldn't come up with any legitimate concerns about my casework.

I confronted her one day about her false allegations. I told her I knew it was all about politics. She got all flustered and said, "You're a liar! Liar!"

Liar? I thought, *I will never cease to be amazed.*

New Management

I was on my own again for about six months when I started hearing news about the Tribe hiring new management for social services. Yeah, Stan was gone by then too, but that's a whole 'nutha story. Now, normally I wouldn't be so eager to have additional management, but as opposed to no management, it seemed like a preferable compromise. Piggy had been promoted from being Lucky's administrative assistant to temporary Director, and I couldn't get her to address any of my concerns. She kept putting me off, saying, "These issues will have to wait until the new director comes on." I could understand if these *issues* were regarding things like purchasing supplies or hiring a new caseworker, but numerous safety matters were going unaddressed, and I was becoming increasingly concerned about the safety and well-being of several of the children and families we served. I couldn't understand why Piggy wouldn't provide *any* direction. I could only guess that it was a combination of her lack of education (she only had a GED) and her total disdain for many of our ICW families–her fellow Tribal Members.

Although the ICW Code seemed pretty simple and straightforward regarding jurisdiction, we had many cases that were open for years at a time in which the Tribe had no right taking jurisdiction. Wildflower's was one such case. She was an enrolled Tribal Member, and she lived on the Reservation, but her children were not eligible for enrollment in any tribe. Our department had intervened in their lives numerous times over the years and provided extensive services for them to address the safety issues and other identified concerns. The Tribe didn't legally have jurisdiction over this family, nor did our department have the resources to adequately serve them.

Wildflower could barely take care of herself, let alone her young children. She could maintain stability for brief periods of time while she had professional workers actively involved, literally coming to her house four to five times a week. However, as soon as services were decreased or discontinued, it was usually only a matter of days before we started getting calls from concerned community members alleging ongoing neglect.

The first time I went to Wildflower's to perform a child welfare visit I found numerous safety concerns throughout her home and property. She seemed entirely oblivious of things that I found distressing. Many of us tried to help her over the years. Throughout the course of her children's cases, she never seemed to gain the needed awareness and understanding of the ongoing safety issues and risks to her children.

Whenever I transported them, she focused all her attention on me. It was very uncomfortable and, at times, unnerving. It didn't seem to matter how many times I redirected her attention back to her children, within moments she would be fixated on me, literally staring at me from the passenger seat while her children were clamoring for her attention in the backseat. She had developed an infatuation with me. I talked to Stan about this situation a few times. At first, he just made inappropriate jokes about me going to see her alone at her house, but eventually he seemed to understand, and he transferred the case to another worker. Of course, in time they all got fired, and I was the only one left to work with her—against my professional judgement.

I'd practically begged Piggy to take an official stance regarding jurisdiction and services for this family, to no avail. Piggy maintained her position for months—nothing was going to happen until we got our new managers. This was the first case I wanted to staff once I got a new supervisor or director. I hoped we could find some solutions with new leadership.

Eventually I heard that both our new director and ICW supervisor were Tribal Members. I asked around among my clients—the adults and the kids—as well as other professionals and Tribal Members to see what the community consensus was regarding my incumbent leadership. I heard from several families that our director was a former Councilman who was removed from Tribal Council for embezzlement. *Great,* I thought, *our new director is known for being an infamous criminal.*

One evening I ran into one of the Tribe's former executives and his family at a pizza place I frequented. He was a highly respected leader in the community. After greeting each other with warm smiles and handshakes, he asked me, "What do you think about your new director?"

Trying to be positive I said, "I'm really excited to have an Elder Tribal Member running Social Services. I have high hopes for our program and our department."

He looked at me real serious and said, "You better keep an eye on your new director—he's smart."

Interestingly enough, but certainly not surprising, my new supervisor was my new director's niece. #1 Rule in Indian Country.

I asked around about her, too. Most people I talked to in the community didn't seem to know much about her. I asked Betsy, a friend who was a Tribal employee at the Health Clinic, and she said, "She didn't grow up around here, but she has a reputation for being rude and arrogant—she thinks she's better than the other Indians on the Rez."

I was walking through the Admin Building one day, and another staff member named Jayden said, "Hey, I hear you guys are finally getting a new supervisor."

"Yeah," I replied, "and she's a Tribal Member. I'm really excited about it."

He said, "I know plenty about her. I'll give you a couple months—you won't be so excited."

The same day another staff member said, "I hear that you guys are going to have ICW run by someone with no ICW experience." I wasn't sure what to say.

The next day another staff I knew shared more negative comments about her, "Odessa Knight's going to be your boss? Good luck. You're going to need it. She'll make a horrible supervisor."

I guess the word was getting around about new management in Social Services. I really was genuinely excited when I first heard about them coming on. Unfortunately, I got increasingly discouraged the more I heard from members of the community. Finally, I asked a trusted co-worker who knew her. He said, "Odessa Knight, huh? Well, she's educated, that's the good news. The bad news: she's really close friends with Piggy."

That was the statement that concerned me the most. If she was good friends with Piggy, well frankly, I was fucked.

I figured that my only chance was to keep doing what I was doing. I needed to keep following my code including doing my job and keeping my head down (an almost impossible combination), and maybe I'd earn her respect over time.

Barney Smith

My new director Barnie Smith started a few months before Odessa. I was eager to meet with him so we could discuss a few pressing issues regarding our Tribal Member clients. I was excited because after all these months I finally had a director who could make some serious decisions that would benefit the Tribal families whom we served.

I went to his office to introduce myself. At first, he perked up and looked at me like a tasty dessert. He clearly liked what he saw. Though once I introduced myself, and he realized who I was, he seemed annoyed with me. He was obviously attracted to me, but he also seemed conflicted, presumably with pre-existing loyalties. I could only imagine what Piggy and others had already said to him. After polite salutations and a little small talk, I asked him, "Mr. Smith, would it be possible if we staffed a case?"

He looked at me as though he had no idea what I was talking about.

I said, "I want to talk to you about one of the families we work with in ICW—the mother to be specific. She's a Tribal Member."

He seemed uninterested and more annoyed.

I continued, "I've been working with this mother and her children on and off for the last few years. I've witnessed several of my co-workers attempt to work with her as well. I'm concerned that the Tribe has neither legal jurisdiction or the resources to serve this family, so I strongly suggest we transfer the children's cases to the State so the family can receive the necessary services and resources to address their ongoing safety issues."

He scrunched his brow as he looked me up and down. He didn't seem to understand me at all. Not just what I was saying, but me in general. He seemed confused as to why I was even talking to him about it. I was also confused. He was the Social Service Director, and he was responsible for the ICW program.

He basically ignored my testimony, and then went on to tell me about his glorious executive banking experience from thirty years prior. I wasn't really sure how this was relevant to our discussion, but I patiently listened as he gloated about some of his past achievements, and then when the opportunity presented itself again, I asked about our Tribal Member client. I again apprised him that the Tribe did not officially have jurisdiction over her children's welfare cases because they were not eligible for enrollment in the Tribe, or any other tribe for that matter. I told him that I was gravely concerned about the children's safety.

With a pretentious, effeminate tone he stated, "I'm well aware of the needs of our Tribal Members. I don't need any additional information from you at this time." He turned and went back to his desk and started rifling through papers, giving me the unambiguous message: our meeting was over.

I knew I shouldn't have been surprised or disappointed. I was sure Piggy had already filled his head with vitriol. But I still kept getting my hopes up with every new supervisor, manager, or director. I kept hoping that each of my new leadership would understand child welfare, ICWA, and the importance of strictly following the Tribe's code regarding jurisdiction in child welfare cases. I kept hoping they would have a heart for doing this work.

Barney behaved as though child welfare work were below him—that our clients were below him. Thanks to Piggy, I was no longer surprised by this attitude from one Tribal Member toward her fellow Tribal Members. Piggy held such disdain for many of the families we served. She didn't hide the fact that she felt they were undeserving of many of the resources they were receiving. I never could understand why she chose to work in social services given her contempt for the people whom we served. She stated to me many times, "You didn't have to grow up with them."

Funny thing about Barney…he brought his own, um, *assistant* with him who he referred to as his nephew. It was funny because everyone else referred to this young man as *Barney's boy toy*.

In a gesture of good faith, I presented both of them with potted plants as welcoming gifts to our department, to our new team. Neither of them acknowledged their gift. Barney looked as though he was suspicious of my intentions, and his nephew just looked confused.

Odessa Knight a.k.a. *Full of Herself*

A few months after Barney started, I heard that my new supervisor Odessa would be starting soon. Although I was feeling pretty hopeless regarding the prospect of things getting any better under his leadership, I still held out hope for Odessa. She had a master's degree, and, well, I just had to keep focusing on the positive. Maybe she'd prove to be an asset to our department and to the families we served.

I also bought her a potted plant and left it on her desk. I attached a simple note that welcomed her to the team and expressed my excitement about having a new supervisor.

On Odessa's third day I showed up at her office at the TANF building (temporary assistance program) and went in to introduce myself. She'd been unavailable her first two days because she was busy meeting other managers as well as the TANF staff whom she'd also be supervising.

I walked to her open door, saw her sitting at her desk, smiled, and introduced myself. She looked at me with a familiarity that suggested she already knew who I was. She seemed disappointed to see me standing at her door. I imagined all the things that Piggy had probably told her over the last four or five years, and then I resolved myself to give her a different impression than the one she already seemed to possess.

She looked toward the floor, sighed, and then invited me to sit down. When she did look up, she caught me eyeing the new plant on her desk, and then in an obligatory fashion, she mumbled, "Thanks for the plant."

I enthusiastically welcomed her to ICW. I told her, "I'm so grateful to have you here. I've been alone for so long; I really need some help. More importantly, there are several issues that require managerial approval."

She sat with her body perpendicular to mine. Her arms were crossed against her chest, and her legs were crossed, not gingerly and feminine, but masculine and guarded. She was pretty with a thick, athletic build. She talked for a while about her family and *everyone* they know in the community. When she was done talking, I went right into staffing Wildflower's case. I told her about Wildflower and her children, and her chronic instability. I apprised her of all the services she'd received over the past few years and all the bizarre behaviors she exhibits. I told her that her children were not Tribal Members, they were not eligible for enrollment in any tribe, and they needed more services and supports than what the Tribe could offer. I strongly encouraged that we transfer Wildflower's cases to the State.

Odessa stood up from her chair, glared down at me, and then stomped out of her office demanding, "We are not referring any Tribal Members to the State as long as I'm running ICW!" Apparently, our meeting was over. I was oh for two with new management.

Well, I thought, *that's not a good sign. What can I do, but focus on my work? Maybe in time she'll understand.*

And that's just what I did. In fact, I worked harder during that next year and a half under her supervision than I had worked any of the previous five years. I wanted my skills and accomplishments to be recognized. I wanted to feel accepted. I figured that maybe if I just kept perfecting my social work skills and continuing to do a great job, then maybe someday she'd recognize what an asset I'd become to the program—really, the Tribe. I'd spent the past five years building relationships with the ICW families and compassionately serving everyone I could in the community. I knew our ICW families better than any other professional at the Tribe, and I'd become relatively accomplished as an ICW social worker. By this time, I'd already reunified dozens of families with their children. Not only had I grown to clearly understand the scope and nature of this work, but I'd also grown to love it.

This would be a great point in the story to have another montage. Imagine if you really wanted to prove yourself to your boss, so you worked non-stop, day after day, being as effective and productive as you could possibly be. I was kind of a maniac when it came to performance. The moment I got in the car in the morning I was on the phone. Throughout the day, if I wasn't face-to-face with a client or another professional, then I was on the phone either talking, emailing, or texting. After every contact, I'd email Odessa with an update. I must have driven her crazy because I was constantly updating her with my activity. I wanted her to see just how active and engaged I was working with the community. I wanted her to know how effective I was at my job. I documented everything. I'd already become accustomed to this practice as a survival technique, but now I really upped my game. I became obsessed with proving to Odessa and Barney that I was an invaluable member of the team. I badly wanted their recognition and approval. Besides, they say, *show, don't tell.* I could have told them how hard I'd worked over the previous years, and how much I'd achieved, but actions speak louder than words. If anything was going to win them over it had to be my actions. That would prove to be a very tough sale.

Sadly, it didn't matter how hard I worked, how much my clients liked me, or how effective I was as a social worker. Barney and Odessa always seemed disappointed to see me. It may have helped if either one of them had *any* social work experience. Maybe they would've appreciated my abilities. Odessa pretended to have ICW experience in the beginning, but the more I staffed cases with her, the more I saw that she really didn't understand the scope of ICW. I finally pressed her one day to get specific details of the previous ICW experience she alluded to. I got the details all right. She was a collateral on cases that involved ICW, but never held any ICW cases, nor would she *ever* hold any ICW cases. In the year and a half she supervised ICW, she accomplished feats that no other ICW supervisor has ever managed to pull off. *She never took on a case, she never removed a child, and she never stepped in court!* How could she respect and appreciate what I was doing for the program when she had no gauge to measure my performance? Besides, she had judged me long before she ever met me.

When I did staff cases with her, she maintained the same closed body language, and she huffed and puffed. I'm not exaggerating. I'd be in the middle of presenting a case, and she'd huff or puff and roll her eyes at me. She was dismissive of anything I had to offer. Many times, she would curtly state with a condescending tone, "I already know all about this family." I found that response interesting since the families she said that about didn't seem to know anything about her. I imagine she knew them just as well as she knew me, *before* we met.

It didn't help that our clients, other professionals from the Tribe, and people in the community were constantly complaining about her. Numerous Tribal staff disclosed to me how they thought she was arrogant, rude, and disrespectful. Well, maybe it did help; at least, I knew I wasn't the only one she treated that way. I encouraged everyone who came to me with complaints, "Please talk to her supervisor Barney about any of your concerns."

Many people responded the same, "Her uncle? What good will that do?"

After months of hearing these same types of reports from numerous individuals throughout the community, I decided I should at least try to bring the situation to Barney's attention. I approached him several times over the next month and asked if we could talk. I told him I was getting a lot of complaints about Odessa from our clients and other professionals at the Tribe. Every time he gave me the same response in his usual effeminate, condescending tone, "I have more important things to deal with." I don't know about other family traits, but they definitely had that *condescending tone thing* in common.

Eventually, I decided I'd take the risk and send him an email detailing my concerns. Given my experience with Stan and Lucky years before, I knew it was a gamble. I knew I'd be violating rule #1 of The Code, but I decided that I, at least, wouldn't violate rule #2 and name the people who were making complaints. I'd keep my message relatively generic and simply inform him that numerous Tribal staff and ICW clients were complaining about her unprofessional behavior, so I'd like to schedule a time to talk to him about it.

I did, however, share specific examples of how she'd been treating me. I told him, "I already asked her if we could talk about the apparent communication issues we seem to be having. I also told her that I didn't feel supported by her." Additionally, I shared the following dialogue that had recently transpired between us.

I asked her, "Do you want me working in this department? I would like to be able to plan for my future."

She responded, "Do you want to work in this department?"

I said, "Yes, absolutely, I love my job. Do you want me to work here?"

She responded, "I can't have an opinion on that."

I said, "Wow! Ok, well I wish you could express your opinion about that. Uh, thanks...bye."

Barney responded to this email by writing me up for spreading gossip. I had followed Chain of Command (as expected) by reporting my concerns about my supervisor to my director. I had even documented numerous complaints about her from our clients and other professionals. Of course, she was his niece. I knew it was probably pointless, but I thought I should at least have the documentation.

For the record, at this point I had worked for over five years in a position where most people didn't last a year. I'd never been put on probation, and my only write-ups were my demotion from Stan (for calling *him* out for his lack of integrity) and Barney's accusation that I was spreading gossip.

Simple Math

I had another issue I wanted to address with Odessa and Barney—my pay. I had numerous justifications. Stan promised me I would regularly receive an annual step-increase. Stan and Lucky had demoted me (punished me, really) for my *Rookie Mistake*. I ran the department by myself for an extended period without a promotion or a pay increase, and during one of my annual reviews, another former supervisor promised I'd receive an additional step-increase. That supervisor was fired before he could fulfill his commitment. In fact, at that time our department went from eight staff including Lucky, Stan, Piggy, said supervisor, a Tribal Member caseworker (the only Tribal Member from the Tribe that worked as a social worker while I was there), a case aide, and an administrative assistant to just me and Piggy. Of course, Piggy didn't do any casework. They were all fired. Now, Stan had an exit strategy; he *was* a politician. But, ultimately, they got him in the end.

Things really did go measurably better when it was just me handling cases. We had way less complaints to Council—way less drama in general. I didn't have to take the fall for Stan's false promises to TC and our clients, nor did I have to clean up the messes created by my co-workers. Well, I did during the transition, but afterwards I was able to establish the tone of the cases, which typically generated way less political backlash. I figured the Tribe was getting quite a bargain with just me as clearly evidenced by how much smoother things ran, and, more importantly, by how many Tribal families were being successfully reunited. That may sound arrogant, but *ICW ain't no joke!* Few people can do it, and even fewer can do it well. Just ask someone who grew up on the Rez. They know.

After my new leadership had been on the job for a few months, I decided I'd attempt to broach the subject with them. I figured it was appropriate timing since I was coming up on another anniversary with the Tribe. I went up to Barney's office at a time I knew he'd be with Odessa. I presented myself at his door, greeted both of them, and then I asked if I could have a moment with them to discuss a work-related issue.

After just staring at me for a moment, Barney offered for me to come in. Odessa never looked up but sighed and mumbled in a gloomy Eeyore-fashion, "Hi, Scott". I told them I had some concerns about my pay, and then I shared some of the details I listed above.

Barney asked, "Well, how much do you make?"

Frankly, in my mind that question wasn't even relevant. What was relevant were the commitments that had been made to me by my former leadership, my duties, my time on the job, and my effectiveness as an ICW social worker. I kind of wished I'd told him that what I was making wasn't relevant, but I figured he and Odessa both had access to that information anyway, so what difference did it make. Besides, I wasn't about to offer any resistance.

When I stated my hourly wage, Odessa abruptly swiveled around in her chair and, for that moment, gave me her *full* attention. It was the most direct and present attention she gave me the entire time we worked together. She looked both shocked and appalled.

Dang, I thought, *that can't be good.*

Barney also seemed a little surprised. He told me he'd look into it, and then he dismissed me.

Par for the course, he never brought it up again. After a few weeks with no response, I decided to take a different approach with him. I knew he had no foundation to appreciate my expertise as a social worker, and similarly, I don't think he cared about the successful work I'd done with his fellow Tribal Members, but I figured with all his *glorious* banking experience he could appreciate the value of a dollar.

I sent him an email entitled, **Simple Math**. I also cc'd Odessa. In it I wrote about a recent training I'd attended at the Tribe.

"Subject: Simple Math…

Barney,

I have taken a couple of the training sessions offered by the Tribe with Smart Sequoia from Woodland Research and Counseling. The last one I took was Supervision 1 back in April. Smart Sequoia talked extensively about the cost of losing an employee including loss of productivity for the entire department, advertising, interviewing, hiring, training, etc., (not to mention the loss to the families who have invested in a relationship with the social worker). Three to six months minimum to get people 'up to speed' (a year in ICW). $$$

The following social workers have left since I started:

[I named nine of my former co-workers including Stan]

(I am probably forgetting at least one).

No two-week notice from any of them. Most were fired.

It's like buying the same house over and over again.

I am like a rental that always stays rented. Rentals require maintenance. Please compare the costs.

Yesterday was my six-year anniversary with the Tribe. I want my two-step pay increase that was promised a year and a half ago.

Lead Social Worker Position (?)

-Scott"

He never responded. I'm pretty certain he read it though. As often as he seemed annoyed with me, he also always seemed intrigued. Barney was clearly conflicted when it came to me. Unfortunately, his alliances with Piggy and Odessa always seemed to win out.

I saw him a few weeks later in the Admin Building, so I approached him and asked about my email. He told me he didn't know what I was talking about. I didn't believe him. I just had a feeling. He promptly closed our discussion with that familiar phrase, "I have more important things to deal with."

Making the Rounds

Although I made numerous attempts to find POCs with Barney, Piggy, and Odessa, I was never successful. It didn't matter if we had things in common or not, as long as they were unwilling to accept me, there was no POC to be had. Eventually, I gave up. Eventually, I hated working with all of them.

However, I continued to love working with the ICW families, *and* I grew to love interacting with many of my co-workers at the Tribe. My job required me to come into contact with numerous Tribal employees from various departments, and I liked connecting with all of them.

The women who worked at the front desk at the Tribal Center were some of my favorites. As I made my rounds each day, these ladies were always friendly and courteous. They also worked way harder than the average Tribal employee. Many a computer screen had the familiar blue and white banner up, as people scrolled through their workdays. It often amazed me that they had so much time to engage in this endeavor (especially when I was always so busy), but not the ladies at the front desk. They were always on; their jobs demanded it. They arrived at the Tribe and started their workday way before most other employees. They only got their regimented standard breaks, and they were always still working long after most employees had already left, especially on paydays when the Tribe literally cleared out well before the end of the workday. I particularly liked the mother and daughter team who managed the front desk for years. I imagine they are still there, smiling, answering phones, and helping whomever presents themselves at their gateway.

I also really liked the ladies at the daycare. I often went there to visit my young clients who attended their program. These women were always professional, enthusiastic, and accommodating. Many a times, I sat with Director Brave Heart in her office and shared our love (our POCs) for serving Tribal children, discussing spiritual growth, and writing.

Additionally, the staff at the Health Clinic, the Youth Center, the Accounting Department, Housing, Law Enforcement, IT, Tribal Court, Maintenance, and

Substance Abuse were *always* awesome! I enjoyed working and connecting with all of them.

When you walk through life with an open heart, you'll meet many people on your path who share this predilection. I was often met with smiles and salutations as I made my rounds each day.

Big Thunder

The first time I saw Big Thunder he was passed out. One of his family members had called me to make a *referral* (a report of child abuse or neglect). She claimed, "Big Thunder and Rosetta are held up in a motel down in South Town. They've been druggin' for days, and they aren't taking care of their children. ICW needs to go down there and tell them their kids are gonna be placed and they need to go to treatment."

Most referrals we received were from concerned family members. Most of them not only included reports about the parents using drugs and neglecting their children, but also directives on what ICW was supposed to do about it. I'd gotten used to it.

The caller gave me the name of the motel, details about the children, and brief histories on Big Thunder and Rosetta. Big Thunder allegedly had a long history of domestic violence and drug abuse. He'd been jailed numerous times for assault, and he'd been hooked on drugs since he was a teenager. Rosetta also had a long history of drug abuse, these were her fourth and fifth children, and she'd never been successful staying clean. Her other three children were being raised by their aunties.

I decided to go to the motel in South Town to see if I could find the parents. I knew if I substantiated serious concerns about them, I'd also need to identify stable placements for the children. I got the directions and headed out there right away. The motel was located in an industrial area in a seedy part of town where the street was lined with warehouses, dive bars, and used car lots. It looked like the kind of motel that would be frequented by drug addicts and prostitutes. I felt like I should have police backup, so I contacted local law enforcement for assistance. Dispatch told me that no officers were currently available, I could wait for an officer (which could take hours), or I could proceed on my own. I decided to go to the manager's office and see what I could find out. After identifying myself as a Tribal social worker, the manager eagerly gave me the room number where the couple was staying.

He directed me into the courtyard and up to the second floor where I found their room. I knocked on the door, and to my surprise, a woman answered right away. I was kind of hoping no one would respond so I could just get out of there.

I said, "Hi, my name is Scott Strider. I'm an ICW worker from the Tribe."

She invited me right in. She seemed to be expecting me. I looked around the room and saw a large man, presumably Big Thunder, face down on the couch. There were no children present. I asked the woman, "Can you please identify yourself and the man on the couch?"

She politely responded, "My name is Rosetta. That's Big Thunder."

I asked, "Do you know why I'm here?"

She lowered her eyes. "Probably 'cause my mom or sister called ICW to report us. They've been saying they would call you guys if we didn't go to treatment and get clean." She kept staring at the floor.

"I understand that you and Big Thunder have two young children. Can you tell me who's taking care of them?"

She looked up. "They've been staying with their cousins 'cause we're so bad on drugs. I suppose ICW wants to take them now."

"I'm here to investigate and get information to help me determine if your children are at risk of abuse or neglect. I did receive a call, as you suspected, but, frankly, I didn't really know what to expect when I came out here."

"Who called you? Was it my sister?"

"That's actually confidential information. People who make referrals to ICW are allowed to remain anonymous."

"Well, our kids are fine. Like I said, they're with their cousins, but I know we need to go to treatment."

"Are you willing to go to treatment?"

"Yeah."

"If your children do need to be placed while you are in treatment, who would you want them to live with?"

"Not any of my family. They'll just hold it over me. And Big Thunder's family won't have anything to do with us. They're all tired of us druggin'."

"Do you know if Big Thunder's willing to go to treatment?" He hadn't stirred a bit.

"You'll have to ask him yourself, but you're not going to get anything out of him today. He'll be knocked out for a while. He's been up for days."

"Ok. I'll try to contact him again soon. I can also talk to the ICW Committee about placement recommendations for your children if they do need to be placed. For now, I want to commend you on being so open and honest. It sounds like you're ready to get some help. I encourage you to go see Elk up at Substance Abuse so he can assist you with treatment. Is there anything I can do to help you in the meantime?"

"No."

"Do you agree with the concerns that were reported about you guys neglecting your kids?"

"I'm not neglecting them. They're with their cousins. It's not like I abandoned them in an alley."

"Ok," I said. "Let me ask you this: are you currently in a position to take care of them?"

"I just told you that we've been druggin'. No, we're not able to take care of them until we get clean."

"Do I have your permission to set up formal ICW placements for them?"

"Yeah, but just until I get done with treatment. Then they're coming to live with me. I know how to be a good parent. Big Thunder doesn't have a clue. He's still a kid himself."

I gave her my card and asked that she call me as soon as she made contact with Substance Abuse, and then I inquired about contact info for her and her children's current caregiver.

"My phone is broke, but you can call my mom or sister—I'm sure you already have their numbers—and they can make arrangements with you for our children."

Rosetta showed me out, and I left.

I called Flower from the ICW Committee on my way back to the Rez and filled her in on the situation. She said she'd make some calls and get back to me. Flower called me back before I reached the office. "I talked to several of the extended family members. Rosetta was right. No one wants to be an ICW placement. Many of them have their own drug issues. They told me, 'We don't want ICW breathing down our backs.' I was able to find placements for the boys though with two local families who really want them. They're both from here, and they already know the boys."

Flower made all the arrangements to have the boys each transitioned into their respective placements. I got the contact information for each, and then called them to introduce myself and make plans to see the boys. I also gave Flower a big heartfelt thanks. She was awesome at quickly finding suitable placements and doing her best to have the least amount of impact on the children.

A little aside…when you think about social work, I'm sure you can imagine the stereotypical, dramatic scene with parents fighting, cops intervening, and the children crying in the back seat of some social worker's car (a total stranger) as they're being *taken* away to some foreign foster home on the other side of town. Erase that image from your mind. It doesn't apply here—not to how I did Tribal social work, anyway. In eight years, I never transported a child in my car immediately after they were removed from their parents or extended family members. I always had family do it. I regularly moved children with established cases to new placements, but by then they knew me. I was no longer a stranger. Often, I was seen as an ally, maybe even a friend.

I never heard back from Rosetta. A few weeks later I found out from Flower that Rosetta had enrolled in inpatient treatment within a couple weeks of our meeting, but then she left shortly after she arrived and went missing. I called Elk to see what I could find out. He confirmed Flower's report, "Yeah, Rosetta came to see me a couple days after she met with you at the motel in South Town.

Fortunately, I was able to line up a bed for her right away in a facility about an hour south of here. She entered the program two days later, but then she started calling me within a few hours of intake saying I needed to find her a bed somewhere else. She had her reasons—said the staff weren't supportive, the other residents had too many problems, you know, the typical excuses our clients give when they aren't really ready to get clean. The next day I got a call from her counselor letting me know that Rosetta had left a few hours after she called me. When I talked to her, I tried to encourage her to commit to a couple more days, at least until she got through the worst of her detox, but you know how it goes."

"Well, I'm grateful for your efforts," I responded. "She seemed like she was ready to get help, but I'm sure it must be hell coming off those drugs and being faced with all your demons. Let me know if she resurfaces, and I'll do the same."

Elk asked, "What about the boys? Where you able to find a placement for them?"

"Yes. Flower from the Committee was able to set up placements right away with a couple professionals from right here at the Tribe. Both boys made smooth transitions into these respective homes. Flower had checked with both sides of the boys' families, and no one was willing to take them, so I think it's a blessing she was able to find Native placements here in the community, especially so quickly. They'll be able to attend the Tribe's daycare, so they'll see each other most days, and both placement custodians are amenable to visits with the boys' parents and extended family."

Doubtful, I asked, "Have you heard anything about Big Thunder?"

With a sigh he muttered, "Not a word."

I commiserated, "I get the impression that he's pretty deep in his use, but we can always hope. I'll see what I can learn about him in the community. Given his M.O., it probably won't be long before he gets arrested again. If nothing else, I can reach out to him once he's back in jail."

Elk agreed, "Yeah, given his record, the police will probably see him before we do. He certainly has issues with meth, but it's his drinking that gets him locked up. From what I hear, all of his assaults have happened when he's been on a drinking binge."

I thanked Elk and ended the call.

I got a call from Elk a couple days later informing me that Big Thunder had come to see him, and Elk was able to set up a treatment bed at a local, all-Native facility. He said, "Big Thunder told me he wants his boys back."

"Great!" I replied. "I'll get out to his program right away so I can meet with him while he's open to it and make arrangements to bring his boys for visits."

I called the facility and left a message for his counselor, and then I headed out there. When I arrived, I saw several men hanging out in the yard. As I was walking up from the parking lot, Hawk greeted me, "Hey Scott, you must be here to see Big Thunder. He's inside. Hey man, I'm doing good...staying clean for now."

We chatted a bit. I gave him recognition and encouragement for being on the *Red Road* and wished him well on his journey. He smiled and hugged me, and then led me inside to find Big Thunder. Hawk introduced me to a couple of the staff and then left. One of them said, "I'll go find him. You can wait here."

After a few minutes I felt the floor begin to shake. It was Big Thunder stomping down the hallway. He trudged up to me, grunted, and then mumbled, "*ICW*". He said it the same way most people did—with scorn.

I introduced myself and told him I wanted to help him to see his boys and get them back into his life. He was somewhat friendly, but also seemed hesitant to talk with me. We went outside and sat at a picnic table on the grounds. He talked about how he'd been through treatment before, how this time was different, and he was going to be a good father to his boys.

At this point in any case, you really didn't know which way it would go. Most of the parents went MIA after ICW intervened. Often the parents seemed relieved; they could just go party now and know that their children were safe. Many of them were raised by their grandmothers or aunties while their parents were off using drugs. It was all too common. The pattern kept repeating itself.

Prior to our involvement, the children were often left with all kinds of unsavory people. Even though the parents had suitable options with other healthier family members, they often didn't utilize them until after ICW was formally involved. I imagine they would have had to take responsibility for their problems if they went to their stable family members, whereas they could remain in denial as long as they left their children with people who wouldn't hold them accountable.

The only families I witnessed achieving success with treatment and family reunification were the ones who first took responsibility for their problems before doing anything else. It was the most crucial step in the process. Otherwise, people would remain in victim consciousness, blaming everyone they could for their situation…everyone but themselves. Not only did I witness this dynamic in dozens of cases, but many parents identified this element as a key component of their success. I remember one father proclaiming, "We've got to own our shit, before we can do anything about it!"

I also knew that timing was, well, of the essence. It was critical that I acted while the parents were open to it. We made arrangements for me to bring the boys to see him two days later.

Big Thunder was all smiles when we came for the first visit. He seemed really happy to see them, and he also seemed grateful for me bringing them. He was way more open and friendly with me during that visit. In fact, he interacted with me more than he did with the boys. This was often the case with parents who had limited parenting experience. They didn't seem to really know how to interact with their children, whereas they were used to shootin' the breeze with another adult. In those situations, I'd either model appropriate interactions, or I'd tell them that this time was for them to interact with the kids, not me, and I'd bring a book or a journal along to occupy myself during the visit. I often had to redirect the parents' focus, especially the fathers, back to their children.

I brought the boys out for several of these visits while Big Thunder remained in treatment. During one of the visits, he gifted me a beaded keychain he made in group. He told me he'd never beaded anything before, and he'd made it for me to show his appreciation for how I was helping him. I was grateful. It's nice to feel appreciated. ICW workers get very little recognition. In fact, we usually got the brunt of the blame. The little bit of recognition we did get usually came from our clients but very rarely from our leadership.

After a couple months, he graduated from the program and moved back to a place of his own on the Rez. He quickly engaged in outpatient treatment at the

Tribe, started looking for work, and maintained his focus on building meaningful relationships with his children. In the beginning visits went pretty well. We would meet up at the daycare and take the boys on an outing in the community. This was typical in many of my cases since many of our ICW children attended the Tribe's daycare.

Big Thunder consistently arrived fifteen to twenty minutes late for our appointments, but he kept showing up, and I kept commending him on his progress. One day I decided I'd show up to the daycare fifteen minutes past our agreed time since he had never arrived on time. When I got to the daycare, the staff told me that my new co-worker Kooky had taken Big Thunder and the boys to McDonalds for their visit since I was late. Go figure, every other visit I'd sit and wait for Big Thunder to arrive, and then the one where I intentionally show up late, he leaves without me. I didn't blame him, but I found it odd that my new co-worker would intervene in my case and take them on their visit without consulting me, or at least letting me know.

She'd recently been hired by Barney. She was a problem from day one. When I asked her how she was able to land a job in ICW without any previous social work experience, she said, "It was simple. Barney said, 'Hey Kooky, you've got a degree don't ya?' and then he gave me the job." No interview, no experience...well, I did find out later that she and Barney were good friends. They do say, *It's not what, but who you know.*

I wondered, *Is that how little he thinks of our program, that he'd just throw someone in without any child welfare experience?* Of course, Odessa didn't have any child welfare experience either. Granted, I didn't have ICW experience when I came to the Tribe, but I did have extensive experience working with at-risk youth and their families, *and* I had a supervisor with tons of child welfare experience, including working with Tribal children and their families *and* doing State social work. At this point, I was the only person in our department, including our director, who had any ICW experience.

Over time, Big Thunder progressed from supervised, to monitored, and then to unsupervised visits. He was able to go to the daycare and pick the boys up himself, and then they'd either walk around the community visiting with relatives and friends, or he'd watch the kids while they played in the little parks around the neighborhood. Big Thunder was proud to be seen out in the community with his boys, and he was receiving lots of encouragement from his friends and family whom they'd visit.

One day after one of their visits, I got a call from one of their caregivers. She said, "Margie [the other caregiver] and I have a request. We'd like you to talk to the boys' father about the snacks he's feeding them during visits. He gives them soda pop and gummy worms and other sugary snacks, and then we have to deal with their sugar meltdowns afterwards. We know that he's probably just trying to keep them happy during visits, but we don't feed them those kinds of snacks at home, and it's really throwing them for a loop after every visit. We don't want to strain our relationships with him, so we thought it would be better if you brought it up."

"No problem," I responded. "I'll talk to him, educate him as best as I can about the benefits of providing healthier snacks during visits—not to mention how that will look for him in court—and I'll suggest some healthier alternatives."

I called him up. I praised him for all his progress with maintaining his sobriety. I commended him on getting a job. I recognized his diligence in following through on his court requirements and being consistent with his visits, and I acknowledged how difficult it might be for him to take it all on at once, when he's not used to that level of responsibility.

Then I attempted to address the caregivers concerns about the sugary snacks without disclosing the source of the concerns. I led him to believe that it was all coming from me. These were both cornerstones of my social work practice: that is, praise before accountability, and let ICW be the bad guy. I'd focus on building up the parents as much as possible by giving them genuine recognition and praise whenever I could, and then, *and only then*, I'd address any concerns. I also made sure (as much as possible) to direct any of the parents' hostilities towards our program vs allowing them to sabotage or strain their relationships with their children's caregivers. Even though it was challenging enough to build my own positive relationships with the parents, I figured it was even more important to protect the relationships with the caregivers. We could be the bad guys. We were used to getting the brunt of the blame, anyway.

Funny thing, well, funny to me…after I attempted to address the sugary snacks issue with Big Thunder, he became agitated and bellowed, "Healthy snacks! That's the White Man's way. All my Indian friends give their kids the same kinds of snacks I give the boys. That health food shit is for White People!"

I giggled inside as I thought, *First of all, these concerns originated from your children's Native caregivers. Second, I thought it was the White Man who brought the processed sugar to the Indians. Isn't it more traditional for Indians to eat healthy snacks?*

Culture can be subjective. We can choose parts of our own culture to accept or dispense with, just as we can pick and choose parts of other people's cultures. Culture can also be forced. Certainly, Tribal people weren't eating processed foods before the White Man came, but that doesn't mean they haven't adapted it as part of their own food culture now. Culture can also be learned, shared, and absorbed, just as many people throughout the world have adopted indigenous practices and perspectives, and others have adopted American hip hop culture. Should people be limited to living within the boundaries of their traditional culture? If people were forced to adapt to a dominant people's culture, should they now revert back to their traditional ways, or continue to include the aspects of this foreign culture that's now their own? How do you separate it? Where do you draw the line?

Well, again, that begs the question of culture. Is culture how we live in the present, or how our people used to live in the past? I think it's both. I know that potatoes are a big part of my diet because I'm American (and part Irish). I also know that even though I didn't grow up eating sushi, I've incorporated it into my current food culture, just like I've incorporated West African drumming into my life. I live djembe culture. It's not appropriation. It's pure love, respect, and admiration.

Once Big Thunder started getting overnight visits with the boys, the caregivers began complaining that they were coming home hungry and exhausted after visits. They said the kids passed out hours before their regular bedtimes, and then it took days to get them back into their normal routines. Additionally, they said they were concerned about the kinds of movies the kids were watching because they were becoming increasingly aggressive, and the oldest boy was having nightmares about *Chucky*, the doll from the horror movies. They were very worried about the impact the visits were having on the children's overall well-being. I empathized with the caregivers, and I said I'd address their concerns with Big Thunder.

I also advocated for Big Thunder and the boys. It was their right to have these visits, and it was our job to support all three of them as much as possible. That included helping to educate Big Thunder about his children's needs *and* working with him to make more appropriate parenting decisions. Additionally, the boys were having normal behavioral reactions to all the recent changes in their lives. I assured these ladies that their concerns wouldn't go unaddressed, but I also stressed the importance of supporting Big Thunder. I didn't want to give him any reason to give up on all the progress he was making.

The next time I saw him, I broached the subject of the movies and the Chucky nightmares. He chuckled about Chucky. Apparently, he'd been using a Chucky doll as a deterrent to keep the boys in their room at night. He was having issues with his oldest son coming out of his room after bedtime, and he knew both boys were afraid of the doll, so he perched Chucky up on the railing of the stairs outside the boys' bedroom. He said it had been very effective, but he agreed that it wasn't worth the cost of traumatizing his son.

As for the discussion about watching appropriate movies, I got the same response as I did about sugary snacks. "All my Indian friends let their kids watch the same movies I watch with the boys." He was resistant to discussing this topic any further. I said what I could. I used my own parenting practice as an example. My wife and I had sheltered our son from violent and scary movies as much as possible. He certainly wasn't watching movies like *Spiderman* and *Batman* when he was a toddler. I realized that many parents, Native and non-Native alike, didn't share these values. In fact, many of my non-Tribal friends let their young children watch these movies. We didn't like for our son to be exposed to so much violence. We were happier letting him watch movies like *Happy Feet* and *Ratatouille*. Of course, it was not for me to push my values on my clients (I shared them, but didn't push or preach them), and Stan had made it clear years before, "*Let the community set its own bar.*"

Nonetheless, I did my best to educate him. I encouraged him to make sure the boys were getting enough to eat (with examples), getting to bed at a reasonable time (with clarification), and that, at least, they weren't watching Rated-R movies. A couple weeks later, I found out he took the boys to see a 10 p.m. showing of *Prometheus*, the prequel to *Aliens*. At the time, I looked it up and this movie was Rated-R for violent, bloody horror. There's even a scene in the movie where the protagonist gives herself an abortion on an automated surgery table to remove an alien fetus—not exactly the kind of movie I thought he should be watching with toddlers. Not to mention, that seeing a 10:00 p.m. movie meant they weren't home until about 1:00 a.m. given previews and drive time. Well, I talked to him about it, but at some point, we have to pick and choose our battles. Big Thunder was still remaining clean, working, and holding down a home. I didn't want to be the one offering any discouragement. He needed all the encouragement he could get (don't we all).

With ongoing encouragement, he improved his parenting practices including getting the boys to bed earlier and making sure they had plenty of nutritious food to eat during their visits. He managed to keep this going for a few more weeks, and then he relapsed and disappeared.

This was a part of my job I really hated. It was hard to see parents make so much progress, and then relapse, and fall so far behind. It was always hard on their children. Often, the kids would just get used to having their parents in their lives with some regularity, and then they'd go AWOL, usually for months, if not longer. It often happened around percap time. Go figure, give a recovering drug addict several thousand dollars, and then hold your breath and hope for the best.

The Tribe did the same thing with the teens. Numerous times I watched our youth come out of treatment after having been on the run for six months or more, only to receive thousands of dollars in percap payments and disappear again. It wasn't part of my code, but it seemed to be part of the Tribe's code: *Don't mess with the money!* Most Tribal Members were adamant, "Don't touch the percap money." Neither the adults nor the children had any requirements, such as holding down a job or going to school, to get their percap checks.

Do you know what happens when you give a drug addict thousands of dollars? They either become a drug dealer or they die of an overdose. Well, they become a drug dealer until the money's gone, the drugs are gone, they've hocked everything but the clothes on their backs, and they get tired of the misery that comes with that part of their lifestyle. Then they end up in jail...three meals and a cot! And the cycle would start all over again. It was hard enough to see the adults go through it. It was literally gut-wrenching to watch our teen clients go through the cycle over and over again. Go to jail, go to inpatient treatment, go to outpatient treatment, relapse, runaway, repeat.

Fortunately, there were numerous individuals who were able to change their lives, end this cycle, and successfully reunify with their families. I never would've lasted in this work as long as I did if not for the dozens of success stories.

Lady

After Big Thunder went MIA, I got a call from Margie, the caregiver of his eldest son, asking for my help. She was concerned because Lady, the Education Director from the Tribe, was pressuring her to start the boy on psychotropic medications. In addition to increased aggression at home, he was also exhibiting anger outbursts and aggression in his Head Start class. Lady felt that drugs were the solution.

Margie said, "He's been through so much already with his mother essentially abandoning him and his father in and out of his life. He's been separated from his brother, and he's living in a new home. It's a lot for any child to manage. I think he needs time to adjust to all these changes. I don't think that medication is the solution."

I agreed. He'd been through a lot, and his reactions were normal. *Of course*, he was angry and confused. Part of my job was educating parents, caregivers, and other professionals about the kinds of behaviors to expect from children in these situations. Another part of my job was instructing them on how to support the children to cope with it and get through it. Social workers and counselors have a duty to normalize such behaviors, not pathologize them.

I'd already worked with Lady on numerous other cases, and we had a good professional relationship. I told Margie I'd call Lady to discuss her concerns, and I'd set up a meeting if necessary. When I called Lady, she was friendly and polite, but I also sensed that she was full of fear when it came to this little boy. We decided to schedule a team meeting at Head Start for early the next week.

I met Margie at the meeting which was also attended by the boy's teacher and her assistant. I don't think that Lady was expecting any resistance. She seemed totally caught off guard when we didn't all agree with her recommendations to have the child medicated.

I addressed the group. "I think we should begin by looking at his diet, his emotional needs, and his coping skills before getting him diagnosed and prescribed medications. Little Thunder is having normal reactions to major life stressors. He's still adapting to all the recent changes in his life. Additionally, we need to consider the ramifications of labeling a four-year-old child with a mental health diagnosis. These labels can follow children throughout their education, often eliciting pre-judgements from teachers and other school professionals. I'm confident in Margie's ability to provide for his needs, particularly his emotional well-being. I'm also confident that as professionals we can come up with a plan to support him with the behaviors he's exhibiting in school."

Lady huffed a bit and stated, "If we don't get this child medicated, he's going to turn into a gang member and end up in jail. I've seen other children with the same behaviors, and they all got into serious trouble when they were older. They all ended up in jail!"

"What type of medication do you think he needs to be prescribed to prevent that from happening?" I asked.

"He needs to be on ADHD medication and possibly a mood stabilizer so he can focus in class and stop these disruptive behaviors."

"You're talking about a four-year-old child," I said. "Do you really think that's in his best interest? All of these medications come with potential side effects. There are numerous holistic and behavioral interventions that should be implemented before simply medicating away his symptoms."

Lady retorted, "What experience do you have regarding these issues? You're just an ICW social worker. You're not a doctor!"

"You are correct," I said. "I'm not a doctor. As for experience, I worked as a community mental health counselor for five and a half years prior to coming to the Tribe. Medication management was one of my ongoing duties in that position. I worked with a team of licensed child psychiatrists. I sat in on my client's appointments with these doctors and received the equivalent of clinical supervision from them. Prior to that job I worked for a year as a children's mental health case manager where I was also supervised by a team of child psychiatrists."

Lady just glared at me. I knew in that instant that sometime soon I'd be suffering her retaliation. In that moment it had nothing to do with the well-being of this child, but everything to do with her pride. My pride was also present at that meeting, but it was harnessed by my duty to advocate for this little boy. Not that I wanted to piss her off or make her my enemy, but I wasn't going to sacrifice doing what was right so she could feel good about herself. *Damn*, I thought, *this will cost me.*

With a stern tone, Lady uttered, "That's all the information we need from the ICW social worker at this time."

She turned to Margie and said, "I will discuss ICW's recommendations with the Social Service Director, and then I'll let you know what we decide."

Meeting adjourned.

Starbright

The first time I met Starbright I was investigating alleged physical abuse from her father. This type of referral was extremely rare. In fact, I only received two referrals alleging physical abuse during all my years at the Tribe. These numbers suggest one of two things: (1) Native people don't beat their children, or (2) Physical abuse doesn't get reported in Indian Country.

Upon our first meeting, Starbright and I made an immediate connection. She wasn't forthcoming about any of the alleged issues with her father, but otherwise she was amiable and engaging. We shared our love for movies and music. We found that we shared an interest in helping young people, and we shared our love for dark chocolate. I really enjoyed meeting her, and I could tell we shared that feeling as well.

Unfortunately, her dad skipped town with Starbright and her brother Moonbeam before I completed the investigation. At the time I was still working for Stan, and he basically told me to *let 'em go*. "They'll show up on the radar soon enough," he said. "You need to focus on your other cases."

I questioned, "Shouldn't we involve Law Enforcement and try to track him down? It can't be that hard to find out where he went. I know the kids have numerous relatives around the Rez. I don't feel right about abandoning this investigation."

Stan was firm. "Buddy, you've got enough on your plate. If there are any serious issues going on with this family, we'll hear about them again soon enough. That's an order!"

Sadly, it wasn't soon enough. In fact, it was almost two years before I would hear about Starbright again when I got a call from a state social worker a few states away. She'd been taken into CPS custody, and her father had been incarcerated for, you guessed it, child abuse charges. I felt sick to my stomach. I didn't even know the details yet, but I knew deep down that it could have been avoided had we fulfilled our duties to this child.

The state social worker Susan contacted me and questioned whether the Tribe's ICW program wanted to be involved in Starbright's case—*of course, we did*. She gave me the contact information for the foster family whom the children were living with, and she invited me to a conference call that was scheduled for later in the week. She also said that Moonbeam had his own ICW worker from the River Tribe.

I called the foster home immediately and introduced myself to Starbright's foster mother, Crazy Jesus Sister (CJS). I called her that affectionately, to her face. She accepted completely; she was, indeed, *crazy for Jesus*. In fact, her entire family was utterly-devout Christians. CJS spoke with such passion and love for the Lord that it felt contagious. Fortunately, I'd already been inoculated for this condition, but I knew how to speak her language, so I was able to express my passion and love for God in words and terms she understood. We discovered numerous other POCs in addition to our love for God, including a shared passion for helping disadvantaged children.

I was pleasantly surprised when I got on the phone with Starbright and learned that she remembered me. "Of course, I remember you, Scott. How could I forget? You came out to see me when my dad got reported for abusing me and Moonbeam."

I was also surprised to hear such joy in her voice. She did not sound like someone who had (allegedly) suffered the horrible trauma she had. After catching up with a bit of small talk about her placement, her brother's well-being, and her progress in school, I said, "Starbright, you don't need to go into any details about what happened, but I do want to check in with you on how you're doing."

"I'm doing great!" she gleefully responded.

More bewilderment ensued on my end. "Oh," I said, "I'm really happy to hear that, but I must admit that I'm a little surprised to feel such happiness emanating from you, I mean, given what you've been through."

"I completely understand," she responded. "You want to know how it's possible?"

"Of course, I do."

"I found Jesus!" she exclaimed.

"Oh," I responded, "it sounds like congratulations are in order. Where did you find him?"

Starbright giggled and said, "Oh, Scott," and then she proclaimed, "Jesus is taking care of me. He's taking away all my suffering."

"Ok," I said.

She continued, "I've accepted Jesus into my heart. He's my *Savior*."

"Go on," I encouraged.

And she did, for quite some time.

"I'm so happy for you, Starbright. I expected to find you in a state of despair. Truly, I'm astonished at the growth and maturity you're demonstrating."

I hoped deep down that she wasn't really masking her grief and stuffing her true emotions.

"Scott, I'm so much happier with my life than when we first met. I'm not even angry with my dad for what he did. I've forgiven him. I pray for him every day. I pray for him to get better. He's very sick, you know."

"Well, actually I don't know a whole lot, but what I did hear from Susan is troubling."

"What you heard from Susan is all true. I gave her permission to give you as much detail as possible so you would know what happened to me. But that's all in the past. Jesus is helping me to heal. My foster family is helping me to know Jesus better every day. I'm so grateful that God brought me to Mom and Dad. God knew exactly what I needed, and He blessed me with their love."

I was genuinely inspired by Starbright. I was also amazed by her ability to have so much compassion for her father, especially given his allegations.

She asked me, "Have you accepted Jesus, Scott?"

I had accepted Jesus, but not in the way she meant. I believe that he existed, *and* that he is a Christ. Shoot, I even welcomed him into my heart. I welcome you, too, if you are willing to help with my evolution, but as you already know, I think his message was corrupted by the Scaredy Cats. Of course, I didn't volunteer that information to Starbright. It wasn't necessary. (Rule #5 …only answer what's asked.)

"I accept that Jesus is a son of God," I said. "I accept that he came here to show us how to have a more meaningful relationship with God."

"That's wonderful," she responded.

"To be honest though, I don't think I have the same kind of relationship with him as you do."

"That's ok, Scott. He accepts you as you are, and you can learn to love Him the way I do."

"Frankly, Starbright, I'm just grateful that you found something, *someone,* to help you through such a difficult time in your life. It doesn't matter to me if it's Jesus or Buddha or Ramtha who you found. I can hear in your voice that this experience has had a profound effect on you, and *that* is truly a blessing."

Starbright also shared how much she loved the private Christian school that she'd been attending. "Scott, everyone at Lordy, Lordy has Christ in their hearts. It's a really wonderful place." She also talked more about how much she loved her foster family. I made sure she knew how to contact me and then asked if she had any questions before we wrapped up the call.

"I do have one question. Will I get to keep living with the Hathaways now that the Tribe is involved? I really want to stay here. Mom protects me like a mother bear, and Dad makes me feel really safe. For the first time in a long time, *I know I'm safe.* I know that nothing bad is going to happen to me as long as I'm with them.

"Being with them has made all the difference in my healing. I love being part of their family. Moonbeam loves it, too. I also really love our church, and just wait to you see my school—you're really going to love it. You are coming out to see me, aren't you?"

"I would love to come see you, meet the Hathaways in person, and maybe even check out your school, but all that has to be approved by my supervisor. Really, it's my duty to come see you, but I haven't had any ICW cases that are so far away, *and* I have a relatively new supervisor, so I'm not sure what she'll allow me to do in this situation. I'll talk to her about your case and get back to you as soon as possible. In the meantime, you have my number, so please use it. You can call me anytime."

"Scott, please ask your supervisor if I can keep living with Mom and Dad, I mean, the Hathaways. That's the most important thing I would like to know."

"I will get right on it," I assured her. We said our goodbyes and hung up.

I headed directly over to Odessa's office to see if she was available to staff Starbright's case. Her car was out in front of the TANF building so I parked my GSA, took a few deep breaths while focusing on Starbright's highest good, and then headed in.

To my surprise, Odessa was way more pleasant and engaging than usual. She was in a good mood, and she actually didn't seem disappointed to see me.

I told her, "I have a case I'd like to staff with you if you have a few minutes."

"Sure," she said, "come on in."

Feeling somewhat tentative, I walked in and sat down in front of her desk. "I just got a call from a state social worker in Union City regarding a Tribal teen named Starbright Meadows. Do you know who she is?"

"*Of course, I do*—she's my cousin." Of course, she does.

"Oh, I didn't know that. Well, Starbright and her brother Moonbeam were taken from their father and placed in foster care in a small town just outside of Union City. Her father has been incarcerated…" I went on to explain the details I'd learned so far, including the fact that the foster family was White. I also told Odessa about the family's history and the father's past allegations of child abuse from a couple years before.

"There's a conference call in two days with various Tribal and state social workers, as well as numerous family members who want to be involved in the children's cases. I plan to be on that call, and I also recommend that I schedule a trip to go out and see Starbright and meet her foster family in person as soon as possible. She asked me if I was going to come and see her. She's been through a lot these past few years, and I really want to show her that she has the Tribe's support."

"I think that's a good idea for you to go and see her and meet her foster family. What does the State want from the Tribe?"

"They want to know what our involvement will be."

"What do you recommend?"

"Well, they already have an investigation in progress, which will likely lead to a trial. There are no family placement options currently available, and the children are stable in this placement. I think we should remain a party to the case, but let the State handle the proceedings for now. We really need to focus on identifying viable family placement options."

"That sounds good to me. Why don't you look at your schedule and see where you can clear a few days during the next few weeks to fly out there. Once you have some dates, you can organize your trip with Accounting. Also, please let me know what's discussed on the conference call."

I told Odessa about Starbright's newfound love for Jesus and how it seemed to be helping her to cope with her trauma. I also told her about the Hathaway family and Starbright's attendance at Lordy, Lordy, the local Christian school.

"That all sounds really nice. Is there anything she needs from the Tribe right now?"

"Well," I said, "she asked me if she was going to be able to stay with the Hathaways. She really likes it there. She feels safe with them. And, of course, she loves that they're all about Jesus."

"I don't see any reason why she couldn't stay there."

"*They're White*," I stated.

"Oh, well, she's a teenager; she has some say in where she's placed. I think it would be fine for her stay with them."

I was very surprised to hear *that* answer. I again wondered if Odessa really understood the full scope of ICW and the ramifications of leaving a Tribal child in a White foster home, especially so far from the Tribe. I told her, "Starbright's been through a lot of disappointment these past few years. I certainly don't want to contribute to her discouragement. Before I tell her anything about the Tribe's position on her current placement, can you please staff this with Barney and Tribal Council to make sure we have their approval?"

"Sure, we have a meeting with them tomorrow. I can bring it up then."

I thanked Odessa for her direction and her support, and I left. I felt somewhat dismayed by her change in behavior toward me. It was refreshing, but I wasn't holding my breath.

Elephant in the Room

Starbright's state social worker Susan had given me a 1-800 number and a pin number so I could access the conference call. I wasn't really sure what to expect since I was coming in a little late in the game (her case had been active for months prior to the Tribe being informed), so I decided I'd do my best to *just observe* as Stan had directed so many years before. When I joined the call, several people were already on the line including Susan, Starbright's maternal grandparents, her maternal Uncle and his wife, a therapist that was contracted by the State, and Moonbeam's ICW worker from the River Tribe.

Susan briefed everyone on the current status of Starbright and Moonbeam's cases. The therapist gave a report. The ICW worker from the River Tribe asked a few questions, and then the children's grandmother took the floor, so to speak. She stated, "I think that Starbright is lying about what her father did. I think that she just didn't want to live with him anymore, so she made up this story. I don't believe he did the things that she has accused him of."

Wow! I thought. I didn't see that coming. I had every reason to believe what Starbright had reported. She was an open book.

No one responded to the grandmother. The conversation turned to the topics of school progress, foster care, medical and dental needs, etc.

Some space opened in the conversation, and the grandmother went on the offensive again, attacking Starbright's innocence. No one said anything. I swear everyone was thinking it, but no one said a word.

India had taught me years before, *Sometimes, things just need to be said. It doesn't matter who says them, but they need to be said.*

We were only on a conference call, but I could feel the Elephant looming. Susan kept trying to change the subject, but the grandmother kept bringing it back to her son's presumed innocence—i.e., Starbright's guilt.

Well, call it a strength, or maybe a curse. I'm that guy. I'm not afraid to address the Elephant in the room; but you've probably already figured that out.

I stated to the group, "As difficult as it may be to imagine, I mean, who wants to think that their own adult child is capable of such acts? As difficult as it is, we all have a duty to err on the side of caution on behalf of the children, at least, until a full investigation and potentially a trial have run their course. No one on this call knows what really happened. Only Starbright and her father know the real truth. Hopefully, the court will sort it all out, but until then, we must protect the children."

Complete silence. Yeah, I have that impact on people sometimes.

Susan wrapped up the call shortly after I successfully alienated myself from the entire group. That probably wasn't one of my better first impressions, but I doubt anyone will ever forget that call. Besides, it wasn't about any of them or what they thought about me. It was all about the safety of the children.

Visiting Starbright

About a month after the conference call, Odessa and I organized a trip to go see Starbright and attend the State's monthly staffing regarding her case. Odessa had confirmed with me that she had, indeed, staffed Starbright's case with Barney and Tribal Council, and we were given the green light to support her placement with the Hathaways. I was shocked. I didn't think there was any chance they'd allow her to stay with a White foster home, especially so far from the Tribe, but I also wasn't about to challenge Chain of Command. Odessa directed me to inform Starbright about the Tribe's position regarding her placement with the Hathaways as soon as possible, "…so we can, at least, reduce this stress in her life."

I updated Odessa on an additional request from Starbright. "Starbright is also asking if the Tribe can help pay for her tuition at the private Christian school. The Hathaways are currently paying for it, but they don't have the money to continue sending her there."

Odessa responded, "Why don't you call Lady in Education. I know they have money for stuff like that."

I hadn't had any contact with Lady since our meeting about Little Thunder. I was a little hesitant to call her, given her obvious frustration with me in our last meeting, but I knew I'd have to cross her path again eventually, and this might be a good opportunity to bridge those troubled waters. Besides, prior to that meeting, we'd always had a good working relationship.

I called the Education Department and was transferred to Lady. "Hi Lady, this is Scott from ICW. How are you doing?"

"I'm great, Scott. What can I help you with?" We were off to a good start.

"I have a Tribal Member teen who is attending a private Christian school out-of-state, and she is wondering if the Tribe can help pay her tuition. I staffed her case with my supervisor Odessa Knight, and she directed me to contact you."

"Oh, ok. Well, we've never done that before, but I'm sure there are ways to help this young woman. I'll need a letter from her stating why it's important for her to attend this school, you know, like why she feels it's in her best interest to go to this school in particular. Once I get that letter from her, then I can proceed with her request for funding."

"That sounds good, Lady. I'll get right on it. Thank you."

I updated Odessa about my conversation with Lady, and then I called CJS and shared the same details with her. Starbright got on the phone and confidently stated, "I'll get right on this, Scott. I can start the letter now, and then I'll have Mom email it to you by tomorrow."

"Copy that!" I enthusiastically responded.

I also told Starbright that Odessa had informed me that she'd be allowed to stay with the Hathaways.

"Scott, that makes me so happy! You have no idea how much this means to me."

I feared that we were only setting her up for more disappointment. I figured it was only a matter of time before tribal politics would put an end to her dream.

The next day I received an email from CJS with Starbright's letter attached. Starbright had made a very personal plea, even sharing parts of her traumatic history. Just as I was finishing her letter, I received a call from Starbright. She said, "I just wanted to make sure you got my letter."

"I just read it," I told her.

"I know my letter is personal, but I really wanted Lady to understand why it's so important for me to continue going to Lordy, Lordy."

"She asked for you to tell her why you feel it's in your best interest. I think that you did a good job doing just that."

"Thank you, Scott. Please let me know what she says."

I forwarded Starbright's letter to Odessa. She seemed touched by her emotional appeal. She directed me to forward it to Lady, which I did.

I arrived at Union City to see Starbright the day before Odessa. It gave me a chance to meet the Hathaways and visit Starbright's school prior to attending the State meeting. When I arrived on their property, Starbright came right out and greeted me with a radiant smile. She eagerly introduced me to everyone in the Hathaway family. She not only appeared to be very connected to *Mom and Dad* as she referred to them, but also to their two teenage children. She was fond of all of them. Moonbeam also looked comfortable in their presence. He was definitely not the withdrawn, timid child I'd experienced years before.

Starbright offered to give me a tour of the home and property. The Hathaways lived in a grand old farmhouse that was surrounded by miles and miles of corn fields. It was one of those quality, turn-of-the-century homes that felt like it would withstand eternity.

Starbright was most excited about their horses. She even had her own horse! She simply glowed while sharing stories about her experiences with the Hathaways. She proudly listed her various chores and duties around the property, which included taking care of her horse. I couldn't help but think that in some ways she was living a more traditional lifestyle than the majority of our other ICW children.

Starbright questioned, "Is the Tribe really going to allow me to stay here? I'd been trying not to get my hopes up, but after you told me that Odessa said I could stay, I've been so happy. I finally feel like I can settle in and lay down some roots."

"Odessa told me that she and our director Barney talked with Tribal Council about you and your living situation here, and Council gave their full approval. To be honest, I was very surprised to hear their decision, but let's not look a gift horse in the mouth."

"Huh?" she replied. "What do mean by that?"

"It's an old proverb about not questioning the value of a gift. It refers to the practice of evaluating a horse's age by looking at its teeth. Basically, if someone gives you a horse for free, don't question the value of this gift by looking in its mouth to see how old it is. Just appreciate the gift. If TC has approved your placement with the Hathaways, let's try not to question it, but simply accept their gift with gratitude."

"No problem there," she proclaimed. "*I accept!*"

After my tour and some light conversation with everyone, I departed so I could check into my hotel and get some rest.

The next morning, I drove out to Lordy, Lordy. The school had a beautiful campus with grand old buildings from an exquisite, bygone era of architecture. As I approached the main building, I saw Moonbeam walking with his class. When he saw me, he ran straight towards me and jumped into my arms. I gave him a big hug and then exclaimed, "Moonbeam, you just made my day!" He smiled as I lowered him to the ground, and then he ran back to join his class.

I identified myself at the office and was quickly introduced to the principal and several of the staff. They all made positive comments about Starbright and Moonbeam. One of the ladies called down to Starbright's classroom and asked that she come up to the office. She arrived a few minutes later with her teacher who introduced herself as Miss Heavenly Sent. She praised Starbright for being a great role model for other students. She said, "Starbright is an absolute blessing to our community—Moonbeam, too. We just love having them here at Lordy, Lordy."

Starbright asked if she could give me a quick tour before returning to class. Everyone in the office was totally enthusiastic about both children. They all genuinely seemed to love having them at their school. I could see why the kids loved being their so much.

Starbright gave me a brief tour of the school during which she continually expressed gratitude for me "coming all the way" to see her. "Scott, I hope that your visit to Lordy, Lordy will help my cause to get funding from the Tribe. I really can't imagine going to any other school."

"Well," I commented, "I'll do all that I can to influence the process, but ultimately that decision lies with Lady, and perhaps TC."

"Ah Scott, just pray for me, and I'm sure it'll all work out."

I was on an emotional high from all the joy that abounded in this community. In all my years doing counseling and social work, I never met a stronger and more dedicated support system than I did with the Hathaways and the staff at Lordy, Lordy. To be fair, I had the same experience when I visited the

Hathaway's church during my second trip to Union City for the trial against the children's father. Everyone at their church was equally supportive and dedicated to the children's well-being. However unlikely, if I ever do decide to join a church, I hope to discover a community just like that one.

After visiting Lordy, Lordy I headed back to the hotel to do some work before driving back out to the Hathaways for the meeting with the State. Odessa arrived to the Hathaways shortly after I did. She had a grave look on her face. She pulled me aside and told me, "There's been a problem."

"What's that?" I asked.

"Well, we have a new directive from Tribal Council. Starbright will not be staying with the Hathaways. We can't leave her in a White foster home, especially so far from the Tribe. We need to work diligently on finding a suitable family placement, preferable closer to the Rez."

I just looked at her.

Part of me—that part that believes in fairness, accountability, and doing what's right—was waiting for her to acknowledge her colossal mistake, to be accountable for how her overconfidence and lack of experience were about to crash down on Starbright's world. The other part of me knew that Hell would freeze over, first.

Right then Starbright came walking over. Odessa smiled and gave her an exuberant, "Hey Cuz!" like they were the best of besties.

Starbright returned an awkward, "Hello." She looked at Odessa as if she were a complete stranger.

One of the state workers got our attention and asked if we could come into the house so they could start the meeting. We all entered the kitchen and took seats around the dining table. Three state social workers attended the meeting as well as the Hathaway parents, Odessa, Starbright, and me.

I did my best to just observe. Susan gave a brief update on how Starbright had been doing, and then her supervisor added a few bureaucratically-infused comments, meaning that she didn't really say anything. Odessa joined in with some inflated political niceties, and then the third worker successfully drained the last bits of joy from the room. Needless to say, it was a typical State meeting…dry and boring and soulless.

Starbright had a puzzled look on her face. She didn't seem to understand much of what was being said, so a couple times I tried to translate the other professionals' jargon into terms she could comprehend. Finally, she raised her hand, waited to be acknowledged, and then asked, "I was just wondering about my placement. Am I going to be able to stay with Mom and Dad, I mean, the Hathaways?"

Susan responded without actually answering Starbright's question. She basically talked around it. Starbright just looked more confused.

Additional dry, seemingly-pointless babble ensued, and then when a space opened up, Starbright asked again, "Am I going to be able to stay with Hathaways?"

This time Odessa jumped in, gave her own version of political doublespeak, and then changed the subject.

Starbright looked more confused. She spoke up and tried to ask her question again, but Odessa and Susan's supervisor just talked over her like they hadn't even heard what she said.

She looked to the Hathaways, presumably for support, but they didn't say anything.

Then she looked to me.

Well, sometimes things need to be said, regardless of who says them. I *am* that guy—the one who is willing to piss off an entire room of professionals in order to advocate for the needs of a child, even against politics.

I cautiously interjected, "I was just wondering if anyone is going to answer Starbright's question. It's obviously important to her to know whether she will remain in placement with the Hathaways or if the team intends on looking for another placement."

First, dead silence. Then, more doubletalk. Yep, they *still* didn't answer her question.

I'm pretty sure that both Starbright and I lost interest in the discussion after that. I couldn't even tell you what else they talked about. All I could think about was that Starbright deserved a straight answer and not one of the other workers seemed willing to give it to her.

After the meeting wrapped up, I walked outside to get some air and ponder the situation. Starbright came out a few minutes later and asked if we could walk down to the barn. She said, "I'm not really sure what happened in there, but after you made that last comment, your supervisor looked at you with daggers. [Notice that she referred to her *bestie cousin* as "your supervisor".] She's definitely angry with you. After you walked out, she made a comment about you to one of Susan's co-workers. I didn't quite hear what she said, but I don't think it was good. What's going on, Scott?"

I stopped walking and turned to look Starbright directly in the eyes. I could feel my emotions welling up inside of me. I felt she deserved to know, so I told her. "Starbright, I have some bad news for you. When Odessa got here today, she told me that you're not going to be able to stay with the Hathaways. She received the directive from Council prior to flying out here. I'm not sure what happened to make them change their decision, but that's it."

I started to wonder if Odessa had even staffed Starbright's case with Tribal Council in the first place. I could see tears begin to well up in her eyes. I had to hold back my own. I really didn't know what else to say to her. We just stood there looking at each other.

Moments later we heard Mother Hathaway approaching. She also looked like she was about to cry. She looked at me with sadness, and then she mustered up a smile for Starbright and embraced her in a big momma bear hug. She whispered encouraging words in Starbright's ear, "It's going to be o.k. Jesus is always with you. Even when we don't understand why things happen, it's all part of God's plan."

I did my best to also encourage her and share an optimistic outlook regarding her future. In my own way, I agreed with CJS's sentiments. I also believe everything happens for a reason. As difficult as this would be for Starbright to accept, it was in her best interest to accept reality as it was and move forward.

I said goodbye to Starbright and Mother Hathaway, and then I walked back to the house to share my salutations with the rest of the group. I had a feeling it was going to be a long trip back to the Rez. Odessa made no reference to what had just happened in the meeting, but simply told me, "See you back at the Tribe."

A few weeks after we got back from our trip, Odessa wrote me up for violating Starbright's confidentiality. Apparently, Lady was the person who initiated the complaint that I had violated Starbright's confidentiality when I forwarded her letter to Lady. You know, the letter that Lady requested, and Odessa approved. I knew Lady would be seeking revenge, but I never expected such a blatant action. I found it additionally interesting that the department managers and directors had had numerous meetings over the years to discuss this very issue. That is, they had meetings to discuss whether the Tribe needed to develop a universal release of information to be used in sharing confidential information about Tribal Members between Tribal departments. They reached the same consensus in numerous meetings: no release was needed since the clients were being served by both departments.

Nervous Beaver

About six months after Odessa started working at the Tribe, she hired a second social worker, a Native woman from Alaska named Nervous Beaver. I liked her right away. She was warm and friendly, and she was passionate about working with Indian children. We hit it off immediately.

Finally, I thought. *Finally, I have a co-worker who can share in some of the cases, and she actually seems open to my friendship and guidance.* Nervous Beaver had no ICW experience, and Odessa wasn't in any position to train her, so that duty fell on me. I didn't mind. I was so happy to have some real help. Besides, I liked training new staff, and she was an eager beaver.

Fortunately, Odessa finally took some action on Wildflower's case and assigned Nervous Beaver to work with her family. I discussed Wildflower's case with Nervous Beaver in depth. I told her about all the services she'd already received as well as my recommendation to get the State involved. Nervous Beaver told me, "I know how tribal politics can go, and I'm not about to rock the boat and refer her to the State when I'm so new here, but I'll do my best to help Wildflower and her children."

She did just that. In fact, for several months Nervous Beaver met with Wildflower at least three to five times a week. She referred her to a home-based therapist who set up additional wrap-around services. They had professionals in her home working directly with Wildflower or her children almost every day of the week. Our program had made similar efforts numerous times in the past (unsuccessfully), but I wasn't about to get in the way. On the contrary, I was literally thrilled that someone in our department (other than me) was making it a priority to try and help her.

Nervous Beaver was really motivated and inspired in the beginning. Wildflower appeared to be making progress with all the support, but she required so much ongoing attention from all the professionals involved, that over time it took a toll on all of them. Wildflower would call everyone on her support team five or six times a day—including all hours of the night—asking the same questions of each of them. She monopolized everyone's time. It would've been difficult enough if she was Nervous Beaver's only case, but her caseload was building, and there just weren't enough hours in the day to manage Wildflower's ongoing crises and fulfill her other casework duties.

It didn't take long for Wildflower's perceived emotional stability to start deteriorating. This had been a pattern of hers for years. She responded well to all the initial attention, and she'd even follow through on many of the professional's recommendations, but she required this intense level of ongoing support to maintain any semblance of stability.

Nervous Beaver certainly did her best, but it was a daunting task, especially once the onslaught of constant phone calls began. Wildflower always seemed to be in some kind of crisis, and she was good at pulling people into it with her. She had such a big heart and so many issues that people often felt sorry for her and tried to help, but they all eventually hit the same wall. No matter how much help and support she received, she couldn't maintain it once the supports were removed. Even with all the ongoing assistance, our department kept getting referrals from concerned community members alleging that Wildflower was neglecting her children and putting them in danger.

Nervous Beaver continued her intensive work with Wildflower for months. Wildflower came by the office to see her almost daily, sometimes several times throughout the day. It was obvious she had bonded with Nervous Beaver.

She told me, "You know, she requires almost constant hand-holding, but like you keep telling me, social work is all about the relationship, and we really are building a beautiful relationship. I think she trusts me, and I really do care about her. She's finally starting to let her guard down."

Wildflower engaged in the process whole-heartedly with Nervous Beaver's support. She even took a stand against her former abusers. She recruited a fellow Tribal Member, and they both went to Tribal Council and called-out her father and eldest brother for abusing her throughout her childhood. From a professional standpoint, her proclamation was congruent with many of the behaviors and symptoms she exhibited. I wasn't surprised at all to hear about her public disclosure. And yes, it was very public. Like I said, have a few burgers at the casino bar...

Ironically, our department finally responded to Wildflower and referred her children's ICW cases to the State! She was shunned and abandoned by the very people who were supposed to support her the most. They didn't want anything to do with the FUS.

Wildflower literally fell apart. She finally had the courage to face her demons (her abusers), and the Tribe shut her down, and kicked her out (figuratively speaking).

Well, she didn't take it lying down. In fact, once she pulled herself together, she recruited more help from fellow Tribal Members, mounted an offensive against our department, and took her fight right back to Tribal Council. It didn't take much to get their attention considering she also called them out for supporting our department in sending her children's cases to the State. It took some time, but in the end, she was successful. In the end, taking her fight public empowered her.

This was when our department created and implemented another jurisdictional loophole utilizing the Tribe's *Adoption List*. They had to do something. They had actually (finally) used jurisdiction as a justification to transfer her children's cases to the State, but now, under immense political pressure, our department was being directed to bring them back. Easy-peasy. Someone in the legal department had a great idea. They simply added a few clauses to the ICW Code stating that if a child is *validly* placed on the Adoption List, then ICW can take jurisdiction of their case. Of course, no one bothered to define *validly*. So basically, all we had to do to take jurisdiction of a child's case was get them placed on the Adoption List—a simple call to the Enrollment Department. Yeah, they had their piece in it, too. At the time, over a third of our cases were not actually eligible for our services. They put them all on the Adoption List in one fell swoop.

Big Ocean gave me the skinny on it. He was an Elder Tribal Member who'd recently joined the ICW Committee. I really liked Big Ocean. He had a strong presence, he went above and beyond in advocating for our youth, and I didn't feel the rejection from him that I often experienced from new committee members. We worked well together.

He frankly stated, "Scott, the Enrollment Department has had the Adoption List for about thirty years. No one has ever been adopted from that list. *Anyone* can be placed on it. Shoot, you could be placed on that list. It's more of an honorary decree. No one's getting adopted by the Tribe anytime soon. There'd be way too much political backlash. It's just not gonna happen."

There's a few more twists and turns to this part of the story. Once our department got her children's cases back, they also finally determined—with the State's help—that her children were indeed not only at-risk, but that there were current safety concerns that warranted immediate removal of the children from her custody. Yes, they determined this with the help of CPS investigators. The only problem—there were no Native homes available to take the children. They'd have to be placed in White foster homes. Guess what Odessa and Nervous Beaver did. Nothing! That's right; they left the children in Wildflower's custody. Odessa's response, "We're not placing these children in White homes as long as I'm running ICW!" Apparently, she thought it was better to leave the children in an unsafe Indian home than to place them in safe White homes. This went on for months. The children were left in this dangerous situation *for months!*

Eventually they did finally remove all of Wildflower's children and place them, drum roll please, in White homes. The children all thrived.

It didn't take long after this experience for Nervous Beaver to leave the Tribe. She had a good heart, and she knew that Odessa wasn't making decisions based on the best interests of the children. She hated working under Odessa. We all did.

Starlight

I worked with Starlight for years. Like many of the teens, she had drug issues, and she had a habit of hanging out with adult men who were horrible influences. They were the usual suspects from around the Rez who preyed on vulnerable children from the community, including their own family members.

Starlight was attending a residential outpatient program with a local tribe out on the coast, and she was doing really well with her treatment. Many of our youth attended this program over the years. In all my experiences with them, I found their staff to be impeccable.

Starlight was ready to graduate. I cleared my schedule for the day so I could attend her graduation and bring her back to the Tribe where she'd be placed with her auntie. During the ceremony, the staff and residents showered Starlight with blessings and encouragement. They all had something sweet and touching to say about her. It was an inspiring and heartfelt experience. It was obvious that Starlight had bonded with many of the staff and residents. She didn't seem to want to leave.

I usually carried a bundle of sage on the dashboard of my GSA. Remember, I'm a hippie. Hippies respect the values and teachings of traditional cultures. Many of us recognize that our traditional culture has been lost, and we look to the teachings of indigenous peoples to help regain forgotten, ancient wisdom.

I believe in the cleansing properties of sage. My Native friend Quasina (Shy Beaver) taught me how to use it more than a decade before I came to work at the Tribe. He was a great mentor and friend. Sometimes I'd use it to clear the space after I transported a client. I also always offered it to the Tribal Youth when I picked them up from treatment or detention. They usually accepted.

Before we departed the facility, I offered Starlight some sage and a lighter. She accepted with a smile, and then *smudged* herself. She seemed appreciative of my gesture. As we were leaving the parking lot, she asked, "Is it ok if we drive down by the water so I can see the eagles one last time before we leave the Nation? We go down there a lot to hang out and watch them. I thought that you'd appreciate seeing them. I want to share it with you."

"Absolutely," I responded, "that sounds cool."

Starlight directed me down some wetland roads to the shore where we walked on the beach and watched the eagles. She passionately shared stories about her treatment experience.

After returning to the car, she looked up at me with a curious gaze and asked, "Are you a Native?"

"No," I responded, "well, not officially, anyway. I may have some Native ancestry on my dad's side, but I really don't know anything about it. Of course, I think that America's a pretty heterogeneous group, and most White people probably have more Native and Black ancestry in them than they realize."

"Oh," she flatly responded.

I became a little defensive. "Is there something wrong with me if I'm not Native?"

"No, no, not at all. Come on, Scott, you know my mom's White. It's just that I made a gift for you, and I was really excited to give it to you."

"Oh." I lightened up. "Well, what's the problem?"

She reached into her bag and pulled out a string of beadwork with a feather attached to it.

"I made this for you. I fastened a baby eagle feather to it. I found the feather just down there by the water. The beads are the color of your car. But you can't have the eagle feather if you're not Native."

"Oh!" I responded. "Now I see why you're asking."

"Starlight, I'm so touched that you made this for me."

She smiled.

"Wow," I reflected. "I don't know what to say. That's one of the most beautiful gifts anyone has ever given me. Geez, let's see. What can we do?"

Starlight brightened.

"Hmm." I thought for a moment. Then I smiled. "How about I just hold on to it for you...indefinitely. You can get it back anytime you want."

Starlight's smile broadened as she reached up and hung the beads over the rearview mirror with the little baby eagle feather dangling below it. Then she sat back in her seat with a look of satisfaction, closed her eyes, and went to sleep.

Where's the Baby?

One late Thursday afternoon, I returned a missed call I had received the minute before from Odessa. She answered and said, "I need you to clear your schedule tomorrow so you can transport baby Ramsey and Arlene up to the Healing House. Arlene is refusing to have Kooky go with her. She doesn't want anything to do with Kooky."

"Ok," I responded. "No problem."

"Baby will be ready at Grandma Clara's at 10:00 a.m., and Arlene will come up here to TANF at 11:30, do a UA, and then you take them to the Healing House."

"Where is it?"

"Just as you get into the city."

"Am I supposed to pick up Ramsey an hour and a half before Arlene meets me?"

"No, Grandma Clara just knows to have Baby ready by 10:00 a.m."

"Ok, will do." Then I sent an email to Odessa and Kooky titled, **Arlene Transport.** In it I wrote, "Address please."

Odessa responded a few minutes later, "Kooky can you give him the address, so he can take baby Ramsey and Arlene tomorrow?"

A little while later Kooky responded with the address. And then Kooky sent an email just to me stating, "I remember how upset YOU got when I did Big Thunder's visit. Told me not to interfere with YOUR case. Just saying. Yeah, I'm upset. I let Dawn [the Healing House Intake worker] know I was coming with Baby and mom. I will help with the transport."

I responded to Kooky and cc'd Odessa. "Kooky, you completely lost me. Odessa told me to clear my schedule tomorrow to do your transport because Arlene was unwilling to have you do it. Therefore, I found it confusing when you offered to help with the transport. To be clear about the situation with Big Thunder, I was upset because you didn't inform me. That's what I told you that day, and I also put it in writing to you afterwards. If you have an issue with Odessa's directive, take it up with her."

I forwarded that message to Odessa and added, "This is not cool. This is why I don't like to team-up on cases with Kooky. I've never had issues like this with another caseworker at the Tribe or anywhere else I've worked. I don't appreciate being reprimanded by a co-worker for following my boss' orders. Please address this with Kooky. -Scott"

Odessa responded, "I will take care of this. Thank you for transporting." A little later she wrote, "Please grab Baby and make sure Arlene does her UA and keep in touch with me, and I'm sure all the stuff will fit. The reason I want Baby to go with her is because she needs any encouragement she can get. We will staff this when I return."

On Friday morning I called Grandma Clara and left a message that I would be over shortly after 10:00 a.m. to get baby Ramsey. I arrived at Grandma Clara and Great Grandma Thelma's about 10:20 a.m., and they told me that Kooky had already picked him up. They were both very concerned that Kooky was involved. They both expressed frustration with her. Great Grandma Thelma stated, "That lady is unprofessional and crazy."

After I left Grandma Clara's, I messaged Kooky and cc'd Odessa, "Odessa directed me to get baby Ramsey. According to his grandma you picked him up (?)" I also got call from Arlene's mother demanding, "You need to come get her from my house (click)."

A little later I messaged Kooky again and cc'd Odessa and Barney, "Kooky, where are you with the baby? Odessa clearly directed me to pick him up and transport him with his mother to treatment. -Scott"

She didn't respond.

I waited for a little while, and then I called her. When she answered, I asked, "Where's the baby?"

She casually replied, "Oh, we're just feeding him and changing his diaper. I'll meet you at TANF at 11:30." She didn't say where she was or who she was with.

This was very concerning to me. Not only was my co-worker obstructing my work and defying direct orders from our supervisor, but I was also worried she was allowing a visit with Claudia Moss, Ramsey's previous placement custodian. Claudia had apparently developed quite an attachment to Ramsey when she cared for him, and recently she'd been harassing Arlene, Odessa, the current family placement custodians, and other staff in our department. Odessa had met with Claudia several times in attempts to set boundaries with her. She clearly informed her that she was not to have any further contact with this child or the mother, as she was interfering in their reunification process. She's the only custodian I've ever worked with who demanded visits with a child after he was returned to his family. I knew that Kooky was friends with Claudia, and after she stated, "We're just feeding him and changing his diaper…", I just had a gut feeling that Claudia was involved.

At that point, I was already sitting in my GSA outside TANF, so I just waited for Kooky to show up. She arrived at 11:45 a.m., but then she sat in her car talking on the phone for about 10 minutes, essentially ignoring me. I stood by her car waiting for her to acknowledge me and get Ramsey. After about another ten minutes, Claudia came walking up. I knocked on Kooky's window and asked if she was going to get him out of her car. She rudely replied, "Get him yourself!"

I proceeded to walk around to the rear passenger door to get him. Claudia followed me, saying "Can I hold him? Can I hold him? Can I hold him?"

I said, "I got him," and I lifted the car seat with him in it and walked him over to my car. I placed the seat on my back seat so I could fasten it in. Claudia kept asking to hold him. The car seat was not adjusted properly, so I had to take him out of it. I acquiesced and handed him to Claudia rather than lay him on the seat where he could potentially roll off. She squeezed him, kissed him several times on the face, and kept telling him she loved him. I quickly got him back and put him in the car seat.

At this point Kooky got out of her car and demanded to know where Arlene was located. I told her, "I'm going to pick up Arlene right now. I was waiting for you to respond and bring Ramsey, so that I could go meet her."

I must admit that it was strange, and yet affirmative, to have Claudia show up like that after I'd just imagined that she was involved. I had compassion for the fact that she loved this child, but she was clearly violating boundaries in this case.

It felt like she was trying to get in her last goodbyes before Ramsey went off with his mother. It made me wonder how many of these secret visits she may have had.

I drove over to Arlene's mother's house to get Arlene. She was waiting in the doorway with her mom. She was wearing her usual mean mug, but she lightened up as soon as she saw Ramsey and quickly came down to the car to get him. For the first time, I witnessed her softer, maternal side shining through that tough, indifferent exterior. Her mother, however, maintained her, *Fuck with me, and I'll kill you* persona.

After greeting them both, I got right to business and asked her about doing the UA.

Matter of factly, she stated "It's going to be hot."

I nonchalantly responded, "I know. You're on your way to treatment. I was directed by Odessa to get a UA at TANF, so I'm asking you for it—that's all."

She responded, "I'm not going up to TANF to do it; I'll do one here."

I wasn't about to give her any reason to bail on treatment. I'd been down this road with Arlene before. The last time I'd literally pleaded with her in a McDonald's parking lot to get back in the car so I could take her to treatment. She dug in her heels, but I kept pushing. I gave her the best motivational/get clean and get your kids back speech I could muster. She did get back in the car, and I delivered her to treatment, but she was gone from the program before I even left the parking lot.

I retrieved a UA test kit from the trunk of my GSA, opened it, and offered her the UA cup and cap. She kissed Ramsey, handed him to her mother, took the supplies, and entered the house, presumably to head down to the bathroom. When she returned, I made sure the lid was on tight, turned over the cup, and then waited a couple minutes for the results. It was positive for meth, opiates, and MDMA. I showed her the results, and she just shrugged.

We packed the car completely full of Arlene and Ramsey's things, and we left.

I called Healing House to inform the intake worker Dawn that we were on our way. She said, "This is frustrating. We have an intake appointment in thirty minutes." I told her I hadn't been apprised of an intake time, and we wouldn't be there for another hour or longer depending on Friday traffic. She grumbled, "Well, we'll have to work it out. See you when you guys get here."

"So, how are you doing?" I asked Arlene.

"How do you think?" she curtly responded.

"If I knew, I wouldn't ask."

"I'm fine."

Trying to lighten the mood a bit, I asked her, "Do you remember what you called me the last time we saw each other?"

She thought for a moment, and then startled giggling. "I called you a little bitch."

"Yeah, I don't think anyone has ever called me that before—not to my face, anyway. I thought it was kind of funny."

She shrugged again and smiled. "Well, you know, if the shoe fits…"

"You act so tough," I told her, "but I'm sure you have a gentler side."

"You'll never see it!"

I grinned as I looked ahead down the road.

"I must say, even though it was your hot UA that got you into this, I want to commend you for even being willing to do it. You didn't have to, and you had to know that it was a risk, being pregnant and all. We wouldn't even have proof that you're using, if you weren't trying to get Horndog [teenage son] placed with you. You easily could have dodged that bullet, and you'd probably still have Ramsey in your custody."

"My son needed me."

"He still does."

She reclined the seat and went to sleep.

I enjoyed transporting my clients to treatment. It's a huge step for any of them, and they need all the support they can get. I took it as an opportunity to really build them up and encourage them right before they got there, to try and help fortify them as much as possible for the challenges that lay ahead. Once I had them in the car, they were a captive audience for my motivational speeches, which centered around making it through that first day and eventually getting their kids back. Many people don't last a day.

After she woke, I gave her a few minutes to gether bearings, and then I asked, "Do you think you're ready this time?"

She flatly responded, "Ready as I'll ever be."

"I'm serious. It takes a lot to get to this point along your path. You've got your baby and all the things you'll need while you're there. Anything else you require, we can bring to you."

"Scott, I know that in some strange way, you seem to care about how I do, but, honestly, I'm taking this minute by minute. I can say, though, that it really helps having Ramsey with me. I've never gone to treatment with one of my boys before, and that feels different to me. Maybe I'll be successful this time."

"We can certainly hope for that; well, and we can focus on it." I smiled at her.

"Whatever, Scott. Are we almost there?"

"We get off in a few exits."

In contrast to the strange morning I'd experienced, or my typical meetings with Arlene, it was a great trip up. Ramsey slept most of the way, and Arlene didn't call me any names or look like she wanted to hit me—not once.

We arrived at Healing House about thirty minutes late for the scheduled intake appointment. Dawn came out to meet us and asked if Arlene had done a UA. I told her she had, and I had it in the car if Dawn wanted it. With a bit of attitude, she asked, "What are the results?" I told her that Arlene was positive for several substances. With pretentious satisfaction she stated, "Then she can't be here. We will not accept her with a dirty UA."

Arlene became distressed. "But I'm here with my baby. We have all our stuff. I've been clean for a few days."

Dawn continued to treat her with insolence, consequently exacerbating the situation. I told her I needed to call my supervisor as I was only directed to get the UA (presumably to establish a baseline) and do the transport.

I called Odessa's work phone but didn't get an answer. Dawn was starting to argue with Arlene, so I went over and intervened. Dawn just walked away. I called her name three times attempting to get her attention, but she just kept walking. I tried to comfort Arlene who was understandably upset.

Then I called Odessa's personal phone because I knew she was at the coast and she had bad reception there with her work phone (maybe both). She answered my call. I told her that Arlene was not allowed to stay because of the UA. I expressed frustration that I was not told she needed a clean UA to be accepted into treatment. Had I known, Arlene's expectations wouldn't have been raised, and we could have avoided the anti-climactic trip to the city in Friday traffic. Odessa directed me, "Take Baby back to his grandmother's home and drop Arlene off at her mom's, and we'll figure it all out on Monday."

I got off the phone, told Arlene that we needed to leave, and we started walking toward the car. Dawn had one of her staff follow us out, presumably to make sure we left.

Ramsey was already strapped in the car seat, and Arlene and I were proceeding to get in the car, when Kooky showed up, seemingly out of nowhere. It was downright creepy. Kooky demanded to take Ramsey. I told Kooky, "I just talked to Odessa, and I'm still following her directive. You're not taking Ramsey."

She proceeded to go around to the rear passenger door and try to take him.

I demanded, "Get away from the car. You're not taking Arlene's baby."

She said, "Well then, I'm taking Arlene. She can't be with her baby."

Kooky's presence was clearly escalating an already tense and stressful situation. Arlene looked like she was ready to blow, and I couldn't believe that Kooky had just shown up at the treatment center after everything I'd already gone through with her in the last twenty-four hours.

I firmly stated, "Arlene, get in the car."

She looked as though she was about to attack Kooky. She hesitated for a moment, took a deep breath, and then got in the car. At the time, I kind of wished I had let her indulge her primal, maternal instincts.

Kooky went around to the back of the car, pounded on the trunk, and yelled, "You're not taking Baby!"

I put my foot on the brake so she could see I was going to change gears. I waited for Kooky to move out of the way of the car, then I put the car in reverse, backed out of the parking spot, and left.

Arlene and I were in shock and disbelief. Arlene stated, "She tried to kidnap my baby! What was she doing there? That lady's crazy!"

Ramsey sat blissfully unaware, smiling in the back seat.

Arlene was so distraught. I felt bad for her. She had done her part. It was a huge accomplishment for her to make it all the way to the treatment program in the city with her baby and literally a car full of their things. She was ready for the next step in her plan, and the carpet was being pulled out from under her. I tried to console her and encourage her not to give up. I assured her that Odessa would get it all worked out.

I could tell that we'd lost her. She wouldn't be going back to treatment any time soon. Baby Ramsey would have to go without his mother, again.

I called Grandmother Clara and said, "Things didn't work out. I can't go into the details, but I need to bring Ramsey back to you. I wanted to make sure that you'll be home."

She responded, "Well, I was going to go to a movie, but I'll be here."

I said, "Ok, thank you so much, we should be back in a couple hours given it's Friday rush hour."

She said, "It will probably be three hours. See you when you get here."

I turned the wrong way when we left, and we ended up coming across a lake that seemed to be obstructing our way. We meandered through a local neighborhood trying to circumvent it. I ended up stopping and asking for directions to the highway, and then I followed the directions through a few turns down some residential streets, which finally led to the entrance ramp. I eagerly pulled onto the ramp only to join bumper-to-bumper traffic.

About thirty minutes after we left, I received a call from a local city area code. I figured it was the Healing House calling to make sure everything was ok. I answered the call, "This is Scott."

The person said, "This is Officer Green with the City Police. Is this Scott Strider, social worker for the #### Tribe?"

"Yes, it is."

"Mr. Strider, you've been reported for vehicular assault and kidnapping, and I need you to return to the Healing House for questioning immediately."

What!?! I thought. *Kidnapping? Is he serious? And he wants me to go back up there after everything we've been through? We just barely escaped as it is. Is this guy insane?*

There was no way I was heading back up there. It was not going to happen. Besides, I thought, *how do I know this guy is really a cop? Kooky could have put him up to this.* Call it denial or shock or whatever you want, but here's what I did.

I said, "How do I know you're a police officer? I only have a local number on my phone. You could be anybody."

He promptly replied, "I'll hang up and have dispatch call you to confirm who I am."

I said, "Ok," and hung up the phone.

Then I turned my phone off. Ok, call it denial. I felt like an ostrich burying my head in the sand, but I needed a moment to digest this information and figure out what I was going to do.

Arlene asked, "Who was that?"

I told her who they *said* they were and what they wanted. She said, "Oh shit! Scott, what are we going to do? We're gonna have cops on us any minute. You need to do something."

She was right. I had to deal with this. I had no intention of going back up to the Healing House, but I did need to face the reality of my, uh, pending charges.

I took a few deep breaths while I considered the worst possibilities. After a couple minutes I turned my phone back on. I had two messages requesting immediate return calls: one from Sargent Sanchez at Tribal Police and one from

911 Dispatch. Before I had a chance to respond to either message, I received a call from Officer Red at Tribal PD who told me that they'd been contacted by City Police. I told him about the call from Officer Green, and he said that he'd call him. I gave him the number, and he hung up.

Officer Red called me back a couple minutes later and said that City Police had put out an *Amber Alert* on me for kidnapping because of what Kooky told them. He said that Chief Rocking Horse put a stop to the Amber Alert, and they wanted to make sure that Arlene, her baby, and I were ok. I told him about the incident with Kooky. He said, "Tribal is handling this, just get everyone back safely to the Rez."

I also responded to the voicemail from Sargent Sanchez at Tribal Police. I texted telling him that I'd already talked to Officer Red, "…did he still need me to call."

He responded, "No thanks. Please just call when you guys are close to the Reservation."

A little while later I received a call from Barney. "I heard what happened. Are you guys all ok?"

I told him, "We're all fine, but Arlene and I both feel like we've been harassed by Kooky. You're not going to believe the day we've had [except that it's your crazy-ass friend we've been dealing with]. I'll call and let you know when baby is back safe with his grandmother."

Odessa called as we were driving through the base, and I told her that we were almost back to the Reservation. She told me, "I've been in close contact with Chief Rocking Horse, and he's handling everything with City PD."

Initially I kind of felt rescued by Tribal Police. I mean, what would have happened had they not intervened? I felt like the Chief really had my back. Perhaps he did. As I thought more about this situation though, I realized that the Tribe had to do everything they could to *keep a lid* on this situation. Imagine how it would have made the Tribe look to the outside world to have one of their own social workers report the other one for kidnapping.

As we were driving through the base, Arlene says to me, "Man, I'm having this vivid memory about a time me and some friends stole a car."

Where's the Baby? - 207

"What?" I responded, "Are you serious?"

"Yeah," she said, "it was crazy. We got chased by the police and ended up ditching the car down by the river."

"No shit?" I exclaimed.

"No shit," she said. "We swam across the river to get away, and then we got chased by some hovercraft thing."

"It was probably a drone from the Army base," I told her.

"This was quite a few years ago," she said. "I doubt they had drones back then."

"Trust me," I said, "they had that kind of technology long before we ever heard about it. That *is* crazy. Damn girl, sounds like you've had some wild experiences."

"You don't know the half of it."

Arlene may never admit it, but we were connecting. We had shared quite a bonding experience. It was definitely a new POC for us, maybe our first.

Once we got back to the Tribe, we met Sargent Sanchez at the front of the Casino in Valet Parking as he was there dealing with a possible DUI. He asked me if I was ok and if Arlene was trying to take her baby. I said, "No, Arlene hasn't been a problem at all. My crazy co-worker Kooky is the one who's causing all the problems. Kooky was the one who tried to take the baby."

He said, "Ok, just wanted to make sure you guys are all right." He visually checked the status of Ramsey and Arlene, and then we left.

It was early in the evening when we arrived back to Grandma Clara's house. She said that Kooky had already called and stated that I tried to hit her with the car and that Arlene had a dirty UA so she couldn't stay at the Healing House (violating Arlene's confidentiality).

Great Grandma said, "Didn't I tell you that Kooky was crazy?"

I just shook my head is dismay.

I stepped out on the porch to call Barney and left a message informing him that Ramsey was back at Grandma Clara and Great Grandma Thelma's house.

When I came back in, the two grandmothers were encouraging Arlene as best as they could. I thanked them, and then we headed out for her mom's house. Once we arrived, we unloaded the car, gave each other a look that said, *What a fucking day*, and then I left for home.

A couple days later I called Officer Green with the City Police. He told me, "Mr. Strider, you had been accused of vehicular assault and kidnapping. I quickly determined that there was no basis for Kooky's claims about the vehicular assault after questioning her. I determined there was no basis for kidnapping when I talked with Tribal Police." He concluded, "The only other issue we had was the Tribal Court Order about the mother and her baby, but that's the Tribe's business to handle. Any other issues please address with your supervisor. They'll be able to help you clear up anything regarding your criminal record and the Amber Alert through the Tribe's legal department."

I asked Barney and Odessa in person and in writing to take the appropriate steps with the Legal Department to adequately clear my record. I don't even know if that was necessary, but it weirded me out to think that I'm listed in numerous databases (State, County, Tribal, FBI) for having an Amber Alert for kidnapping. They both gave me the Indian no... *no response*.

By the way, Kooky did get fired. Another one bit the dust!

Big Thunder Returns

I stopped at RezGas one day to get a drink. When I turned from the cooler, Big Thunder was blocking my path. "I want to see my kids," he told me.

"Hey," I said. "Long time. How are you doing?"

"I told you I want to see my kids!" he demanded.

I put my drink down. "Hey man, this is not the place to discuss your case. Let's, at least, go outside so we can have some privacy to talk." I headed for the front entrance, and he followed me out to the side of the building.

He angrily stated again, "I want to see my kids!"

"Big Thunder, no one's stopping you from seeing your kids. Have I or has anyone else told you that you can't see them?"

"*Fucking ICW!* I want to see my kids now!"

"I'm happy to help you set up a visit as soon as possible, but face it, you left. You were doing great, you were seeing your boys regularly, and then *you* disappeared. It's not my fault or anyone else's fault that you haven't seen them."

He continued to escalate. "It's their mother's fault. She's the one who lost them. None of this is my fault!"

"Look, like I said, I'm happy to set up a visit. We can do it as soon as you're calm. However, this hostility that you're directing at me is misguided. I've only ever tried to help you."

He yelled, "I want to see my kids! It's not my fault!"

Perhaps I should've been more concerned for my safety given Big Thunder's escalating hostility and his history of violence, but I was actually kind of embarrassed for him. I mean, here he was, standing outside the busy RezGas, pretty much yelling at the top of his lungs at an ICW social worker. He was drawing a lot of attention. I felt very uncomfortable. *So much for confidentiality,* I thought. I figured he was likely coming off a drug binge. He looked horrible, and he was clearly combative. I'd experienced similar behavior from other clients before, but never in public. Of course, this was his community. Perhaps he felt comfortable expressing himself in this place; and perhaps he didn't care.

I attempted to de-escalate him. "Big Thunder, I understand you're angry. Hell, this is the angriest I've ever seen you. Just answer me this: have I helped you in the past?"

"Yeah," he bellowed.

"Have I ever gotten in your way when it comes to seeing your kids?"

"No."

"Do you have any reason to believe I won't help you now?"

"No," he said again.

"I need you to try and take it down a notch so that we can talk about this rationally."

"Fine."

"This is the first time I've seen or heard from you in months. How can I help you if you're not in contact with me?"

"I don't know."

"Is it fair to say that you disappeared for a while?"

"Yeah."

"Ok, well now you're back. So, let's pick up where you left off. I told you before you can see your children as long as you don't show up to visits under the influence of drugs or alcohol. Is that fair?"

"Yes."

"Are you under the influence of any drugs or alcohol now?"

"No. Not since last night."

"Is it safe to assume you've been on some kind of binge?"

"Yeah."

"Have you been to see Elk yet?"

"No. I just saw you inside, and I wanted to ask you about seeing my boys."

"Ok, now we're getting somewhere. What do you think should happen next?"

"I need to go back to treatment."

"Well, you've done it before, so you know you can do it. Your boys are certainly going to be happy to see you again. I'm sure it's been hard on them going from having you in their lives to not seeing you at all. Let's focus on setting up visits again, and maybe you can also get up to see Elk at Substance Abuse when you're ready."

"I could probably get up there in a few days."

"Is there anything gettin' in your way?"

"I'm just pissed about the boys' mom. She's seeing Harvey now. I heard that she's pregnant again. That shit pisses me off. *Fuckin' bitch*. None of this would've happened if it wasn't for her."

I had other thoughts about this perspective, about him putting all the blame on the boys' mother, but now was definitely not the time to get into *that*. I asked, "Do you still have a phone?"

"No."

"Where are you staying?"

"I'm still at my sister's place."

"Do you still have my number?"

"Yeah."

"Ok," I said, "why don't you call me tomorrow morning, and we'll schedule a visit."

"Ok," he said, and he turned and walked away.

I didn't hear from him. This kind of thing had happened before when I randomly ran into ICW parents in the community. I think that when they saw me it brought their issues to the forefront. I imagine it's hard to remain in denial about neglecting your children when your ICW social worker is standing right in front of you. It gave them a reason to act. I'm sure they missed their kids, but I imagined that it was probably easier to approach me in public than to pick up a phone and call. It's easy to talk ourselves out of making a phone call or taking other proactive steps, but when the ICW social worker (opportunity) appears in front of you, it's time to act.

We had a court review a few weeks later, and to my surprise, he showed up for court. He looked haggard, and he seemed just as agitated as the last time. I was glad the focus wouldn't be on me. That day, the judge would get to handle Big Thunder.

The judge called court into session (different judge, by the way). The Tribe went through a bunch of judges, too. The judge went through the normal proceedings including naming the children, referencing my case management report, and asking the ICW Presenting Officer what he had to say. The judge also asked Big Thunder's assigned attorney for his input, and then she turned to him. He stood up and said, "I want to see my kids."

The judge replied, "Mr. Thunder, it's nice to see you back in court again. I understand that you've been absent for a while."

He stated it again, "I want to see my kids."

The judge continued, "Mr. Thunder. I understand from Mr. Strider's case management report that you've been out of compliance with your substance abuse treatment and your visitation schedule. Can you please explain to the court what efforts you've made to come back into compliance with the Family Reunification Plan (FRP)?"

With a thunderous roar he yelled, "*I WANT TO SEE MY KIDS!*", and then he stormed out of court.

"Whew", was the common sentiment in the courtroom.

The judge looked perplexed. She asked, "Was it something I said?"

His attorney reassured her, "I think that had very little to with you, your Honor."

"Ok, then," she said. "Well, I see from the case management report that Little Thunder is having some behavior issues at home and in Head Start. Mr. Strider, I understand from your report that Head Start in bringing in a specialist to have him assessed."

"That's correct, your Honor."

"It also appears that the boys see each other on almost a daily basis at daycare, as well as for other scheduled visits, and the youngest boy is doing well in his placement."

"Yes, your Honor."

"And the mother has not been in contact with your program or with her children since the case started?"

"Yes, your Honor."

"Is there anything else that needs to be addressed at this time?" she added.

"Your Honor, I just want to assure the court that I will do my best to re-engage Mr. Thunder in the services detailed in the FRP. I will also continue making active efforts to try and engage the children's mother. Additionally, I want to inform the court that we're very happy with the care that's being provided to both boys in their respective placements, as indicated in my report, and I recommend that the boys continue to reside in these out-of-home placements."

"Thank you, Mr. Strider. If no one else has anything to offer, then we'll adjourn. The next Review Hearing will be in three months unless there's activity on this case that would warrant coming back to court sooner."

I headed toward the door that Big Thunder had just excited to see if he was still in the area. I was met at the door by his younger son's caregiver, a director from the Tribe. She said, "Scott, we need to talk. I'm really concerned."

"What's going on?" I asked.

"Have you seen his social media posts?"

"No," I responded, "I'm not on his site."

"It's very concerning. He's been making disparaging remarks about the ICW program and the people that work there for weeks. He recently posted a picture of a guy in the same Batman mask that was used in the Colorado movie theater killings. I think it's a death threat. I think it should be taken seriously as a death threat. The caption said, 'The Tribe's Reckoning', and he wrote, 'They haven't seen this side of Big Thunder yet!' Given his history of violence and drug abuse, not to mention his immaturity and impulsivity, I'm gravely concerned. I'm concerned for my own well-being, but, frankly, I'm even more concerned for yours."

I thanked her for informing me. Now I was also concerned for my safety. This was right around the time of the Colorado Batman Shootings. It was disturbing news, indeed.

I immediately called Odessa and left a message informing her of the caregiver's report and asking for her direction. Keep in mind, this wasn't only a report from a caregiver, but also a report from a Tribal Director.

Then I emailed Odessa and cc'd Barney and the Tribe's CEO. I marked it with a red flag.

In the email, I wrote:

"A few minutes ago after court, Gazelle told me that Big Thunder posted a picture on #### [social media service] of a guy in the same Batman mask as the killer in the Colorado shootings, the caption said, 'The Tribe's Reckoning', and then the message, 'They haven't seen this side of Big Thunder yet!'

This sounds like a potential death threat. Please look into this.

Scott Strider

Tribe's ICW."

Remember "Chain of Command"? I was freaked out, but I also knew I had to be careful how I proceeded if I wanted to keep my job. I wasn't giving them any reason to fire me. I was afraid that if I went directly to Law Enforcement like my two former co-workers who went directly to the Tribe's legal department, I was setting myself up.

I didn't get a response to my phone call or my email. I waited for 45 minutes and then I sent another email to Odessa (I also cc'd Barney and the CEO again), and I called Barney (no answer).

This time I wrote:

"Big Thunder yelled at the Judge today and left court extremely agitated.

Do I alert Law Enforcement? This is concerning given his history and

Gazelle's report.

-Scott

Tribe's ICW."

A few minutes later I sent another email to Odessa and the ICW Presenting Officer. I also cc'd Barney again.

In that email, I wrote:

"Please File Immediately. I want to be taken off Big Thunder's Cases as of court today. Please see forwarded emails from me and file them with the Tribe's Court.

-Scott Strider

Tribe's ICW."

I forwarded the messages referenced above to the court to be filed.

I didn't get a response from anyone, *ever*. My leadership never acknowledged my reports or my concerns. The court never acknowledged my report. I was never taken off Big Thunder's cases.

To be clear, I don't know if his messages were intended as death threats or not. I do know that neither my supervisor, my director, the court, nor the Tribe's CEO ever responded to me regarding this alleged death threat.

It probably had something to do with Big Thunder being directly related to Barney and Odessa. #1 Rule!

Runaway Randy

It's common practice for teens in ICW to run. They didn't run in the traditional sense of the word. They usually weren't actually running away from home, but rather, running away from ICW. In fact, many of them ran to be with their parents. For them, they were running home.

ICW means accountability. If an ICW worker is worth half their salt, then they hold their clients accountable—the parents *and* the children. First, they build relationships with the family members (if they let them), always being as helpful and supportive as possible, and then they hold them accountable for their actions.

Did they go to treatment? Did they make their visits? Are they following the court-ordered plan? Unfortunately, many of these questions pertained to the children as well as the adults. Some of our teens had as many court orders to fulfill as their parents.

Herein lies the art of social work. No one wants to be held accountable for their actions—not you, not me, not anyone! Imagine trying to have a rational conversation with an addict about their parenting deficiencies, and all they can think about it getting high. Or perhaps they're all tweaked-out after being up for a week straight, and all they want is to crash, for days. For them, you're the problem. Running away or going AWOL means leaving *your* jurisdiction.

So, how do you keep people engaged? How do you get them to keep showing up, no matter what? *You* keep showing up; hopefully, with your judgements in check.

If people are going to accept your help, they need to know that you care about them, or, at least, care about their well-being. They want to know that you're not judging them—you accept them as they are. Your relationship with them is key. In all my social work success stories, developing meaningful relationships with the family members was one of the most important factors. The other one, of course, was ownership. They needed to take responsibility for their situation before they could rectify it.

Randy was one of my teen clients who had a history of running. To be fair, most of them did. He'd already completed treatment numerous times, but he couldn't maintain sobriety once he got back to the Rez. Sometimes he'd do really well when he first got back, consistently going to school and attending outpatient treatment, but he always ended up running within a few weeks—if not days—of being back on the Rez.

When our kids ran, it was our practice to petition Tribal Court to issue a pick-up order to have the child taken into custody and detained. That's a nice way of saying that warrants were issued for their arrests. Many of these youth would remain on the run for three to six months or more before they were finally brought in. When they did get detained, it often seemed like they allowed it; they were burnt-out from the druggie lifestyle, and they needed a break. Even the kids would say, "Hey man…three meals and a cot." So, they allowed themselves to get picked-up. Sometimes they even turned themselves in. Often, they did it just so they could get their percap check and take off again.

Randy was detained in juvie. The Tribe contracted with a juvenile detention center in another county. Many of my male and female teen clients had been detained at this facility. They were always brought there by the police, but they were released to a family member or their social worker—usually their social worker. I had visited and picked up youth from this facility numerous times over the years. I'd made connections with many of the detention staff including intake, education, medical, and administration.

The kids were usually detained for two to three weeks while their social worker found beds for them at various local treatment facilities. There were a couple all-Native facilities where we sent youth from the Tribe, but they didn't always have openings. None of the treatment centers *always* had openings. One of the skills of a good social worker is building quality relationships with the intake workers at various treatment programs. That way, you are way more likely to get a bed for one of your kids when you really need it, and we often did.

Per the Tribe's contract, this facility would hold our kids for as long as we requested without question. Usually, a facility like this would require a judge's order stating that the youth was serving time for a specific criminal offense, like stealing. When it came to the Tribe, there were never any questions asked. The

Tribe always seemed to get exactly what it wanted in their dealings with government entities. I know that this dynamic is a far cry from the history of tribal government and U.S. government relations, but it *is* the new standard.

Randy was ready to be picked up and taken to treatment. I had worked on and off with him for years. Whenever I got a new co-worker, his mother Terri would request that her children's cases be transferred. She knew she could take advantage of inexperienced staff. She told me so! Since my co-workers always got fired, I would inevitably end up with her children's cases again. I had the same experience with several of the families who were chronically involved with ICW.

Many people were not ready to change; they didn't want to be held accountable. I was a stable force of accountability in our department. If you had me as your social worker, you could be sure that I would keep showing up with a keen focus on building our relationship and helping you to move forward in your life. Some people just aren't ready for that, even when they know deep down it's exactly what they need. Some people just want to be left alone. Most of us need prodding sometimes. *Sometimes,* we just need a good kick in the ass.

I often prodded people to be more involved in their children's cases. Sometimes I pushed hard. I'm sure that sometimes my clients felt like my push *was* a kick in the ass. Often, they thanked me later. People say that ICW, well social work in general, is a thankless occupation. I strongly disagree. The thank-yous didn't come often, but they surely came (usually years later), and when they did, you knew it was for real.

When I arrived at the detention facility, I buzzed the staff from the intercom just outside the sally port. Once I identified myself, they raised the gate to let me in. I parked the GSA near a couple police cruisers, and then walked up to the Intake entrance. After getting buzzed through the vestibule, I entered the intake area and waited for one of the detention officers to retrieve Randy. After a few minutes, Randy shuffled into the intake area wearing his detention jumpsuit. He appeared somber, but he looked way healthier than when he was incarcerated a few weeks earlier. He'd put on a few pounds, and his skin was clearing up.

Randy was a regular at this facility. He'd experienced numerous extended stays over the last few years, and most of the staff knew him well.

One of the officers teased him with a raspy, Southern drawl, "Now come on Randy, as much as I like hearing your jokes and seeing those pretty brown eyes, I really don't want to see you here again." She continued, "You know what we've talked about. The only way you're gonna keep out-a-here is if you stay in school and keep away from them drugs!"

Randy's demeanor lightened up a bit. He gave her a coy smile. "I know, I know. Don't worry, I'm gonna do good this time."

I greeted him, "Hey Randy, nice to see you again. You're looking good, man. You look rested."

Randy gave me a nod, and then one of the staff handed him a plastic bag containing his clothing. He took the bag into a small changing room and then emerged a few minutes later dressed in a pair of black Dickies and a white t-shirt. One of the officers called him over to sign for his other personal belongings. She gave him a few papers and a comb. I asked if they could send him with a lunch, so we didn't have to stop anywhere between juvie and treatment. I didn't want to give him any chance to run before we got there. I'd lost a few kids in the past during that transition. We couldn't lay hands on them (fortunately) so if they wanted to run, there wasn't much we could do.

I thanked the detention staff. One of them asked when I'd be back to pick up one of the other Tribal youth who was detained in their facility. I told him I should be back to get her within the week, and then we departed.

When we got to the GSA, I reached into the car and grabbed my bundle of sage off the dash as well as a lighter from the driver's door compartment, and then walked around the car to Randy. "Would you like some sage?"

He accepted, so I handed the items to him. He broke off a small piece of sage from the bundle and returned the rest. Then he lit the sage and smudged himself. Afterwards, he handed me back the lighter, and we both got in the car to go.

"Where am I going for treatment?"

"I'm taking you up to the city to the facility where your cousin went last time."

"How long do I have to be there?"

"It's a 30-day program. I hoped to get you into the 90-day program at the Lodge so you could be with other Tribal youth, but all their beds are full, and I didn't want to leave you sitting in detention any longer."

"Thanks."

"So, I lost count. How long were you in juvie?"

"25 days."

"And how long were you on the run?"

"I think about six months."

"That's quite a bit of time in my book."

Randy shrugged.

"You should know that I'm considering recommending to the judge that youth serve a day for a day after they've been on the run."

"What do you mean?"

"If she agrees, and you run again, then you'd be serving one day in detention for every day that you were on the run."

"What?" he exclaimed. "That's crazy!"

"It may sound crazy to you but consider this: would you have remained on runaway for so long if you knew you had to serve a day in detention for every day you were on the run?"

"*Hell no.*"

"Exactly," I responded. "Keep in mind, my job is to look out for your well-being. So, you were gone for about six months then, right?"

"Yeah."

"Well, that was six months that you weren't getting an education. It was also six months that you were probably using drugs every chance you got, right?"

"Well…yeah."

I continued, "Before you ran, you got your percap check for almost $5000. What do you have to show for that money?"

"Huh?"

"What did you spend it on? Do you still possess any of those items?"

"I bought a bunch of clothes and a Play Station. I also bought some stuff for my mom and my grandma."

"Ok, so perhaps you do have something to show for it, even if that's just a good feeling from knowing that you helped out your mom and your grandma."

"What about your PlayStation and the games that went with it?"

"I pawned 'em."

"What about your clothes?"

"They're gone."

"All of 'em?"

"I have the clothes I'm wearing. But, hey, you went shopping for me, didn't you?"

"Yes, I did. Take a look." I motioned to the large black duffle bag sitting on the back seat. "I was able to get $600 released from your percap funds so I could shop for you. That's why I asked the detention officer to have you make a list of the things you needed for treatment. If you don't mind me asking, what happened to all the clothes you bought before you ran?"

"You know. When I'm on the run, it's hard to hold on to things. I woke up after partying one night, and my shoes were gone. Another time it was my sweater. I traded a bunch of my stuff away, too."

"If I understand it correctly, I imagine those clothes and video games and things all become trade goods for you while you are on the run."

"Yeah."

"I also imagine that it's one of the reasons you're able to stay gone for so long. I mean, shoot, if you didn't have $5000 worth of new stuff, how long would you have made it on the street?"

"I wasn't on the street. I stay with people."

"I know, I didn't mean it like that. I hear about sightings of you throughout the community. I have a pretty good idea where you've been staying, at least for part of the time."

"You do? Well, where's that?"

"Well, I know you've been at your grandma's house, and you've been staying with your Auntie Xena."

He didn't respond.

"So, let me summarize."

"Huh?"

"Let me review…you were on the run for six months. You went through $5000. Other than helping out your family a bit, you have nothing to show for the money."

I continued, "Because of the pick-up order, you can't show up at Tribal events, and you can't be seen around the Rez, at least during daylight hours, so you're pretty much disconnected from the Tribe. You can't go to school, so in addition to missing out on your education, you don't get to see many of your friends and family. Oh, and then, of course, there's all your drug use and the harmful effects it has on your life. Is that a fair assessment?"

"Yeah."

"How do you feel about missing so many cultural events? And don't you get tired of always having to watch your back? I mean, having a pick-up order on you and all."

"It gets kind of old, but I get used to it."

"And Randy, I'm sorry to say it, but you looked horrible when you got picked up by Tribal. I can only imagine what havoc those drugs wreak on your body. You know your liver and kidney and other organs must work really hard to get that shit out of your system. Don't you ever worry about how it affects your health? Come on, you see how the chronic drug users around the community look."

"I don't think about it too much."

"I wish you would. I wish it were something you'd consider. When you get back to the Rez, check out some of these guys in their thirties who've been living the same life you do when you're on the run. They've been doing the same stuff since they were young. Their skin looks horrible. Their teeth are rotten. Many of them suffer from numerous ailments due to their drug use. Is that the kind of life you want for yourself?"

"No."

"Is that the kind of life you want for your brother or sister? How about your little cousins? Do you want them following down the same path?"

"No."

"I don't mean to be hard on you. I'm asking you these tough questions because I want you to think about these things. I've seen you make some great decisions over the years, looking out for your mom, and your sister and grandma. I've also seen you at Tribal events, and to me, you look right at home.

"Randy, what I really want for you, more than anything else, is for you to learn what it means to be a traditional man from your tribe. I want you to learn as much as you can about your culture, become a leader in your community, and share what you've learned with younger Tribal Members. Culture *is* the cure. Can you see yourself doing something like that? Is that something you would be interested in?"

"I don't know. I guess if I stay clean."

"You may be surprised to hear me say this, I don't say it to everyone, so please don't think I'm blowing smoke."

"Yeah, what?"

"I see you being on Tribal Council someday. I see you becoming a great leader in your community, someone who people can really look up to. Have you ever imagined your life being like that?"

"No."

"Can you imagine your life being like that? I mean, stop me now if you think what I'm saying is crazy, but I just have a feeling about you. I see you doing great things for the Tribe someday."

Randy sat back in his seat and smiled. "Can we listen to some music?"

"Funny you should ask," I stated. "That brings up another topic I want to discuss with you."

He gave me a look that said, *Oh brother, now what?*

"Do you remember the last time I picked you up from treatment?"

"Yeah."

"Do you remember what music we listened to? You had a cd that you burned from one of the other residents in that program."

"Oh yeah. That was some good music. Man, I wish I still had it."

I sarcastically questioned, "Another casualty of being on the run?"

He didn't respond.

"Sorry man, but really, it must be hard to keep track of your stuff when you're living like that.

"So, here's the thing I want to share about that music—well, really about music in general. One of the artists you played literally left me feeling sick. Now don't get me wrong, I don't say this to criticize you or your taste in music, but I do want to make a point."

"What's that?"

"In that one song, he rapped about raping women, killing people, stealing, and doing drugs. He used the N-word dozens of times. My point is this: what kind of effect do you think that kind of music has on your consciousness, your thoughts?"

"It doesn't have any effect. I just like to listen to it."

"Well, I'm proposing that it does have an effect. What we think matters. What we focus on matters. What we expose our brain to matters. If your brain is repeatedly getting those kinds of messages, then it will have an impact on how you think...on how you approach life."

"That isn't the only kind of music I listen to. I listen to hip hop artists who have a positive message, too."

"I'm glad to hear it. I'd like to listen to some of that music. Some of that stuff you played last time definitely had an effect on me. My head was aching after listening to it. It just worries me to think that those behaviors I mentioned are being glorified or promoted in your music."

"My grandma doesn't like it, either."

"Of course, I'm sure my parents felt the same about music I listened to when I was your age. Shoot, I still listen to some of those same bands. Take Metallica, for instance. I'm sure my mom didn't care for songs like 'Am I Evil?' or 'Jump in the Fire'. 'Jump in the Fire' is basically the Devil's song about how he performs his dirty deeds. To me it's masterful poetry. I love that song. Although, I'm sure to some, it's heresy."

"I like Metallica."

"You do? Well, there's something we have in common. I've loved them since I was sixteen years old."

"I'm almost sixteen."

"Right on, that's cool. Well, to be fair, I fell out of love with them for over a decade, but I fell back in love with them over the last year or two. It wasn't that I didn't like them during that time in my life, I was just really focused on World Music...you know, African drumming, classical Eastern Indian music...stuff like that."

"I don't know any of that music. Do you have the *Black Album?*"

"As a matter of fact, I do. I'm pretty sure it's down in the door beside you."

Randy looked down into the side compartment and pulled out the cd.

"Funny thing about that album," I said. "When it first came out, I hated it."

"Really? Why?"

"Well, at the time, for die-hard Metallica fans like myself, it felt like a sell-out."

"How come?"

"It was much more commercialized than their previous albums and way less sophisticated. MTV was huge, and songs like 'Enter the Sandman' got constant play. Really, it was their crossover album into the mainstream. I wanted to like it. I couldn't wait for it to come out. Their album before that was ...*And Justice for All*."

"That's the one with 'One'?"

"Yep, and frankly, I didn't really care much for that album, either; it just seemed so dark. But I had more tolerance for it because it was their first album after they lost their bassist Cliff Burton. That man was a virtuoso anomaly. I don't know if you know their history, but he died in a bus accident. I figured that they deserved more compassion given their loss. I think you can really feel their pain on *Justice*."

"I did hear about their bass player dying. Yeah, that must've been rough on the other band members."

"Well, I guess you can say I was a selfish fan. I wanted more music like *Master of Puppets* or *Ride the Lightning*. I couldn't understand why they would change so much, especially after *Master's* monumental success."

"I didn't know that album was so big."

"It was for me. It's the first one I fell in love with."

"So, how did they change after *Master of Puppets*?"

"James' vocal style changes significantly on their later albums. I'm sure part of that was production, but it feels very different to me. Also, the compositions are way more technical, maybe too technical. Of course, how could they be the same without Cliff? He was instrumental in their success."

"I mostly just know a few songs off the *Black Album*, and that song 'One'. I didn't know that they went through such a big change. It's really sad when you think about it."

"Yeah, it is sad. So, anyway, at the time, I didn't allow them to evolve. I can say this, though; over twenty years later, I've grown to appreciate the *Black*

Album—especially 'Nothing Else Matters' and 'The Unforgiven'. Those songs just aren't on the same level as the other albums."

"I like 'The Unforgiven'. Can we listen to that?"

"Definitely. Can I share one last thing about it, and then I will be quiet so we can listen to it?"

"Sure. What's that?"

"Ironically, the thing I really like about 'Unforgiven' is how James contrasts his rocker voice with what my friend Foldy calls his *pretty voice*. He changes to pretty voice in the chorus. I think it's the first time he shares that voice with us. He gets a bit softer on 'Fade to Black', but I think he shows us another side of himself on 'The Unforgiven'. Anyway, let's check it out."

Randy pulled out the disc and put it in. I made a point to note the parts of the song where James Hetfield changes his voice back and forth from rocker voice to pretty voice. Randy giggled or smiled each time I did it. After that, he reclined his seat and went to sleep.

The Worst Thing You Can Do

I attended numerous trainings over the years that focused on supporting Tribal families with healing from Generational Trauma and recovering from drug addiction. One such training was held at the newly-constructed yurt right next to the Community Center. The facilitator of this training was Lone Wolf, a man I very much admired and respected. We had attended numerous trainings together in the past, but this was the first one that Lone Wolf led.

I always enjoyed his company, and I appreciated his passion for working with at-risk youth. He's a charismatic individual with an interesting life story. He primarily worked with the Tribal Member youth, and like Black Silk, he had a natural ability to engage the kids. The adults liked him, too. Whenever training participants would break off into groups, people always wanted Lone Wolf in their group. I was excited to see that he'd be facilitating this training.

As usual, when we broke into small groups at this workshop, all of the participants seemed to want Lone Wolf in their group, including myself. He was kind of a hot commodity.

For lunch we all went over to the casino to eat for free at the buffet. The Tribe offered food at most of their events, and trainings were no exception. If the Tribe didn't provide food right at the event location, then we were often allowed to eat for free at the casino buffet. In fact, many of our department meetings also took place in the grille next to the buffet. Although I'm not a big fan of buffets, who can complain about free food? I always appreciated this perk of working at the Tribe.

After lunch I headed into one of the casino restrooms. When I walked in, I saw Lone Wolf standing at one of the urinals. As I walked past him, I felt an urge to reach up and tug on his ponytail. You know that feeling you get when you're about to commit an act, and just before execution, you get a strong sense that you shouldn't do it? But it's too late because your action is already set in motion. Yeah, I had that feeling right before I touched his hair. Well, jeez, we were in the bathroom. He was in the middle of peeing for God's sake.

After I did it, I kept moving, but watched as he peered over his shoulder. He didn't look too happy. *Dang,* I thought, *nice one, Scott. What were you thinking? Just keep walking.* I felt very uncomfortable and, frankly, like kind of an idiot.

When I was leaving the front entrance of the casino, I saw Lone Wolf coming towards me. I felt a little scared. I knew he was a trained boxer, and I also got the sense he'd seen some hard times. He walked right up to me and stared down with a mean look. "If we were in prison, you could get killed for touching an Indian man's hair!"

I pathetically apologized. He just turned and walked away. *Well,* I thought, *at least we're not in prison.*

I was filled with regret for indulging my hair-tugging impulse, in the bathroom of all places. I wasn't sure what to do. I didn't really want to go back to the training.

I saw Gentle Owl walking across the parking lot. He was a Tribal Member Elder whom I also greatly respected. I approached him and asked for his counsel. I told him that I just unintendedly offended an Indian man whom I very much admired, and I wasn't sure what to do about it. I asked, "Should I bring him some tobacco or sage or something?" I had a fresh bundle of sage on my dash.

He said, "Well, those things would be fine, and you can always give him money."

I thanked Gentle Owl, and then decided I would head back to the training to face Lone Wolf. I didn't want to give him money. That felt like paying him off. He wasn't a schoolyard bully. I wanted to make a culturally-appropriate gesture to show him that I was sincerely sorry for my actions, while also honoring him at the same time.

I drove back to the Community Center and looked around for Lone Wolf. He was standing in the yard in front of the yurt. I grabbed the bundle of sage and straggled up to him. He stood hard with his arms crossed. He had a stern look on his face. I reached out with both hands to offer him the sage. In a regal tone, I said, "Lone Wolf, I'm very sorry for my actions back at the casino. I by no means meant to offend you, and I feel terrible for violating your personal boundaries and touching your hair. I hope that you can find forgiveness in your heart. As a symbol of my sincerity, I offer you this sage."

He just stood looking at me for a moment. And then he softened a bit, reached out his hands, and accepted my gift. His face slowly turned from a scowl to a smile. He leaned down and put his arm around me and said, "A wise Indian man once taught me that the worst thing you can do to someone is ignore them." He looked deeply into my eyes as he chuckled, and then he shook his head and smiled. *"You weren't ignoring me."* I nodded and giggled, and then we walked toward the yurt together.

The White Table

It's a strange thing to go to Thanksgiving dinner at a tribe, especially as a White person—well, a socially-conscious White person, anyway. Frankly, I find it odd that any tribe would celebrate Thanksgiving.

Like most Tribal events, I arrived at the staff Thanksgiving dinner well after it started. If you arrive pre-event, then you're likely to find yourself lingering, making small talk. When a function has already started, it's easier to pop in, get seen, make a few connections, and move on. That day was no exception, except that my desire for acceptance was much stronger than usual.

When I walked in, I saw Barney standing in the center of the gym holding a microphone. Apparently, he was MCing the event, and he was trying to engage people in the festivities. When he saw me, he excitedly announced over the loudspeaker, "Hey, Scott. Welcome. Come and get some food."

I thought it was strange since he usually did his best to either ignore me or make it clear that I wasn't worth his time. This was the second time he'd identified me on the mic during a staff dinner. It didn't feel genuine. It felt like he was putting on a show, falsely portraying our relationship.

After he announced my arrival, I meandered through the tables a bit, hoping to receive a welcoming smile or friendly gesture to sit down and join someone's table.

No one looked up at me. No one invited me to sit down at their table. I realize that I was probably overreacting, but I felt dejected. I really wanted someone to be excited to see me and invite me to join them. As I walked through the dining hall, I looked across the room to the very last table way off in the corner—The White table. *No,* I thought, *I'm not going to sit at The White table.*

I humbly looked around for what I perceived as acceptance. Other than Barney recognizing me, no one else seemed to even notice me. I felt dread well up inside me...dread that I'd have to sit at *that* table.

Alas, in the end, I relegated myself to go and sit with the (other) White people.

I wondered, *Is this how people feel when they sit at "Only" tables?* I always assumed that if people sat at the Black table, or Asian table, etc. that they did it because they wanted to, not because they felt restricted to sit there. Now granted, when I think about the dork table in middle school, I'm pretty sure those poor kids didn't want to sit their (no one did). But when it came to ethnic groups, I'd always assumed that they wanted to sit with people from their group. I had never considered that minority people may experience the same kind of dejection in similar situations. I'm sure that most White people have never considered this or experienced it for themselves.

Of course, you have to wonder: how much of it's going on inside our heads? The only way we'll ever know is if we're courageous enough to approach some of those seemingly unapproachable tables. I'm pretty sure there were many people at that dinner who would have welcomed me had they known that I desired an invitation. I wanted to feel included. Most people do.

Another Grand Opening

I was feeling pretty reluctant about participating in any Tribal events. I'd been working under Barney and Odessa for over a year, and it was taking its toll on me. Even though I was really good at my job, especially connecting with the families and the kids, they didn't see it, and they didn't seem to care. When it came to the ICW children, unless the kids were directly related to their family, then they weren't important.

At that point, greatly due to Barney, Piggy, and Miss Full of Herself, I was at the height of feeling dejected by the Tribal Community. I'd been there six years, and I was struggling to feel like I had a place.

Of course, a good portion of this was all going on in my head. Even though I was still having great interactions with most people in the Community, I was becoming more and more focused on the rejection from my direct leadership. I allowed their treatment to affect my judgement.

It did help to lower my expectations of them, though. As India likes to say, *When people show you who they are, believe them.* Why should I expect anything different from them than what they'd consistently shown me?

The Tribe had completed yet another multimillion-dollar construction project (Deja vu?). This time, it was for the Tribal Administration Building, and, par for the course, they had another grand opening ceremony with plenty of hoopla, fanfare, and, of course, gifting of Pendleton blankets.

It was a beautiful sunny day, and people were gathered on the unfinished, gravel lot in front of the new building. Like the grand opening at the jail, people seemed generally enthused about participating in the event. I even arrived in time to catch the ribbon-cutting ceremony and a few of the speeches.

I walked around the gravel lot while I listened to different leaders praise themselves for their roles in the project's success. As I meandered through the crowd, I saw Lester hanging out. He gave me a nod. I saw Kooky. She turned as though she didn't see me. Then I saw the ladies from the daycare. They all smiled at me. I saw some of the staff from Substance Abuse. They smiled, too. I saw more familiar faces…more smiles. Everywhere I looked I felt witnessed and appreciated.

After the speeches, people broke off to explore the new building before gathering in the old administration building for lunch.

There were a couple Tribal staff handing out commemorative bandanas, so I joined in line to get one. I watched the two young boys in front of me fold their bandanas and wrap them around their heads, so the graphic of the new building was centered on their foreheads. I was inspired by their example, so I followed suit.

Just after I finished securing my bandana, I turned and almost bumped into Red Deer, a Tribal Elder I knew. I had met him years before after seeing him perform on his traditional flute at the local fair-trade café, the same one where Sasha got so high on ice cream. We hit it off the first time we met.

Red Deer is a traditionally-trained *Pourer* from a local tribe. He facilitates invitation-only Sweat Lodges at a nearby farm. His Lodges are the controversial kind—the kind that allows White people. I'm sure he gets plenty of flak from the Tribal Community, but he has a huge heart, and he's a great teacher. He invited me to his Lodge the first time we met. He invited me several times over the years.

I tried to go one time. I packed up Shiva with the recommended supplies including offerings of tobacco and firewood, and I drove up to the farm one day of a gathering. Although the lodge was constructed just up the hill from the parking area, I didn't hear people gathered by the fire, and I didn't see any trails, so I left. In hindsight, I realized that, apparently, I wasn't meant to be in Lodge that day.

When Red Deer saw me, he exuberantly exclaimed, "Hey! How ya doin'?"

I shared his enthusiasm. "Hey, how are you doing?"

We hugged, and then he said, "*Vision Quest!*"

I looked at him with surprise.

He told me the date, and then he turned and grabbed a piece of paper from a nearby table and spread it out on the table in front of us. He quickly scribbled directions to the Vision Quest site while describing the location in finer detail. He also wrote down details for the Lodge.

He continued, "Come to Lodge next month so you can start preparing. I want you to be ready when we go to the mountain for Vision Quest." He gave me a big smile, and then he was off.

I thought I knew what a Vision Quest was, but I honestly had no idea if he was inviting me to do my own Vision Quest, or if he was inviting me to help support others with theirs. It didn't really matter to me, though. I had always been interested in participating in one of Red Deer's Lodges, and this felt like the perfect opportunity. I committed myself to going to the next Lodge.

I was on an emotional high. I was having such a great experience at this event.

I heard drumming and singing coming from the new Administration Building, so I headed over. The Salmon Family was gathered in Tribal Council's new chambers. I entered TC's chambers, and then walked over and stood next to one of the male singers. I placed my hands out in front of me with my palms up in a receiving gesture, closed my eyes, and began singing. Every once in a while, I opened my eyes to see smiling, welcoming faces. After singing for a little while, I headed over to lunch.

I continued to feel elated. Everywhere I looked, I was greeted with a smile. I was met with acceptance. Everywhere I turned I saw families whom I had served, and who seemed to be generally grateful for my help.

Councilmen Flowing Waters invited me to sit at her table. We had worked on a case together in the past. I sat and had lunch with her and her family. As I looked around the gym, I saw more of my current and former clients. Everyone looked at me with a comfortable familiarity. I felt like I belonged.

The Lodge

I was really excited about participating in a Vision Quest. As you can probably imagine, that's right up a hippie's alley. Come on…fasting, inward spiritual journey, magic visions…that's got hippie written all over it.

I'm pretty sure I first learned about Vision Quest from Matthew Modine (a *White Man* of all things) in the movie *Vision Quest*. To be fair, his Native friend Kuch (Jake from *Sixteen Candles*) first introduces the idea, but it was Louden Swain who exemplified it. It was his story that resonated with me all these years.

Vision Quest is a great movie, by the way. Matthew is very inspiring, and, oh, Linda Fiorentino (big childhood crush). You may also remember her as a spy in *Gotcha!*, also from 1985. Great flick.

Speaking of childhood crushes, I'd be remiss if I didn't mention Ornella Muti, Princess Aura from *Flash Gordon* (bigger crush), and Meredith Salenger (the biggest). Oh, and let's not forget Heather Thomas. My poster of Heather in her pink bikini took up more real estate than any other picture on my bedroom walls. Somewhere in my preteens, it replaced that huge poster of the white kitten and the goldfish.

They say you should put up a picture of the thing you most want to manifest, like a fancy car or new home, so you will see it every day and strengthen your focus. I wasn't aware of this concept back then, but Heather was the first image I saw every morning and the last image I saw before I went to sleep. Tell me that didn't foster some burning desire in my mind's eye. If only we could harness the power of teenage hormones.

Heather was in *Zapped!* with Scott Baio, the first R-rated movie I ever saw. I remember sneaking into the movie with my buddy Otis and spending the entire movie crouched down in the seats, fearful we'd be discovered. Who says adolescence wasn't fun? I can't reference *Zapped!* without mentioning Scatman Crothers (no other than the voice of Hong Kong Phooey). *He* was one of the best! I know he did a bunch of other movies and shows, but I knew him as Dexter Jones and Penrod Pooch. Good stuff. It's all about finding our POCs, *y'all*. I digress.

I'd participated in a few different sweat lodges run by White people, but I'd never participated in a traditional Sweat Lodge run by a Native person, let alone a Vision Quest. I made sure to attend Red Deer's next scheduled Lodge. I brought all the recommended supplies including water bottles, towels, tobacco, firewood, and food to share afterwards.

I arrived at the site early in the morning. The lead fire tender Sam was the only person there. I eagerly jumped in to help. I carried wood, split it, and piled it near the fire pit so it was readily available for the fire tenders. I also carried buckets of water up from the barn. Red Deer arrived while Sam and I were preparing. He naturally took the lead and began instructing us on preparations for the Lodge. [I differentiate between the Lodge ceremony and the lodge structure by using a capital L for the ceremony and a lowercase l for the structure.]

The lodge was constructed on a hill up in the trees behind the farm. Once you parked near the barn, you had to meander down a bumpy, winding path across a dry creek bed, and then up past a 300-year-old, grandfather maple to a hill that led directly to the lodge site. From the outside, the lodge looked like a domed hut covered in tarps. Under the tarps there was a layer of blankets that covered a wooden frame. Blankets are also spread across the floor of the lodge for added comfort and as moisture-absorbers.

There's a small door facing the fire pit. Earth is dug from the center of the lodge floor to create another small pit where the heated rocks known as *Ancestor Spirits* are placed. The Pourer scoops water from the bucket and pours it over the rocks during or after prayers; hence, the steam and the sweat. The dirt from the pit is piled outside the lodge door between the lodge and the fire to create an altar. The threshold connecting the fire, the altar, and the lodge becomes a sacred boundary. No one, but the fire tenders and the Pourer are allowed to cross this threshold.

Offerings such as sage, tobacco, sweet grass, and money are left at the altar. Each participant is smudged with sage before entering the lodge. They are also instructed to acknowledge the four directions by spinning three times at the door of the lodge. Very specific protocols exist for each step in the Lodge process including locating the site, harvesting the trees to build the lodge, and building the fire and altar. Sage is offered each time a tree or branch is cut.

The Pourer is the facilitator of the Lodge, much in the same way as the Master Drummer is the facilitator of the Drum and Dance ceremony. Red Deer studied with traditional Pourers before he was granted the right to pour, much in the same way as C.K. served apprenticeships with Master Drummers and Dancers before he was given the stick. Red Deer's position in the Lodge reminded me of C.K.'s position in our drum and dance troupe. C.K. was revered by our group members. Similarly, Red Deer was respected by all the members of the Lodge and clearly recognized as the leader of the group. We used to call C.K. "Uncle C.K.", as a term of respect and admiration. I also called Red Deer, "Uncle Red". There were many parallels between these great teachers.

Being a fire tender is hard work. By the time the other participants arrived, we'd already put in a couple hours of intense labor. In addition to all the preparations and the ongoing fire-tending, the fire tenders also lift the rocks from the fire with a shovel or pitchfork, dust them with a branch such as fir tree, and then deliver them to the doorway of the lodge where they are lifted from the forks with antlers and placed into the pit or *womb* of the Lodge.

Members welcome these Ancestor Spirits, and they are offered sage themselves. Sometimes a rock would fall off the pitchfork as it was being moved, and Lodge members would say, "Look, that ancestor is not ready to enter the lodge." I thought that their comments were kind of funny because it always just looked like a rock falling off of an unsteady pitchfork.

There are four rounds to the Lodge ceremony. Each round represents a different direction, a different age group, and *a different nation!* All peoples are represented in the Lodge ceremony. I asked Red Deer, "Where does the symbol of the medicine wheel and the four directions originate?"

He taught me, "It's a universal symbol. No one tribe can claim it. By its very meaning, it's owned by all people."

I chose that symbol for the cover of this book because, to me, it perfectly embodies its central message... *we're all in this together.* Coincidentally, it was also Uncle C.K.'s primary message. He used to say, "If you get to know your neighbor, then you can learn to understand your neighbor." He would continue, "The best way to learn about another people's culture is to learn their language. Their culture is in their language."

He'd often elaborate, "People all over the world have drum and dance. We can all relate to that. We can get to know each other through our music and dance because we all have that in common. Through this connection we can work together to accomplish any task."

I've been drawn to fire-tending my entire life. When I was a child, I was always mesmerized by a fire. I still am. We had fires when we went camping, my grandfather always had a fire burning in his fireplace at his *Up-North* cabin (even in the heat of July), and throughout my youth, we spent most of the summer at the lake, where I would build a fire practically every night. When I was a teen, I'd always break off from daily swimming and boating activities to wander through the woods gathering fallen limbs and branches for that evening's campfire. Additionally, my family has utilized a wood stove as our primary source of heat for almost twenty years.

There's nothing like wood heat. It warms you right through your bones, down to the core. A nice fire creates such a cozy, inviting space. Of course, you're also heated when you cut, stack, split, and carry the wood prior to the flame ever being lit.

After entering the lodge, we'd circle around the pile of rocks, uh, Ancestor Spirits, in a clockwise direction leaving space just to the right of the door for the Pourer. Some Lodge leaders teach that circling in this clockwise direction represents the Earth circling around the Sun. Similarly, we used to perform dances with Uncle C.K. where the dancers would circle around the drummers for the same symbolic purpose.

At the beginning of the first round, really the *First Door*, Red Deer would acknowledge *Father Sky* above, *Mother Earth* below, and then the four directions, *East, South, West,* and *North,* respectively, with smudging of sage medicine, pouring, and prayers. The first door to the East represents the *Red Nation*, children, and love. Each door also has a spirit animal associated with it. In the case of the First Door, it is the *Red Deer*.

The *Second Door* represents the South, the *Yellow Nation*, teenagers, and growth. Its spirit animal is the *Golden Eagle*.

The *Third Door* represents the West, the *Black Nation*, middle age, and maturity. Its spirit animal is the *Black Bear*.

Finally, the *Fourth Door* represents the North, the *White Nation,* Elders, and wisdom. Yep, White people are represented in the sacred Lodge as well. Its spirit animal is the *Bald Eagle.*

Red Deer told us that each of these spirit animals sat outside the door of the Lodge for their respective rounds. Now, granted, I'm open to anything—*all* things are possible—but really, I saw these spirit animals more as symbols than actual beings. I mean, I really didn't think that an invisible Red Deer, Golden Eagle, Black Bear, or Bald Eagle was actually sitting outside the door each time their respective round was happening (in all Lodges all over the Earth). Just like with Jesus I say, "Don't they have better things to do?" Call me a pragmatist. It *is* possible to be a pragmatist *and* an idealist at the same time. It's all about balance. And, perhaps like the mythical DMT Goddess (we've never met), these omnipresent entities come whenever they're summoned.

Once those initial rites were performed, Red Deer would open up the round for prayers from each of the participants. He'd say something like, "Creator, please honor the prayers of my sister (uncle, nephew, brother, etc.) sitting to my left. Please listen to their prayers or look in their hearts…" When it was your turn, you were encouraged to speak about what was on your heart, or you could simply say that you wanted to say your prayers in silence. When you were done, you would say, "All my relations." If it were your first time in Lodge, you would introduce yourself and acknowledge your parents, your grandparents, and your ethnic lineage. At the end of the round, after everyone had their turn, Red Deer would proclaim, "All my relations, open the door!"

We'd follow him out of the lodge in the same clockwise direction we'd entered. After the last round, we'd form a line outside the door, and then each participant would greet and thank all the other participants after they exited, and then join in the line until the last member had passed. Afterwards, everyone shared offerings of food, and generally discussed what a great Lodge it had been.

There's still more work to be done including gathering up the sweaty blankets, spreading out the coals from the fire, putting away tools, and covering the wood pile. Oh, and you still need to carry all your stuff back down to the car. Needless to say, between the preparations, the actual Lodge ceremony, which can be incredibly intense, and then the clean up afterwards, I always felt completely exhausted when it was all over. I felt exhausted, but, more importantly, I felt physically and spiritually cleansed, which, overall, was an incredibly-rewarding experience. I always felt grateful to be part of Red Deer's Lodge. Even when it didn't go so well.

Vision Quest

It turned out that I wouldn't be participating in my own Vision Quest, but rather supporting several Questers as a fire tender. I learned that it took at least a year of preparation. Questers have numerous commitments including making gifts for their *Giveaway*, spiritual preparation, and financial obligations—lots of expenses.

Uncle Red had a location up near the mountain that he liked to use. There was plenty of room for the lodge to be constructed in its own space and for the Questers to have their own isolated areas. Additionally, there was room for a kitchen, camping areas for everyone else, and privacy from any camping neighbors. There was a head fire tender, a head cook, several supporting fire tenders, and numerous other people who came for emotional and logistical support. There was plenty of work to be done.

We constructed a new lodge from small trees we cut down in the near-by riverbed. The Lodge fire had to burn 24 hours a day for the entire period of the Vision Quest. Fire tenders worked out a schedule, so there'd always be one of us keeping the fire going. Uncle Red's Nephew Tall Timbers came down from the North to serve as the head fire tender. Ultimately, keeping the fire going was his responsibility, but there were several of us who took shifts throughout the day and night to support the effort.

The perimeter of the Lodge also needed to be walked regularly throughout the day and night. This boundary was established partly to keep animals away, but also to clearly delineate the Vision Quest territory. Apparently, this would create a kind of energetic barrier to keep out any intruders, including malevolent spirits.

The weekend of the Vision Quest was particularly significant to me: my maternal grandmother had recently passed, and her funeral was to be held that same weekend. I had reservations about not traveling home to be with my mother's family for *that* ceremony, but I'd received my mother's blessing, and, besides, my grandmother is not her body. She had already left. I thought it was way more likely that I'd have an intimate visit with her while tending the late-night fire than I would if I'd gone to the funeral. In fact, I welcomed it!

I honored my grandmother's passing in my own way throughout the Vision Quest experience. I even volunteered to take the 3 to 6 a.m. fire-tending shift, as this is a very auspicious time for such endeavors. I imagined how cool it would be for her to come join me at the fire, kind of like Obi Wan came to see Luke in the forest on Dagobah. I longed for such an experience. I would love to be able to tell my mother that her mother came to visit me around the Lodge fire. Alas, she may have come for a visit, but not in the form I was expecting. I do realize that her ethereal visit might just have scared the b-Jesus out of me, but I still welcomed it, nonetheless.

During breakfast on our second morning by the mountain, Tall Timbers excitedly proclaimed that *he* had been visited by Bigfoot while tending the fire late that night. I was instantly jealous. I didn't think it was fair that he would get an unannounced visit from Bigfoot when I had clearly sent an open invitation to my dearly-departed grandmother.

Uncle Red gave Tall Timbers special recognition several times over the next few days for being honored by such an illustrious visit from the big hairy guy. It would be months later before I found out that *Bigfoot* was actually just a tree dancing in the wind. Red explained, "Well, none of the other trees were dancing. That was surely Bigfoot."

Oh my God, I thought. *That's surely Bigfoot just as that rock that fell off the pitchfork is surely an Ancestor Spirit.* I must say, any remaining feelings of jealousy quickly subsided when I heard the real story.

Overall, serving Questors was incredibly fulfilling. Uncle Red facilitated numerous Sweat Lodges during the week of the Vision Quest. My favorite was sharing in a Lodge with just Uncle Red, his sister Red Doe, and Tall Timbers. It was such an honor to share that experience with three Tribal people, and no one else. I felt like they were my Indian family... *they were*.

At the end of that Lodge, I covered my naked body in ash from the fire pit and ran down to the river to bathe. Tall Timbers seemed inspired by my actions as he also took off running behind me and then surpassed me. He slipped in some mud near the shore and came crashing down to the Earth. Imagine a giant oak smashing to the ground with exquisite grace, and then you can imagine what I witnessed of Tall Timbers fall. He didn't seem fazed at all, but rather leaped up in stride and kept going. We bathed in those fresh mountain waters, and then returned to camp together.

Barney's Confession

And poof! Just like that, Odessa was gone. Apparently, she went on extended leave to care for a family member. She certainly didn't tell me about it. Although I was really looking forward to going on leave myself, I was happy to accept this new reality. The benefits of getting a permanent break from Odessa far outweighed the temporary relief from taking a break from ICW. *Ding Dong, Odessa was gone!* I was afraid to hold my breath. Was it real? I mean, I knew she wouldn't last, no one did, but was she really gone?

After a couple weeks went by, and she didn't return to work, I started to believe my good fortune. I had spent the worst year and half of my professional career working under her, and, frankly, I felt a bit traumatized. It almost didn't matter what came next. If I could weather her storm, I thought I was prepared for anyone.

It would be months before we had any replacements (again). I knew it would be easier without Odessa, but I still had to deal with Barney. I figured my best bet was to stay clear of him and Piggy. Unless, of course, one of my cases was going to complain to Tribal Council—he'd want to know about that.

A few weeks went by without a word from Barney. Then I started hearing rumblings throughout the community about him being angry with Odessa. No one seemed to know what he was angry about, but they knew he was mad at her, that was for sure.

I saw him one day out in the parking lot. He walked directly up to me until we were standing face to face. After quickly scanning the area around us, he leaned in, peered over his glasses, and said, "Odessa made a mess of ICW. She hated you. She's been blaming it on you for over a year, but now that she's gone, I'm seeing that it was actually her fault. I've had many complaints about her from other managers and directors at the Tribe. Apparently, they feel that she's arrogant and condescending. *Apparently*, she's a horrible supervisor."

He paused a moment. "Well, that's fine. When she comes back, I'm putting her on a two-year training program. She's going to spend time working with numerous departments so she can learn how to manage people. I can't have her taking over for me when I retire if she doesn't learn how to get along with people."

He turned to go, but then paused and looked back. "You know you never would've gotten a raise under her. You make too close to what she did."

And then he was off.

Snake Eyes

Nervous Beaver had just returned to the Tribe to take the position as my supervisor. I heard that the Tribe had also hired another social worker, a young Indian woman from a tribe on the other side of the state. I was relieved. I'd been by myself again for months, and I welcomed the help, albeit cautiously. At least with Nervous Beaver I knew what to expect. I'd trained her as an ICW social worker, and I had a feeling I was about to train her as my supervisor. She had a good heart, but she was so timid.

By this time, I'd been with the Tribe for over six years. I'd seen many people come and go from my department. The families saw many workers come and go. I felt a false sense of security in my seniority as a case worker. I felt like it was *my* department they were coming to work in. I had all the cases. I knew all the families. I had built relationships with all of the children.

But alas, I was not the supervisor, nor was I the "new face of ICW" as I heard Barney proclaim. My new co-worker from the tribe on the eastern side of the state was the *new face of ICW*. Barney said she was a very traditional looking Indian. She'd be way less threatening to our clients than a White Man. I understood. She could be the new face of ICW. That was fine with me, as long as she took on some cases.

One morning Nervous Beaver came to my office and said she wanted to introduce me to my new co-worker. I smiled, stuck out my hand, and said, "Hi, I'm Scott. Welcome to ICW."

She took one look at me and then recoiled in disgust. She gave new meaning to The Look. I call her look, *The dirty toilet paper look*. Imagine the look you'd have on your face if someone tried to hand you a piece of soiled toilet paper. That's the look she had on her face when I reached out my hand and introduced myself. *Oh boy*, I thought, *here we go again*.

I resigned myself to follow my code and do the same thing with her that I did with every new member of the team. I offered my help but, otherwise, I gave her space. I did my best to mirror her in all of our interactions. If she ignored me,

I didn't say anything. If she looked at me, I acknowledged her. I kept our interactions as brief, simple, and work-focused as possible.

One day when I came into the office, Nervous Beaver and my new co-worker were hanging out, smiling, and talking about music. I engaged in the conversation and asked them what types of music they liked to listen to. My new co-worker, henceforth known as Snake Eyes, solemnly replied, "I like hip hop," without looking at me. The closest things to hip hop I listened to at the time were Mariah Carey and Justin Timberlake. India had recently picked up JT's *20/20*, and we were listening to it like crazy. I shared my excitement for this new music and offered to burn copies for each of them. Nervous Beaver smiled shyly and said, "That would be nice." Snake Eyes didn't say a thing.

The next day I brought in copies of the cd for each of them. When I reached out to hand Snake Eyes her copy, she glared at me with a look that said, *How dare you*. Imagine a servant trying to give a gift to a royal. Then she looked at Nervous Beaver before scowling back at me. She seemed pissed that she would be obligated to accept the gift. Her body language spoke volumes. She did accept it, with apparent resentment. I thought, *Man, I just need to give up with this woman. There's no getting through. It doesn't matter how friendly or cool I am if she's not willing to accept me*. Later I thought, *Maybe it was a bad choice to share music from a White artist*. It didn't matter. I'd try not to make any further gestures of good faith. I'd do my best to *leave her alone*.

Fortunately, we didn't come into contact all that much even though we all eventually had offices in the same modular building. Usually when I saw her, she would look down her nose at me. I just tried to avoid her.

One day I got a call from one of the grandmothers I used to work with. She called to express concern because she thought that her young granddaughter was being molested by her older brothers. She said that her granddaughter had exhibited numerous explicit signs that she'd experienced sexual contact, and it was alleged by a close family member that the brothers were involved. I commiserated with the grandmother, and then I told her that her grandchildren's cases where now being handled by my new co-worker. I said I'd tell my supervisor about the grandmother's concerns. I also informed her she could call the Clinic for Sexual Violence and the children's new social worker directly, and I gave her numbers for both.

Later that day I told Nervous Beaver about the grandmother's report. She told me to tell Snake Eyes what had been reported since they were her clients. I went to her closed door, knocked, and announced myself. "Come in," she answered. I opened the door and asked if I could discuss some reported concerns about one of the families on her caseload. She gave me a look that said, *Do you really have to?*

I sat down in front of her desk and proceeded to tell her about the phone call I'd received. She kept her head down with her eyes fixated on her desk. I told her about the grandmother's concerns that her granddaughter was being molested by her brothers. Snake Eyes didn't say anything. She didn't look at me. She appeared completely disinterested in what I was saying, but I know she heard me.

I awkwardly finished, "Well, ok, Nervous Beaver directed me to apprise you of the grandmother's concerns so you can perform an investigation, inform Law Enforcement, or make a referral to the Clinic for Sexual Violence."

I sat there awaiting her response. After a brief silence, she looked up with an expression that said, *And what the fuck do you want me to do about it?*

I said, "Ok, thank you. I just wanted to make sure you knew about this referral," and I left.

I went back to Nervous Beaver's office and told her about my interaction with Snake Eyes. "She seemed totally disinterested when I told her about the sexual abuse allegations. I'm afraid that she won't do anything about it."

Nervous Beaver responded, "I'll follow up with her on it."

Neither Nervous Beaver, Snake Eyes, or anyone from ICW would ever investigate this report. I later heard from the girl's grandmother that when she called and talked to Snake Eyes about her concerns, she got the same response I did—no response.

Snake Eyes had experience working with young gang members in the criminal justice system. She approached social work with the same mentality, that is, more like a probation officer than a social worker. She complained numerous times that she thought our program was too lenient on the parents.

She thought we should be arresting them and punishing them for neglecting their children.

I said the same thing to her that I told Odessa over a year before when she expressed similar sentiments about punishing the parents. "There are natural consequences built in through the court system. If parents don't do what they're supposed to do in terms of treatment and other court-ordered services, then they don't get to reunify with their children. Besides," I told her, "we're here to reunify families, not punish them. It's our job to encourage them and lift them up, to help them believe in themselves. It's not our place to tear them down; they've had enough of that."

Snake Eyes clearly didn't think that being separated from their children was a stiff enough consequence. She berated our practices numerous times both to me and Nervous Beaver. She frequently compared our program to the last program where she had worked, often implying that we were doing things wrong. It always amazed me that she'd speak with such condescension to Nervous Beaver. I was no longer surprised by her behavior toward me, but I thought she'd, at least, treat our supervisor with some respect. One day she pulled me aside and said, "I have absolutely nothing to learn from our supervisor." I was kind of surprised that she disclosed that to me of all people, but then, there it is.

I can honestly say that she's the most outwardly racist person I've ever met in my life. There was a stark difference in the way she interacted with White people and Native people. I witnessed her introductions to many people from the Tribe, and there was always a significant contrast between Tribal and non-Tribal. With Tribal people she smiled, put out her hand, asked them where they were from, showed genuine interest in them, and interacted in a very pleasant manner. In the numerous introductions I witnessed with White people, she always recoiled and gave the dirty toilet paper look. *Well,* I thought, *at least she didn't just do it with me.*

I talked to Nervous Beaver about my concerns numerous times during that first year Snake Eyes joined our department. I told her how I felt harassed and discriminated against by Snake Eyes, and I gave numerous specific examples. I talked to her in person about Snake Eyes' behavior towards me, and I sent her texts and emails. She never responded to any of my written correspondence on the subject. In person, she would listen, but rarely say anything back.

Nervous Beaver never did *anything* about it. I'm sure she was afraid to do something. She told me it was too loaded. "Advocating for a White employee against an Indian one in Indian Country would not be tolerated." No one was going to listen. I understood, but I still tried to get her to do something about it. I felt it was the right thing to do. I also had that false sense of security.

One day during Sweat Lodge, I told my Lodge family about the treatment I received from Snake Eyes. A couple people asked where she was from. After I told them, one responded, "Oh, no wonder; they're really racist there." The other said, "Yeah, those are really racist Indians." Now that was something for me to hear two Indian people say that other Indians were really racist, a whole tribe for that matter. Everything is relative, and that's really saying something. At least, I felt affirmed.

One day, Snake Eyes and I were staffing our cases with Nervous Beaver in her office. After we finished, Nervous Beaver said she wanted to staff a few things with us. One of them involved issues she was having with investigations. In the middle of her discourse, Snake Eyes interrupted and declared in a condescending tone, "If we had an investigator with some backbone, we wouldn't have all these problems!"

Nervous Beaver was the investigator. Although I was surprised that Snake Eyes would talk so derogatorily to her supervisor, in front of her co-worker even, I had to admit to myself, *She's right.*

One of our colleagues referred to Nervous Beaver as a "wet noodle." He said, "She doesn't stand up for anything." This was a professional who'd witnessed countless presentations by Miss Beaver in court. She'd cower whenever faced with conflict—not a very strong quality for an ICW supervisor. That's not a strong quality for anyone working in ICW. The job description should read, "Backbone required."

Of course, Barney and Piggy already knew this about her when they brought her back to ICW as the supervisor. Everyone knew it. They also knew that even though Nervous Beaver and I had a good working relationship, she'd eventually have to turn on me. They knew she'd never support her White co-worker over her Native superiors. They could easily get her to carry out their dirty work.

In that meeting Nervous Beaver also discussed some issues she was having with Many Troubles' case. Many had a long history with our department, and she could barely take care of herself, let alone her children. Many had a new baby, and the baby's White father was totally capable of parenting the child, but Nervous Beaver didn't want to dismiss the case, as the code dictated, because she felt bad for Many. I told her, "The code clearly states that if we have a fit biological parent who's capable of raising their child, and they want their child, then we don't have a case. This precedent has already been established in Tribal Court. Frankly, you're violating the rights of the father and the child."

"I know," Nervous Beaver meekly responded, "but my heart really goes out to Many. If this father gets full custody, she may never see her child. I don't have to tell you what serious problems she has."

I continued, "It's my professional recommendation that the court give custody of the child to the father and dismiss the case. Otherwise, it appears that you're unfairly supporting the Native mother against the White father. This may be Tribal Court, but he still has rights, and more importantly, the child has rights. Once again, let me go on record as saying, we shouldn't even have this case. The child is not eligible for enrollment, *and* we have a fit and capable parent."

To my surprise, Snake Eyes chimed in with support. "Yeah, I agree," she said. "Scott's right. I don't understand why you're enabling the mother. This case should be dismissed."

Nervous Beaver lowered her head and mumbled, "You guys are right. I just feel so sorry for Many. I really want to help her." After a few moments, she concluded with, "Ok, that's all I have for today."

Snake Eyes and I got up and walked out of her office. We both headed down the hallway to the kitchen area. In an attempt to make a connection with her, I looked back, smiled, and enthusiastically said, "Hey, it seemed like we were in agreement back there. I think we may be more alike than we know." I saw this as an opportunity to make a point-of-connection. I considered it a compliment.

She scowled at me. She looked offended, as though I'd just insulted her. I know. I thought, *How dare I compare myself to her?* Odessa gave me the same look before in response to the same statement—a similar attempt at connection. I knew better than to even try. It was a mistake. It's one of my issues. I keep having hope that given the opportunity to rise, people will change. I keep thinking that they will follow suit in taking the higher path. I gave up.

A Different Set of Rules

No one wants to hear about a White Man's experience with racism. Most people don't even believe it's possible for a White person to be the target of racism. Even White people don't want to hear about it. It makes them uncomfortable. It makes everyone uncomfortable—especially *People of Color*.

I continued attending Lodge and learning about fire-tending from Red Deer long after the Vision Quest. I love going to Lodge. It's many things for many people, although the common consensus is that it's a healing experience.

Lodge participants are encouraged to speak from their heart, to share their challenges and their struggles authentically and transparently, and to humbly ask Creator for help, either with their own struggles, struggles of their loved-ones, or the struggles of all Nations of the Earth. Under the appropriate guidance of a traditionally-trained Pourer, the participant can surely experience a major catharsis—physically, mentally, and spiritually.

I felt comfortable with my little Lodge family, perhaps too comfortable. I started sharing some of the minority experiences I was having at the Tribe (I never actually referred to them as minority experiences).

During the different rounds of the Lodge, I told them how I felt discriminated against by some of my Native co-workers. I shared how I felt I was being harassed by Snake Eyes and treated poorly by Barney and Piggy. I could tell that my feelings were not accepted by anyone, even the White people. They looked at me like I should know better. *Don't rock the boat, man. You're gonna fuck it up for the rest of us.* I felt justified in my behavior. I'd spent years serving Tribal people. Didn't I deserve to express my feelings about it? Didn't my experience count?

It didn't. Even Red Deer, or perhaps I should say, *especially* Red Deer became increasingly uncomfortable with my prayers.

A few times when it was my turn in the round, I specifically prayed for my Lodge brothers and sisters to have the strength to be more open and accepting of my perspective, of my stories. I even named one of my Lodge sisters during one prayer, basically asking Creator to help her to be more open and tolerant since I could see that she was struggling to accept what I had to share, from my heart, I might add. She couldn't. None of them could, but no one ever said a word about it. And I mean not one word, good or bad. No one was able to witness me. I decided to stop sharing those kinds of experiences with them.

As long as I kept it somewhat superficial and routine, then my prayers were accepted. A couple times I shared one of White Light's songs in the Lodge. That was acceptable. People seemed to appreciate it. I could pray for my family's well-being or a friend's struggles with their health, but if I even broached the subject of feeling marginalized by people at the Tribe, forget it, it wasn't welcome.

During one Lodge, months after I'd made my decision to keep my minority experiences to myself, I felt compelled to share about a challenge I was having because it was weighing heavy on my heart. Essentially, India felt like I was smoking too much weed. I know that it's powerful medicine, but I tend to overindulge. India often reflected about how dull and distant I became under its influence. Who would know better than my wife? She once commented about how my friends who smoked weed had a grayness about them. Once she said it, I couldn't unsee it.

I immediately felt judged by Red Deer. At first, I didn't understand why he was so put-off by what I shared. After the final round was over, he even commented on how "dirty" this Lodge had been. He seemed so disappointed. He looked right at me when he said it.

Then I got it. He wasn't upset or uncomfortable with me sharing about my weed use; he was, however, upset with me for all the things I'd shared previously about my experiences with racism, and this was an opportunity for him to express his frustrations with me. I could see right through it. I'd witnessed Native people share about all kinds of stuff in that Lodge. Everything from serious drug addiction (meth and shit) to suicidal ideations, to their views about the racist White World, but it wasn't acceptable for me to share about my marriage or my weed use(?)

Of course, it was acceptable for me to share about my relationship in Lodge; hell, it was even acceptable for me to share about my love of ganja, but it wasn't acceptable for me to share anything about race. Red Deer had a different set of rules for White people vs People of Color. I knew exactly what was going on that day. It hurt, and it angered me. When I left Lodge, I didn't say goodbye, and I was pretty sure I wasn't coming back.

As time went on, I missed going to Lodge. I liked seeing my Lodge brothers and sisters. I missed being a fire tender, even the hard labor. I missed learning from Red Deer. Well, I hadn't been kicked-out; I just hadn't returned.

Over a year passed before I decided to go back. I checked in with Red Deer online to make sure I was still welcome. He responded right away and told me when the next Lodge was happening. I felt somewhat cautious. *Once bitten, twice shy*, I thought, but I really missed it. You might say that my spirit was calling me back.

I attended the next few Lodges. Everyone seemed genuinely happy about my return. I kept it clean. I didn't go into any of my concerns about feeling judged or rejected by people from the Tribe. I enjoyed my experiences there, I met some new Lodge members, and I felt generally welcome.

I apologize to Red Deer for disclosing what I'm about to share. It's important to me to tell this part of our story. Lodge is sacred, and I recognize that.

During the second round of one of those Lodges, Red Deer stated in a melancholy voice, "White Doe [his partner] is worried that Trump is going to cause a civil war here in the United States…" He went on to elaborate about their shared concerns. What instantly struck me was that he sounded like a victim, i.e., poor me.

He continued with that same whiney voice, "I'm just an Indian. He doesn't care about me…blah, blah, blah, blah, blah." I own it. I felt judgmental and reactive.

When it came my turn to speak, I was compelled to share what was on my heart (and my mind). After easing into my prayer with some acceptable talk about personal growth and all, I said, "There's already a civil war going on. It's going on inside each and every one of us. This war is between fear and love. When we succumb to fear, we become the victim, we exude a 'Poor Me' mentality—"

"Your turn is over!" Red Deer interrupted. I wasn't allowed to finish sharing what I had to say. He was clearly offended and frustrated. He knew I was referring to him. I was frustrated, too. Once again, what I had to offer was not acceptable. Granted, it was his Lodge, he was the Pourer, and he felt disrespected by me. I wasn't intending to disrespect him, but I felt it was important to address the consciousness of his thinking. He *was* being a victim. However, it wasn't my place to address it.

I shut up as directed, but I was riled-up inside. I couldn't stop thinking of getting my message out. I couldn't wait until the next round, when I would get my turn again so I could finish what I had to say, and then some! Once again, I felt like he was rejecting what I had to offer because I'm White. Perhaps he was, perhaps he wasn't. That's not the point of me sharing this story. I've accepted that I disrespected Red Deer with my words and actions. I've also accepted that it wasn't my place to offer a teaching in his Lodge.

I also left that Lodge angry, this time vowing never to return. Red Deer and I exchanged numerous unchoice words via private messages. I actually started the communication with a public apology to Red Deer and the rest of the group. He didn't accept my apology. He chastised me, cut me out of the online Lodge group, and even blamed me for him losing a job because he was so upset by my behavior.

I attempted to reason with him and appeal to his higher nature. I encouraged him to recognize that we never stop learning, and we can all learn from each other. I shared my favorite Metallica quote, "Open mind for a different view."

He responded, "I'm an Elder. I don't have to have an open mind. I've already studied with Traditional Pourers so that I could run my own Lodge. If you want to teach others, then create your own circle. This is my circle!"

I gave up.

Sadly, I was officially done with Red Deer's Lodge.

Over a year past before I would see Uncle Red again. I ran into a Native friend at the co-op one day, and I shared a little of what had transpired with Red. I also shared that it was on my heart to reconcile with him, but I wasn't sure how to proceed. He recommended that I bring him sage. He said, "He's a Traditional Indian. He'll respond positively if you offer him sage and a genuine apology." I thought he was being a bit naïve, given my history with Red Deer, but I took his advice, nonetheless.

A few months later, I took one of two bundles of sage India had at the house, as well as some of my favorite food on the planet—blueberries from the best source around, a local organic nursery just south of town.

I couldn't remember exactly where Red lived, but I knew the neighborhood. I did some breathwork to center myself during the drive over, and then I parked at the local park. I thought I knew which house was his, but I didn't see his truck, so I wasn't sure. I knew he had an alley behind his house, so I walked down to the corner of the street and went around back to see if there was one. Just then I saw a man come out from the corner house. I said, "Hello, how's it going? I wonder if you can help me. I'm looking for my friend Red, and I believe that he may be your next-door neighbor."

He gave me a puzzled look. "I'm not really sure. I don't know that neighbor."

"He's an older Indian man."

"Oh, yes, I do believe that would be him."

I thanked him and walked back around the corner to Red's house. Just as I was approaching the yard, I saw Red coming out the front door. He came down the sidewalk from the front porch and unlocked the car parked in the street. He noticed me just as he was about to get in the car. My hair was longer than the last time he'd seen me, and I had sunglasses on, so I wasn't sure if he recognized me. With a big smile, I joked, "Run! Get away as fast as you can."

He quickly jumped into the car and started it up. Yeah, he recognized me.

I walked up to the driver side door and stood with outstretched hands revealing my gifts of sage medicine and luscious blueberries.

With a huff, he rolled down his window.

I said, "Hello, Uncle Red. I've come to apologize to you for my behavior in Lodge. I brought you gifts of sage and blueberries."

He angrily stated, "I'm not accepting anything from *You*!"

I continued, "Red, I'm very sorry for my behavior. I'm so sorry for how my actions affected you and the Lodge family."

He curtly stated again, "I'm not accepting anything from *You*! You don't respect anyone! You don't even respect yourself."

I smiled and calmly said, "Red, you should know that this is the end of *our* story. It's going in my book."

His face became sterner, he squinted his eyes at me, and then he faced forward and drove away.

Well, I thought, *I tried. I can't force him to accept my apology or my gifts.*

I've been accused numerous times over the years of always going back (for more). I go back when I feel a situation is not resolved. I certainly did not feel understanding or resolution with him.

Unfortunately, I texted him, "I just want to point out that I came to you with love and gifts, and you met me with hostility and rejection."

He responded later, "Do not come to my house. Do not approach me or my family if you see us in the community."

I conceded, although in my heart I really didn't feel like we were done. I wasn't angry nor was I harboring any resentment, but I knew we weren't finished. I just had a feeling. Deep down I felt like Creator had more work for us to do.

The next time I saw Red he was coming out of my favorite weed shop across the street from the co-op. I didn't even go over there to get weed (I was on a break). I just felt compelled to walk over there as I was leaving the co-op. When I saw Red exiting the building, I knew why. You might say that Creator *did* have a plan for us. I think so. I just stopped in my tracks and watched him get in his car. I was curious to see if he'd notice me.

He was on his way out of the lot when he finally saw me. Once he did see me, he couldn't get out of there fast enough. He almost ran into me. I'm pretty sure he wasn't trying to hit me. He was just trying to get out of there as fast as he could, and I was in the way.

I hollered, "I see you." I didn't even go into the store. I just stood there and laughed. I knew his "dirty" comment wasn't about weed. I just had a feeling.

Sunshine Who Walks in the Clouds

She was raped by her cousin. He raped his sisters, too. She was also molested by her uncle. Her sister was raped by a neighbor. He was never prosecuted. None of them were ever prosecuted.

Sunshine had a thirty-some year old "boyfriend" when she was thirteen. His fifty-something year old mother personally threatened to kill Sunshine if she ever told anyone about their relationship.

Many of Sunshine's cousins were on my caseload. She contacted me numerous times over the years to offer information about her family members. She told me who would be safe placements for her cousins. She let me know who was on drugs and who was doing well.

One day she came to my office and asked if we could talk. I invited her in and closed the door. She paced around for a minute, wrenching her hands. I offered her a seat, and then asked what was on her mind. She sat down, but she seemed uncertain about sharing what was bothering her.

I held the space.

After a few moments, she said, "You've been a good caseworker for my family. I've watched you over the years. You listen to what the family says, and you always try to do the right thing."

I thanked her.

She continued, "There's something I'd like to tell you."

She had my full attention.

"Last weekend when I was hangin' out with Beast, I think he drugged me up and let his friends run a train on me."

"Oh my God!" I stated. "What are you talking about?"

"I kept waking up with different guys on top of me, and I could see Beast standing there watching."

I didn't know what to say. I was completely stunned.

I asked, "Are you ok?"

Sunshine started crying.

I asked her, "What can I do?"

"I don't know. I just wanted to tell you. I'm afraid to do anything about it. Beast is very dangerous. His mother's also dangerous. I'll be ok. I just wanted to tell you. I needed to tell someone who I trust."

"Have you told anyone else?"

"A few of my friends know. It's happened to some of them too with other guys. But I haven't told any adults, well, other than you."

I empathized, "First of all, I'm very sorry to hear what happened to you. I'm not really sure what to say. You must be feeling violated, hurt, and betrayed. I also imagine you're feeling very angry for what has been done to you and your friends."

Sunshine lowered her eyes. She had a darkness about her.

I continued, "I'm honored that you trust me enough to tell me. I'll do my best to help you as it's my duty to act with your best interest in mind." I paused to ensure I had her attention. "Sunshine, as the Tribe's social worker it's my duty to report this information to my leadership."

"What do you mean, 'Report it to your leadership'?"

"I mean my bosses. I need to discuss this with my bosses, and likely report it to Law Enforcement."

A worried look spread across her face. "Scott, I didn't tell you so you would do something about it. I'm not asking you to do *anything*. I just wanted to tell you. There's nothing that can be done."

"I can't promise you I won't tell anyone. I really am honored that you felt safe enough to talk to me about what happened to you, but I need to be clear that it's my duty to report this kind of information to my supervisor, manager, and director. I must follow Chain of Command. I'm not sure what they'll do with it, but the police should be notified immediately."

"Do you mean Tribal? They won't do anything about it. They never do. Nobody goes to Tribal about stuff like this."

"Scott, I'm scared. These are very dangerous people. You don't know who they're connected to."

No, I thought, *I don't know who they're connected to. But I do know that everyone is related, so even if this family is not directly connected with TC or Barney, they'll still somehow be connected.*

I knew what I had to do, and I knew it was risky business.

"I understand you're scared. Honestly, I'm scared, too. I told you when we met that I have a duty to help protect the Tribal Member children. I don't want to do something to put you in worse danger, and I need to consider that potential, but it's now my responsibility to help you. I'm your Tribe's ICW social worker, and I take my job very seriously."

We both knew it was unlikely I'd accomplish anything by going to my leadership, but I knew I had to try. I had to do the right thing.

I went to Nervous Beaver and told her what Sunshine had disclosed to me. She quivered. "I'm too terrified to do anything. One of the men implicated is a father on my caseload. You know that he's dangerous. Why the police can't seem to do anything about him is beyond me."

"Yeah," I agreed, "especially after they found him with all that meth recently, and nothing came of it."

"He should be excluded from the Rez at a minimum!" she exclaimed.

"You and I both know that *Exclusion* takes an act of Council, and I don't see that happening—not with his family connections."

I didn't expect her to do anything about it, but I had to follow Chain of Command.

My next step was to talk to Piggy. Now on Piggy's behalf, I must admit that the majority of times I'd staffed cases with her over the years, I don't know that she actually listened to anything I had to say. I say, "...on Piggy's behalf," because it's quite possible that she didn't actually hear or register a word of my concerns that day. For all her issues, I do think she has a heart, however cold and jaded it may be. And then again, she may have heard every word of it, and still chose to do nothing.

Piggy always responded to me in the same way. She would matter-of-factly state, "We will take care of it."

Well, unless she was mad at me. In that case, she'd either become verbally aggressive, or she'd respond with emails in all caps and exclamation points.

Remember the plant I got for Barney? Well, when he went on vacation, I emailed Piggy and asked her if she could please water his plant (since it *was* right behind her desk) and, well, I was worried about the plant dying while he was gone.

She replied that she was frustrated, I was not her superior, and I should never, ever send her a request like that again. Another time she yelled at me during a staff meeting, "Scott, you're making my blood boil!"

When I went to Piggy's office and told her about Sunshine, she never looked up from the papers on her desk. I told her what Sunshine had said about being drugged and gang-raped. I told her the names of the men involved. I told her the names of other young Tribal Members who allegedly had the same thing done to them.

As usual she said, "We will take care of it."

A couple weeks went by, and Piggy never said another word about it, so I went directly to Barney. I presented myself at his office and asked to speak with him. He agreed, and invited me in.

I told him I had a young, female, Tribal Member child who reported that she had been drugged and gang-raped by adult Tribal Members.

He seemed genuinely interested in what I was saying, maybe even concerned. *At last*, I thought, *finally someone is going to pay attention to my concerns so we can get this poor girl some help.*

He leaned towards me, looked me in the eye, and asked, "What's her name?"

He was hanging with anticipation.

When I stated, "Sunshine Who Walks in the Clouds," he immediately lost interest. And then he completely changed the subject. He went on to tell me the story of how he lost his virginity at seminary school. I couldn't understand why he was telling me that given what I'd just told him.

After sharing his devirgination story he ushered me out of his office in his usual manner. He never gave me any direction or any implication that he was going to do anything about my report.

I went back to his office a few weeks later. With resolve I asked him, "Mr. Smith, do you have any direction for me regarding my report about Sunshine being sexually assaulted by adult Tribal Members? I'm following Chain of Command. Do I contact Law Enforcement?"

He stood up from his desk and just looked at me for a moment. Then he walked around the front of his desk, stood face to face with me and said, "Me and my siblings were all molested growing up. I was the only one who got help. The rest of them are still messed up from it."

I didn't know what to say. I wasn't sure where he was going, but that was all he said, and then he turned and went back to his desk and started shuffling through papers.

With determination I asked him, "Is anything going to be done to help Sunshine?"

He looked up at me with a scowl. He got up again, walked back around his desk and stood facing me. Looking extremely agitated, he leaned in, peered over his glasses, and grumbled, "Indians deal with things differently than White people. *I'm taking care of it.* If you value your job, you will leave me alone to do mine. I have more important things to do."

Gentle Owl

While attending one of the Tribe's Sobriety Dinners, I saw Gentle Owl sitting at a table by himself so I asked if I could join him. I had some questions that were troubling me, and I hoped he would indulge me with his unique perspective as a traditional, respected Tribal Elder. After I sat down, he asked me, "How's your work going in ICW?"

My casework's going great. I really love working with the children and families, and I'm making great progress building relationships with some of the teens on my caseload, the kids who no one seems able to connect with. I'm also seeing success with many of the parents. Many people are accepting my guidance and taking more responsibility for their lives."

"It's good you're so committed to helping our people. I've heard good things about the work you're doing."

"I'm committed, and I feel good about my role in the community. I just wish that my leadership could see it. I'm really struggling to get their approval and support."

"Do you require their approval to be effective at your work?"

"No," I said, "but it sure would be nice. I guess I'm kind of sensitive. At some level I do care what they think about me. I keep thinking they'll change their attitudes toward me once they understand how much I'm helping our clients, their fellow Tribal Members, but they don't seem to even care, about me or about the families we work with."

"Would it make a difference in your work with the families if your bosses showed you recognition and appreciation?"

"No, I suppose it wouldn't. I'd do the same work for my clients whether my superiors appreciate me or not. My heart is in my work, regardless."

"So, why do you want their recognition? Why do you need to be accepted by them?"

"Don't we all want to be accepted? I mean, working in ICW is hard enough, with very little recognition; it would be nice to know that I was at least supported by my own department. Instead, I feel discriminated against by them. Frankly, they treat me pretty horribly. It feels like they think I deserve it because I'm White. I know I could leave, but I really do feel called to do this work, here at the Tribe, and, besides, if history is any indicator, they'll be gone before I am. I've outlasted everyone in my department for years."

Gentle Owl casually nodded.

"I really haven't given them any reason to treat me the way they do. At least, not that I'm aware of. I keep performing well in my job and treating them with dignity and respect. I don't get that in return. Mr. Owl, please forgive me for saying this, but for some of the Tribal Members here, especially my bosses, it doesn't seem to matter if I have good character and love in my heart. The only thing that seems to matter is that I'm White. If you judge and hate me simply because of *what* vs *who* I am, how's that any different than any other form of racism? For me racism is racism. There's no justifying it. It feels like they think they have a free pass to treat White people any way they want because of the past. Do Indians get a free pass?"

"My people are stuck in the past. None of us gets a free pass—Tribal or non-Tribal. If I was abused, it does not give me the right to abuse others. You are right. If I treat you badly simply because you're White, then I'm just as guilty as someone who treats an Indian or a Black person badly because of their race. Racism only goes one way—from the racist to the person they are discriminating against. It doesn't matter who's doing it. In fact, if I try to, as you say, justify it and say that you deserve it because you're White and your people have hurt my people, then I'm just as guilty. If we are to be judged at all, it should be on the basis of our character, and it should be by the Creator, not by our fellow man."

"Mr. Owl, speaking of free passes, do you think the tribes are abusing their power?"

Gentle Owl stared at his clasped hands for a few moments. He seemed to be in deep contemplation. I couldn't tell if he was upset by what I asked. I hoped I hadn't offended him. Finally, he responded, "The tribes know the entire world feels a deep sense of guilt and responsibility for what has been perpetrated against indigenous peoples. They know the governments feel obligated by the pressures of our more and more politically correct world. There are Tribal people who take advantage of this. They feel entitled, and they use their entitlement to justify their greed for power. They feel the world owes them, especially the White world, and they'll do whatever they can to recover their debt.

"The problem is that some of them don't seem to care who they hurt in the process—even if it's their own people, their own family members. We have so-called leaders here at the Tribe who've been caught embezzling money from their own Tribal Members, and yet they remain in positions of power. They think they're getting away with this behavior, but the Creator knows, and so do their fellow Tribal Members. This community is too small to get away with that kind of behavior. In the end, they will suffer for what they've done no matter how entitled and justified they feel. The Creator is forgiving, but we all have to answer for what we've done."

My Second to Last Day on the Rez

I went to Nervous Beaver's office and asked if we could talk. I wanted to discuss a few cases, and I wanted to express my disappointment with her not responding to any of my concerns about Snake Eyes. No montage, just the sad reality that Snake Eyes continually treated me as though I was beneath her, *and* I had evidence of her manipulating situations in an attempt to get me in trouble. Fortunately, I always had supporting documentation. I chose not to share those stories because they really weren't all that interesting.

She was sitting at her desk. "Come in," she said, "what's going on?"

I entered her office and sat down in front of her desk. "I just wanted to check in with you about the boys and a couple other issues."

"Where are we at with the boys?"

"I have treatment facilities lined up for both of them, but it'll be at least two weeks for Tony and up to three weeks for Randy before they can get beds. I hate to leave them sitting in detention, but when I consider the alternative of them going back on runaway and hanging with their adult, drug-dealing gang leader, I prefer they stay where they are. At least we know they're safe, and they're going to school."

"I agree with you," she said, "we can't take the risk of having them out on the streets again, getting into who knows what."

"Well, we've tried their families' way before, placing them with their grandma or auntie until their bed is ready, but they always end up running. I know their auntie would at least attempt to hold them accountable, but you know their grandma's thoughts on things. She says that the traditional way is to not discipline them. I think discipline is exactly what they need vs enabling them to do more harm to themselves."

A little aside...we had one Tribal Elder, the Bloodhound, who didn't agree at all with this position on tradition and discipline. She was the older Native woman I met on my first day of work who averted her gaze when either of us spoke. Jah Lion and I affectionately called her "The Bloodhound" because she had a special talent for sniffing out trouble. Numerous times over the years she assisted our department in locating runaway youth and MIA parents.

She expressed many times to different members of our team that she thought the ICW children needed more discipline. She was definitely not all talk. In fact, she got a lot of flak from the community for tying two of her misbehaving nephews to a tree when they were young. She once told me, "Our culture says we must do whatever is necessary to teach our children and keep them safe. If that means tying them up to a tree to keep them out of trouble, then so be it!" I can't say I agree with her methods, but I imagine had she been able to raise those boys they would have turned out much better. I could write an entire book on that family alone. Thank you, Miss Blood.

When Tony was brought in by law enforcement this last time, he'd been staying in a local hotel with his adult girlfriend Sneaky—in a room that was paid for by his grandma Vera. To her credit, it was actually Snake Eyes who acquired this information from the hotel. She had received a report from a concerned community member, and then she did the necessary investigation to follow up and get the details. She was even the one who set up our stakeout at the hotel.

Grandma Vera was in the process of dropping Tony and Sneaky off at the hotel when we spotted them. Tony ran as soon as he saw us. I cautiously tailed him in my GSA so he wouldn't escape before the police arrived to arrest him. He took off across the hotel parking lot and then ran behind a long strip mall. I drove around behind the building and saw him standing near a dumpster looking disoriented. I pulled up beside him and got out of the car.

He looked at me with huge black pupils. I pleaded, "Tony, please stop so we can talk. Continuing to run from us isn't going to accomplish anything good for you."

He took off again, so I followed him on foot. My intention was to merely shadow him, so we didn't lose him. I told him, "Look man, I'm in great shape. I could follow you all day. You're not going to outrun me."

He kept running, so I kept tailing him. While I followed him, I also kept in communication with Snake Eyes so she could direct the police to our location.

Tony ran over to a nearby gas station where we did two loops around the building. I gave him a little space but didn't lose sight of him. He ducked down and tried to hide beside a bush while he remained in plain sight.

I told him, "Tony, I can see you plain as day. Come on man, you obviously aren't doing well. I can see from your eyes that you're high as hell, and you're panting like a dog. I'm not even out of breath. I'm telling you; I could do this all day."

After taking a moment to catch his breath, he started running again and headed back to the hotel where two Tribal officers were waiting for him. They cornered him and then took him down on the sidewalk. Sneaky, Snake Eyes, and Grandma Vera were standing close by. Sneaky sobbed. "I love you, Tony."

He began to cry and shouted back to her, "I love you, too."

Grandma Vera stood there and watched.

Tony and Sneaky kept professing their love to one another while the police handcuffed him and put him in their cruiser. It was all quite dramatic. From there they'd take him to juvie.

No one said a word to Grandma Vera or Sneaky regarding their respective roles in all of this.

This was clearly another example of Elder Immunity. Everyone in our department and Tribal police knew that Vera had harbored Tony during his runaway and that she supported his relationship with his adult "girlfriend", and yet, she was not held accountable for her actions. I wasn't surprised. I had witnessed this dynamic for years. However, I was getting tired of fighting this uphill battle. These kids had enough challenges without their own adult family members contributing to their delinquency.

I digress.

Nervous Beaver responded to my comment about discipline, "All of these kids need more discipline."

"So, anyway," I continued, "once the boys get through treatment and are stable in their respective placements, then I plan to go on my leave. As much as

I need to take it, I wouldn't feel right leaving until I know they're stable. I'm afraid if I go now, they'll fall through the cracks."

"That sounds like a good plan," she replied.

"So," I said, "I hate to bring this up again, but I need to ask if you plan to take any action regarding my reported concerns about Snake Eyes. She's been here for almost a year and a half, and I've done my best to stay away from her. I have to say, though, I'm getting really worn out with her ongoing harassment. I know I don't need to go into details again, but I'd like to know if anything is ever going to be done."

Nervous Beaver looked down at some papers on her desk, and then meekly mumbled, "Not sure I can do anything."

In a defeated tone, I said "Ok, well, I'm not sure what else to do. I've tried numerous times to set boundaries with her verbally. Those attempts were unsuccessful, so I've also attempted to set boundaries with her in writing, so at least I would have the documentation, but her behavior hasn't changed."

Nervous Beaver didn't say anything else, so I left her office.

Needless to say, my attempts to advocate for Sunshine and set boundaries with Snake Eyes backfired.

You already know how my last day on the Rez went.

Aftermath

I was fired on a Friday. The following Monday I showed up at the Tribe's Human Resources Department and submitted a written request for a copy of my file. They put me through a few different hoops including submitting additional paperwork to Accounting, and then ultimately never delivered.

Since Nervous Beaver had already told me she couldn't do anything, I also went up the chain and called Barney. He hung up on me as soon as he heard my voice. I decided I would continue up the chain and contact the Tribal Chairman. I'd spoken to her several times before at Tribal gatherings. She knew who I was, and she was well aware of my history with the Tribe. I sent her three emails.

In my first letter I praised her for her administration's accomplishments. I told her how much I loved my job and the families I served and that it was breaking my heart to be going through this with the Tribe. I told her I had serious concerns regarding my former superiors, and I wanted to meet as soon as possible to discuss them. I told her I was writing a book that was inspired by my experiences at the Tribe, and I was giving her an opportunity to help me *right* the ending on behalf of the Tribe.

I went on to acknowledge how upsetting it must be to receive a message like this, but I promised her that Barney, Odessa, and Piggy were the ones she would be angry with in the end. Of course, she's related to all of them.

She didn't respond. I wasn't surprised. My feelings of anger, hurt, and betrayal deepened and intensified. I wanted to be acknowledged. I longed to be heard. I wanted her to hold Barney accountable for not helping Sunshine and the other Tribal Member children. They deserved justice. No one from the Tribe was standing up for them. I also wanted her to undo the wrongdoing that had been perpetrated against me. I didn't deserve to lose my job. I knew I was a good social worker, and I was effective at helping the Tribal youth and their families.

Unfortunately, I made myself into a victim. *I resisted reality.* I couldn't see my responsibility in the equation. I blamed others for my creation. I resented Barney and Piggy and Snake Eyes. Even though I could see myself falling into the victim-consciousness trap, I couldn't seem to change course. I became increasingly resentful of my former leadership. I became obsessed with gaining recognition from Tribal leaders.

Two days later I sent a second email to the Chairman where I disclosed that I'd felt harassed and discriminated against by my former superiors and co-workers for years, and that my previous requests for help were ignored or retaliated against. I referenced my book again, shared a few stories, and then wrote about my passion for serving Tribal Communities. I suggested to her that I had earned street credit for effectively serving in ICW for over eight years with one tribe. I referenced some of the corrupt politics of the court, and I warned her that I'd share my stories publicly, without the Tribe's input, if they continued to ignore me.

I wrote, "I know a little about your culture. I know that one of your biggest fears is looking bad to other tribes. I know that a much greater fear is looking bad to the outside world. Even worse yet, is making other tribes look bad to the outside world. Looking bad in Indian Country…being the tribe that set off this kind of movement. Jeez, I wouldn't want that responsibility."

I told her I was being as patient as I could, but I really hoped to hear from her soon because I wanted to handle my concerns directly with the Tribe. I was clear that I wanted recognition for my service. I was also clear with her that I didn't want to piss off all of Indian Country in the process. Really, I don't.

She didn't respond. I sent her a final letter. In the end I told her:

"I didn't want to fight. I sincerely wanted you to 'right' the ending with me.

Deep down, I also wanted to have faith in humanity, faith in you…faith that there are people who will do the right thing in the face of adversity.

Finally, I needed to be able to prove to myself and others that I gave you every opportunity, so I could say that I did, and you couldn't say that I didn't."

Yes, I know, how dramatic; but there you have it.

Regal Eagle

When I went up to Accounting to pick up my last check, there was already a long line of people. I joined the line but was quickly redirected by one of the staff to wait on the other side of the room. She said, "Someone will be out to talk to you shortly."

I already felt uncomfortable being on the Rez. I was sure word had gotten around about me being fired from ICW. That was a pretty juicy piece of gossip. Being singled-out at Accounting didn't help. Although I saw no one staring, I imagined the worst of their thoughts. I feared what lies they'd been told. I feared their judgements. They didn't know my side of the story. Would they ever?

I just wanted to get my check and leave. Until then, I wanted to be invisible.

I sensed someone approaching. I looked up and saw Regal Eagle coming towards me. He was a Tribal Member Elder whose family I'd worked with for years. He walked right up to me and stood grand and tall before me.

I straightened up and faced him.

He stood there for a few moments just looking at me.

The longer he stood there, the quieter the room became, and the more eyes I could feel upon us.

Finally, he spoke. "I've watched you over the years. When you came to us, you didn't know where to stand. You didn't know your place in our community."

I nodded.

"I've watched you, and I've seen you grow. I've seen you help many of our people. You've helped me with my own children."

My eyes started to well up.

"I want you to know that your efforts haven't gone unnoticed. I see what you've been doing for our community."

He nodded, and then he left.

First Acknowledgement

About two weeks after I sent my last letter to the Chairman, I received the following email from the Tribe's lead attorney entitled, **No contact**.

"Scott,

Do not attempt to contact Tribal staff and elected officials. I am not sure how many times I have written to you, but that message obviously has not sunken in. This is no longer a personnel issue. Because of your ongoing threats it is a criminal investigation. All of your messages have been forwarded to The Tribal Police Department.

Sincerely,

Little White Monkey

Office of Tribal Attorney

The Tribe"

∞

Little White Monkey earned his name because of that email. It was bait. He was trying to elicit a reaction so that he'd have confirmation I received his warning. He didn't need to lower himself to this tactic though. I was annoyed. I thought, *He'll do anything for peanuts, just like a little white monkey*.

You see, Little Monkey hadn't communicated with me since long before my termination, and it was always regarding ICW matters. He certainly never wrote to me about not contacting Tribal staff and elected officials. He was playing games, and he was being deceitful in the process. By their fruits you will know them.

The only "threat" I had made was to take my stories public if the Tribe did not respond. I was the one who brought my letters to Chief Rocking Horse at Tribal Law Enforcement. Up to this point, the Tribe had completely ignored me. Although I found it annoying that Little White Monkey was playing games like this, I did appreciate the acknowledgment *his* letter represented. It meant the Chairman had indeed received my emails, and they were being read, likely by her, but, at a minimum, by their lead attorney. It was kind of funny, really. He tried to bait me to give him a response, and, yet he gave *me* a response in the process.

However, other than White Monkey's letter, no one else responded to me. The longer they ignored me, the more focused and determined I became. I owed it to the children. *The Tribe owes it to their children.* I didn't want to bring up the child rape cover-up, but I felt like I had no other option to get their attention and shift the focus to the corrupt practices of my former leadership.

I sent an email to all of Tribal Council, Chief Rocking Horse, and several other Tribal leaders and staff calling out Barney and Piggy for child rape cover-up. I told them how I went up the chain of command trying to get help for the children. I told them about my letters to the Tribal Chairman requesting a meeting to address my concerns. I strongly encouraged them to help the children and start investigating my allegations by interviewing all the Tribe's teens privately and confidentially as not to single anyone out. I expressed my concerns about the leadership in social services, I referenced some of the corrupt politics of Tribal Court, and then I finished with a plea for their help in holding their Tribal leaders accountable.

Exclusion

Five days later I received an email from Little White Monkey entitled, **Exclusion**. He had submitted a Petition to exclude me from the Tribal Reservation. That's a big deal, folks. He listed numerous "facts" to support his Petition including my favorite #7 "Because of his ongoing threats, many staff members no longer feel safe at their workplace or in their homes."

He was really reaching on that one. He provided no evidence for any of his allegations. I'm pretty sure people still felt safe in their homes and workplaces even with me still at large.

I have to admit, this email made me laugh really hard for the first time through all of this. They'd finally given me an unequivocal response. They were no longer ignoring me, that was for sure.

Five days after that I received another email from Little White Monkey also entitled, **Exclusion**. That one made it official. It was the last official communication I ever received from the Tribe.

It kind of amazed me that TC considered me to be more of a threat to the Tribe than their local pedophiles and gang members who normally don't get excluded from the Reservation. It takes a lot to get someone Excluded. It takes an act of Council. They had to put me on the agenda, discuss my case, and vote. I'd like to believe it was a long deliberating process, but I'm sure that in reality they probably voted and moved on in less than a minute, unless, of course, people wanted to complain. In that case, it may have gone on for quite a while. I doubt their focus was on Barney, though. Interesting counterpoint here: Barney was promoted to CEO of the Tribe after all of this. Tribal Council excluded me and promoted him.

That part about people being afraid of me just seemed ridiculous. I never gave anyone at the Tribe reason to believe I'd harm them. Well, except Lester. I wanted to knock him out on a few different occasions, and he knew it. Of course, I'm sure he wanted to knock me out just as many times. We never gave up on each other though, and our relationship grew because of it.

Ultimately, I was grateful, and my heart lightened a bit. The Tribe was no longer ignoring me. In fact, they were officially cutting me off from everything they owned, and that took some focus and attention. It kind of made me feel important. I was looking for acknowledgement, and they gave it to me. It certainly wasn't the acknowledgement I wanted, but it was acknowledgement, nonetheless.

My Personal Call to Action

I felt my own call to action. I couldn't rest knowing what injustices had been done to these children. I couldn't rest knowing what atrocities continued to be done. My Omni was Blood Red. I didn't want blood, but I did want justice. I wanted these corrupt leaders to be held accountable.

It doesn't matter if it's a racist White cop, a greedy corporate billionaire, or a corrupt tribal director—they all need to be held accountable. If we don't do it, no one will. They're all banking on the former.

I committed myself to action. First, I consulted a trusted advisor who recommended I contact the U.S. Attorney's Office. They wouldn't touch it. The woman I spoke with actually deferred me to the Department of Labor. Next, I contacted a highfalutin law firm from the city. They didn't respond. I persevered. I contacted an FBI agent I met through the Tribe, *King5 News*, *the Associated Press*, and *Democracy Now!* (a few times)…nothing! I even told Amy Goodman about it when she came to town for *Coffee with Amy*. She said, "We get a lot of stories." I understood. None of them wanted to have anything to do with it. None of them were going to challenge the Tribe.

Next, I contacted a local Native attorney who's known as *Mr. Indian Country*. I sent him an email laden with passionate discourse regarding the wrongdoings of Tribal leaders against their own children. I invited him to join my cause to help these vulnerable youth. I implored him, "Tribal leaders have become the Oppressors of their own people. The Oppressed have become the Tyrants."

I continued, "I have a vision of a White Man (non-Tribal) and an Indian Man (Tribal) coming together to fight against the oppression of this tribe (maybe others, too)." I finished with, "The heart, the higher path, knows that this fight is not about race or color. It's about doing what's right against tyranny."

He never responded. I called him almost a year later, and I was finally able to connect with him. He wouldn't touch it either. I can't say that I blame him. He's built his practice and reputation on helping to defend the tribes. He would have been biting the hands that feed him. Although, I had a much bigger vision than merely sustaining his bread and butter. I imagined him as a world-renowned legal activist who helps Native children and exposes the cover-up of child exploitation. Perhaps he still will be.

I followed up our phone conversation with an email thanking him and acknowledging what a difficult issue this is for any community to face. I also acknowledged his potential conflict of interest given his work representing tribes. I told him, "In my vision, you could have a conflict of interest with every tribe. In my vision, we were fighting corruption together, a Tribal Man and a White Man, for the good of the people—for the good of the Tribal people, especially the children, the aunties, and the grandmothers."

Smoke Signals

For what it's worth, I know that I have grandiose visions. I think that deep down, we all do. I'm on the path to manifest those visions, and I welcome everyone to join me. By *everyone*, I mean the entire stinkin' Universe, and then some! You know what Universe means, right? *One verse*. Everyone singing together. Everyone pursuing their own unique vision, together.

You see, my vision is so grandiose that I'm sending smoke signals out to every being in existence. This isn't just about us. It's about the unfolding of Consciousness itself. We all have a stake in this game, and we need all the help we can get.

So, what do we do? Where do we start?

We start by forming alliances with everyone we can. We find POCs with everyone. We start by breaking down cultural and racial barriers. That's why I reached out to Mr. Indian Country, because just like doing social work on the Rez, we've got to go to work in the trenches, on the front lines, where the real fight is happening.

It's easy to hang out with like-minded people and share common visions about how the world should be. It's another thing to build alliances with people from the most diverse and challenging walks of life we can discover.

So, my (our) journey continues. I'm setting a tone here; hopefully, leading by example. For my next grandiose attempt, I reached out to a famous Tribal author right here in the Pacific Northwest. You might say I sent him smoke signals. Well, I sent smoke signals in the form of an email. I attempted to appeal to his higher nature (just like I did with Mr. Indian Country) by sharing my vision for our potential allegiance. He didn't respond either. Perhaps I was just sending smoke seeds. I have a feeling my book will eventually cross his path. Hopefully, by then, those seeds will have germinated. We may build that alliance just yet.

My Last Communication to the Tribe

For my last communication to the Tribe, I sent an email entitled **Truth is** to numerous people including Council Members, Tribal staff, and trusted former co-workers. I chose to keep it a little lighter and not make any references to the cover-up perpetrated by my former leadership. Following are excerpts from this email:

"I thank the Creator for bringing me to The Tribe. I thank the Tribal Members for allowing me to serve them for eight glorious years.

Truth is, I loved my job. I loved working for the Tribe. I loved serving the Tribal Members. It was an honor.

I took my job very seriously. I became really good at it, and I helped a lot of people. I felt that it was my spiritual mission and duty to help the Tribe's children. *It was.*

When I lost my job, I felt set-up and betrayed by my former supervisor Nervous Beaver and co-worker Snake Eyes.

Truth is, I was wrongfully terminated, and then, unfortunately, in my desperation, hurt, and pain, I reacted and sent those letters to the Chairman and Tribal Council. I pressured Chief and Crow and others to help me.

After over two months of anguish and desperation, I finally pulled myself together, accepted the situation, and started moving forward.

It's been over five months now. I accept what happened. It still hurts, but I accept it.

Thank you for an amazing eight years. I will never forget my time at the Tribe. There are literally hundreds of people whom I really care about in the extended Tribal Community, and I miss all of you. I wish you all the best.

Sincerely,

Scott Strider"

Moving Forward

When I finally pulled myself together and decided it was time to move on, Dudley Flannigan was the first person I called. He was a state social worker who had assisted me on some of my tribal cases. Calling him was completely motivated by intuition. I had no logical reason to do it—I just had a feeling.

He didn't respond.

I figured that finding a new job would be easy; it always had been, so I wasn't too concerned about it. Well, that would prove to be a very humbling experience. After five months of job hunting and zero interviews, I received a letter from the State informing me that my unemployment was going to run out in a month. I didn't see that coming. I'd never been on unemployment before (I'd never lost my job before), but I knew people who had been on it for years, and I assumed I'd receive the same benefits. Apparently, my federal funding was expended. I learned the only option for me to extend unemployment was to go to school. Frankly, going back to school was the last thing on my mind, but fear can be a great motivator, and I was afraid of being broke.

At the time, a friend of mine was encouraging me to become an IT recruiter like him. He worked from home, he earned an impressive income, and he was willing to teach me his craft. I seriously considered this path and even started training with him, but it never really resonated with me. Ultimately, it felt like a sales position, and although I have pretty good people skills, I've never been very good with the close.

Well, although he didn't sell me on IT recruiting, in the process, he did sell me on the need for more IT professionals. Consequently, I started studying computer programming and networking at our local community college. I kept looking for work while attending school. I even called Dudley again; I just had a feeling. He still didn't respond. During those first eleven months of job-hunting, I only got one interview. Now granted, I hadn't really lowered my bar in my job search. For the most part, I was only applying for comparable professional social work positions, but I was getting increasingly discouraged.

My confidence dwindled. It proved to be one of the most stressful periods in my life. I woke up every morning with a sick feeling in my stomach. I dreaded facing each new day. I still held resentments for my former leadership at the Tribe. I blamed them for my situation. I was still being a victim.

I didn't give up though. In fact, when I felt my most desperate, I performed what my network-marketing buddy refers to as a *blitz*. I applied for jobs like crazy. It was all I focused on every day for weeks. Like I keep saying, focus creates reality. I went from one interview in eleven months to six interviews in one week. One of those interviews I call *Finding Closure*.

Finding Closure

My third interview during my marathon-interview week was for a case aide position with the Cool Creek Tribe's ICW program. They're a sister tribe to *the* Tribe. By the way, my sixth interview that week was with Dudley Flannigan. I didn't even know I was interviewing with his team until he introduced himself; we had only ever talked on the phone. That feeling I had about Dudley was dead-on. I rocked that interview and got the job!

My interview with the Cool Creek Tribe was scheduled for 10:10 a.m. My HR contact Shelly had directed me to go to their Administration Building for the interview.

I thought I knew where I was going. I drove down near the health clinic off Casino Blvd. I saw an older Indian man getting out of his truck, so I pulled up beside him and asked where the Administration Building was located. He said, "Go around the building behind us, and you'll see the main entrance."

I drove around the building and parked. I got out and took a moment to put my tie on, using the car window as a mirror. I was right on time for my interview. I went inside and saw another Indian man standing in front of a sliding window with a sign that said Human Resources. I told him I had a job interview, and he gave me a blank look. I said that the Human Resources lady told me to go to the Administration Building for the interview. He directed me to head up the stairs behind me.

Upstairs I saw a big sign that said "Administration", but it looked old, and the room looked like a reception area for a medical clinic. The older man I had seen down in the street came walking in and told me to check in at the desk. I responded, "Oh, ok, I wasn't sure. It looks like a medical clinic."

"That's where you check in," he assured me.

I presented myself to the receptionist, and she directed me to go back downstairs to Human Resources. When I got back down there, a woman came out and asked what I needed. I told her, "I'm here for an interview for the case aide position with ICW." She didn't seem to be aware of this, and then another woman came out to inquire why I was there. I gave her the same info. She directed me to go back to Casino Blvd., turn right at the light, and then I would see the big brick Admin Building on the right.

Now I was running late. I raced down there, parked, and then ran to the rear delivery entrance of the building. I quickly passed through to the front reception area and announced myself to the man at the desk.

He stared at me for a moment as if he were sizing me up, and then he leaned over the desk and looked down at me. With a demeanor that reminded me of my first meeting with Todd Smoke, he curtly stated, "They're waiting for you. Go down the hall." He leaned in even closer. "All the way down the hall...*all the way*."

Jeez, I thought. *What am I heading into?* He seemed like a character out of a Hitchcock movie.

I followed his directions which led me to another little reception area, and I saw a placard with "Shelly" inscribed, presumably for the HR rep who had scheduled my interview. I introduced myself to a younger White woman sitting at the desk, and then she walked me into the adjacent office. An older Indian woman sat at the head of the table with two younger Indian women flanking her sides. Shelly joined the woman on the left side of the table, leaving the seat opposite the older woman for me, and then she introduced them.

The two younger women were social workers and the older woman, Blue Tiger, was the Director of Children's Services. Blue Tiger was slender and attractive with long dark hair. Her eyes reflected blue and green hues from her dangling turquoise earrings. She maintained a commanding presence as she looked into my eyes. I could feel her evaluating me. I straightened my posture, took a deep breath, and then humbled myself to these four women.

First, Shelly asked me general questions about things like my driver's license, CPR training, and pertinent certifications. Then she explored my knowledge about maintaining boundaries and confidentiality with ICW clients. She proceeded to question whether I had any limitations doing this type of work, and then she got into questions about my education and experience.

I shared some of my experiences at the Tribe. I told them I trained three supervisors and several caseworkers, and I ran the department alone several times for extended periods. I told them about Elaina and the story of the Harvest Festival at the Long House. I told them how doing great social work was all about the relationships we build with our clients, and I shared how much I loved working with the children, aunties, and grandmothers.

When they asked me about my experience working with difficult clients, I told them about Lester (not using his real name, of course). I told them how we'd really challenged each other over the years. I also told them how he was one of my greatest teachers, and that I'd called him up one night and told him so. He gave me one of those deep belly laughs in response.

In my opinion Lester is the most traditional Indian Man you'll meet on the Rez. He understands his people, he understands traditional and current Tribal culture, and he walks the path. When you witness *his* creations, you know he has goodness in his heart, and he's working on developing himself. Of course, he has his issues, but, undeniably, he's a good person with a huge heart, and he cares for the well-being of the Earth and her people.

The two social workers took turns asking numerous questions regarding my understanding of Indian Child Welfare and my ability to support the ICW caseworkers. I tried to shine a bit here with my knowledge and understanding of ICWA and best social work practice while also remaining humble to the fact that I was interviewing to be their assistant. I gave numerous examples of ways I could support them in fulfilling their casework duties.

Blue Tiger sat quietly and listened during the entire interview. At the very end she looked across the table to each of her staff, and then she looked at me. "I have just one more question for you…why did you leave the Tribe?"

Aw, man! I thought.

I responded, "I had a feeling I was going to be asked this question. I was hoping that instead I would be asked, 'How on Earth did you last eight years at one tribe doing ICW?'"

I paused, took a deep breath, and then told them about Sunshine Who Walks in the Clouds. I told them about how after working with this young teen's extended family members for over five years, she came to me and disclosed that she was drugged and gang-raped by adult Tribal Members from her own Tribe.

I started crying.

I apologized for becoming emotional.

I said, "I went to my supervisor about it, and she told me she was too terrified to do anything because one of the alleged rapists was a father on her caseload, and he was a well-known local bad-boy…gang leader, drug dealer, pedophile, you name it."

I told them, "My supervisor also said she was afraid of losing her job."

I kept crying. I was having difficulty getting my words out, but I knew exactly what I wanted to say.

"I was afraid of losing my job too, but I had a duty."

By that point I was sobbing.

I told them how I went to the Assistant Director (Piggy), and she said she'd take care of it.

I told them that after two weeks of not hearing anything from the Assistant Director, I went to the Director twice, and in the end, he told me, "Indians deal with things differently than White people. I'm taking care of it. If you value your job, you will leave me alone to do mine. I have more important things to do."

I kept sobbing.

"A month later I was given notice."

"I loved my job, and I felt betrayed by my leadership."

I took a few more deep breaths.

I composed myself, apologized again, and then I told them I wanted to finish on a positive note.

"I'm a very spiritual person—not religious, but spiritual. I believe that we are all mirrors, and I hope you can relate to some of the things I've shared with you today."

Shelly handed me some tissue. I'd been eyeing the box for a few minutes. Then she thanked me for being honest.

Blue Tiger raised her hands in front of her with her palms facing each other, and then she did a couple slight turns with her wrists so that her palms swiveled towards her face. Her actions suggested acknowledgement and understanding. It felt as though she was giving a prayer. I felt like she had both accepted my testimony and cleansed the space with that simple, powerful gesture.

I excused myself and got up to go. I stopped in the doorway and said, "I've needed to cry for a long time. Thank you." And then I left.

I continued crying as I drove away to my next job interview.

I felt a deep sense of relief, as though I'd just released a huge burden. Those women held the space and listened to what I had to say. They witnessed me, and they accepted me. I felt blessed and honored and grateful. I knew *that* was the real reason I'd gone to this interview. It certainly wasn't for a job. I knew they weren't going to hire me. But they knew Indian Child Welfare, I had worked for their sister tribe, and they recognized and accepted the authenticity of my story. I hadn't yet realized the enormity of the burden I'd been carrying until I shared Sunshine's story with those women. I will always be grateful for their gift.

I have so much to share. There are so many stories to tell. I've barely scratched the surface here, but this is how I end it.

The Code

How to survive on the Rez.

1. Everyone's related.

2. Don't name names, even in praise.

3. Know your job. Do your job.

4. Keep your head down; don't attract attention.

5. Treat it like court—be professional and only answer what's asked.

RhythmQuest

Autobiography of a Drummer

(Intro from my forthcoming book.)

Fall 1991

Arizona State University

"Cake Building"

MUP 387, African Drumming

I arrived early for my first day of class. I was so excited about having the opportunity to study West African Drumming, especially since I was an engineering student, and I hadn't had many opportunities to take interesting or exciting classes. I had recently been turned on to this traditional style of drumming at a Grateful Dead show. Drumming was always present in the happenin' parking lot scenes at their shows.

The previous Spring quarter I had witnessed a local group performing drum and dance on the lawn above the campus library. At the end of their performance, their leader, Ethnomusicology professor Dr. Mark Sunkett (great teacher), announced that he was offering a West African Drumming class in the Fall. What I didn't know at the time was that he wouldn't be the one teaching the class. I knew it was definitely for me, so I signed up as soon as I could.

When I entered the corridor adjoining the hallway to my classroom, I was met by quite an extraordinary gentleman. He appeared to be from Africa, as his skin was dark, and he wore colorful traditional clothing. He was about my height, although much stouter, and he appeared to be about thirty years my senior.

He greeted me with a friendly hello and a gleaming smile. He had a regal presence that immediately commanded my attention. He looked wise. The two of us shared this quiet, empty space for several minutes before anyone else arrived. Although we only spoke a few words, I clearly understood the significance of this moment. I knew that I'd met my *Master*. His name was Cornelius Kweku Ganyo, aka "Uncle C.K."

www.ingramcontent.com/pod-product-compliance
Lightning Source LLC
LaVergne TN
LVHW041539070426
835507LV00011B/824